3/16

Beginning
Microsoft Office Live

Build Your Own Web Site
Quickly and Easily

Rahul Pitre

D1530658

Apress®

Beginning Microsoft Office Live: Build Your Own Web Site Quickly and Easily

Copyright © 2007 by Rahul Pitre

ISBN-13 (pbk): 978-1-59059-879-5

ISBN-10 (pbk): 1-59059-879-2

Printed and bound in the United States of America 9 8 7 6 5 4 3 2 1

Lead Editors: Tony Campbell, Chris Mills
Technical Reviewer: Sanjay Padhye
Editorial Board: Steve Anglin, Ewan Buckingham, Gary Cornell, Jonathan Gennick, Jason Gilmore,
    Jonathan Hassell, Chris Mills, Matthew Moodie, Jeffrey Pepper, Ben Renow-Clarke,
    Dominic Shakeshaft, Matt Wade, Tom Welsh
Project Manager: Richard Dal Porto
Copy Edit Manager: Nicole Flores
Copy Editor: Nicole Abramowitz
Assistant Production Director: Kari Brooks-Copony
Production Editor: Kelly Winquist
Compositor: Linda Weidemann, Wolf Creek Press
Proofreader: Liz Welch
Indexer: Ron Strauss
Artist: April Milne
Cover Designer: Kurt Krames
Manufacturing Director: Tom Debolski

Distributed to the book trade worldwide by Springer-Verlag New York, Inc., 233 Spring Street, 6th Floor, New York, NY 10013. Phone 1-800-SPRINGER, fax 201-348-4505, e-mail orders-ny@springer-sbm.com, or visit http://www.springeronline.com.

For information on translations, please contact Apress directly at 2855 Telegraph Avenue, Suite 600, Berkeley, CA 94705. Phone 510-549-5930, fax 510-549-5939, e-mail info@apress.com, or visit http://www.apress.com.

The source code for this book is available to readers at http://www.apress.com in the Source Code/ Download section.

Contents at a Glance

Contents

PART 2 ■■■ Building Your Site

■CHAPTER 6   A Crash Course in Web Design 101

PART 3 ■■■ Being Your Own Webmaster

About the Author

RAHUL PITRE has worked with web sites and the World Wide Web in a professional capacity since 1996, when the version number on most web software read 1.0. He's been a server administrator, a webmaster, and an architect of several web-based applications.

Rahul runs Acxede, a company that builds web-based applications for small and medium-sized businesses. He holds a master's degree in business administration and a master's degree in computer information systems.

Acknowledgments

Only my name appears on the cover, but several people lent me a hand in creating this book. I'd like to take a moment to gratefully acknowledge their help, support, and advice.

First, I'd like to thank Sanjay Padhye, technical reviewer, for diligently checking the manuscript's accuracy and keeping me honest. Thanks to Larry Blake for volunteering to read the first draft of the manuscript and offering valuable feedback. Thanks to Liz Ross for suggestions on improving the text and to Stefan Kanfer for invaluable advice on writing style. Thanks also to Will Shortz for insight into the process of writing a book.

You wouldn't be holding this book but for the valiant efforts of the folks at Apress. Thanks to Tony Campbell and Chris Mills, lead editors, for their advice and suggestions throughout the writing of this book. Thanks to Richard Dal Porto, project manager, for pretending that "the dog ate my manuscript" and many of its variations were excuses he'd never heard before and for taking the consequential delays in stride. Thanks to Nicole Abramowitz, copy editor, for ably translating the manuscript from *my English* to English. Thanks to Kelly Winquist, production editor, for keeping the book on schedule even after I missed quite a few deadlines. Thanks go to Linda Weidemann, compositor, for transforming the manuscript into a clean and pretty book. Thanks to April Milne for making intelligible illustrations out of my doodles, and to Liz Welch for proofreading the pages and locating errors that everyone else missed. Thanks to Ron Strauss for indexing the book, and to Kurt Krames for designing the cover on short notice.

Finally, I'd like to thank three people who contributed the most to this book even without reading or writing a single word of it. Thanks go to my son Rohan, 12, for offering to buy my book with "his own money." Thanks to my daughter Ruhi, 8, for supplementing Rohan's offer with "even if nobody else buys it." And finally, thanks to my wife Minal, for staying married to me even after I went missing from her life for about six months while I wrote this book.

I'd always wondered why authors thank so many people. Now I know.

Introduction

Microsoft Office Live is *not* an online version of Microsoft Office. It's a complete web solution for individuals and small businesses. It includes domain-name registration, web hosting, built-in web-design tools, custom domain e-mail accounts—such as you@yourbusiness.com— and a few other knickknacks to boot.

Office Live comes in three versions: Basics, Essentials, and Premium. Basics is the base version, which boasts all the features I just mentioned plus one that I haven't—it's free. That's right. Free. Complimentary. *Gratis.*

Essentials and Premium are Office Live's beefed-up versions. They include everything that Basics does, and for a small monthly fee, they throw in a few business applications and collaborative tools for building intranets and extranets.

Intranets and extranets are fiefdoms of larger organizations. Small businesses don't usually have the technical expertise or the network infrastructure to build and maintain them. Office Live is Microsoft's attempt to close the gap. With Office Live, the little guys can manage key elements of their businesses—such as e-mail, customer relationships, marketing campaigns, and employee expenses—just with their browsers.

The ability to build a public web site, however, remains the crown jewel of Office Live. *Anyone* can build one with Office Live's easy-to-use tools. But just a tool, no matter how sophisticated, isn't enough to build a great web site; knowing how to use the tool effectively is, perhaps, even more important.

This book is a concise guide to using Office Live effectively. It teaches you the basic Internet concepts and Web terminology. It gives you a clear understanding of what Office Live is and explains what you can and can't do with it. It goes on to show you how to plan a web site from scratch and build it with Office Live. Along the way, it introduces you to the best practices you should incorporate into your site design, and it goes on to offer advice on how to attract visitors to your web site. By following the advice in this book, you'll be able to build an *attractive*, *usable*, and *easily maintainable* web site.

If you've never built a web site before, this book will help you become a *workable* webmaster quickly. If you're already a webmaster, this book will help you become a *respectable* one!

How This Book Is Structured

This content of this book is divided into three parts.

Part 1, "What's Office Live, Anyway?," introduces you to Office Live and helps you sign up for the service, if you haven't already done so. It explores Office Live's features and capabilities, and it shows you how to fulfill your administrative responsibilities as an Office Live account owner.

Part 2, "Building Your Site," introduces you to the best practices in building good web sites. It walks you through building a skeleton of your web site. It shows you how to create web pages and populate them with good content, and it follows it up with a few tips and tricks to make your site more appealing and easier to use. Part 2 concludes with a few hacks that'll help you make the most of your web site.

Part 3, "Being Your Own Webmaster," gives you a taste of your new career as a part-time webmaster. It begins with a final checklist for "going live," then it walks you through Office Live's Site Reports and shows you how to use them to analyze the traffic to your site. It covers the basics of keeping your web site looking fresh and updated before giving you an idea of the maintenance tasks you'll have to perform on a regular basis as a webmaster.

The content often builds on the skills and vocabulary from earlier chapters. As a result, you should plan on reading this book sequentially if you're new to Office Live. However, each chapter of the book covers a distinct aspect of building and maintaining a web site with Office Live, so you'll be able to use it as a reference guide after you master the basics.

System Requirements

To build and maintain a web site with Office Live, you'll need the following:

- A subscription to any version of Office Live

- A computer running Windows 2000, Windows XP, Windows Server 2003, or Windows Vista

- Internet Explorer 6.0 (with the latest service packs) or later

- Internet access, preferably via a broadband service

- Super VGA (800 × 600) or higher-resolution display

Although you can *view* a web site built with Office Live on any computer using any browser, a computer running one of the versions of Windows and one of the versions of Internet Explorer previously mentioned is *required* to *build* a web site. Translation: Office Live isn't compatible with Apple Macintosh or Linux-based computers.

Companion Sites

Office Live is quite a feature-rich package. I've only covered its site-building features in this book. If you want to learn to use the e-mail service that comes with your account, download and use Windows Live Mail as your e-mail client, download and install the free accounting program Microsoft Office Accounting Express 2007, or explore one of Office Live's more advanced features, please visit this book's companion site at http://apress.com/book/bookDisplay.html?bID=10331.

In addition to the bonus companion content, you'll also find articles about Office Live, a forum for your Office Live–related questions, and tips, tricks, and hacks for tweaking your web site at www.acxede.net/books.

Contacting the Author

If you have questions or comments about this book or the content on its companion sites, please send them via e-mail to bookcomments@acxede.net.

What's Office Live, Anyway?

CHAPTER 1

■ ■ ■

Introducing Office Live

The World Wide Web was invented for sharing research papers among particle physicists. Scientists and nerds were really excited. The rest of us yawned. After all, what can you possibly do with an invention that encourages you to read incomprehensible reports filled with Greek letters?

Just about everything, it turns out.

The Web is perhaps the most versatile invention since the wheel. Geeks, big corporations, small businesses, institutions, governments, presidential candidates, artists, poets, astronauts, conmen, pornographers, and terrorists—they all have web sites these days. Even my elementary-school-going children have inquired about the possibility of having their own web sites in exchange for good behavior.

Just a few years ago, building web sites was like brain surgery—mere mortals couldn't do it themselves. You had to hire geeks with goatees and long hair to get a web site up and running. These people usually wore Coke-bottle glasses and spoke only in acronyms. Not only did you have to pay them a king's ransom, but you also had to pick up the tab for their pizza and Coke, which often made their pay look like a real bargain.

Not anymore.

Now anyone can build his or her own web site, thanks to sophisticated yet easy-to-use site-building tools. A recent addition to such tools is Microsoft Office Live, the subject of this book.

In this chapter, I'll give you an overview of Office Live. I'll explain how Office Live spares you pain and suffering by performing a good deal of work behind the scenes. I'll go on to compare its three editions and discuss the features and strengths of each. Finally, I'll help you choose the edition that's right for building your web site.

But you can't really appreciate what Office Live does for you unless you know how you would build and publish web sites with your bare hands. So that's where I'll begin.

Building Web Sites with Your Bare Hands

To build and publish a web site, you need to do a lot more than simply create web pages. The process consists of six steps:

1. Register a domain name.

2. Build web pages.

3. Find space for your site on the Web.

4. Set up e-mail accounts.

5. Publish your site.

6. Point your domain name to your web server.

Registering a Domain Name

A *domain name* is really the address of your site on the Web. If you want people to type `http://www.yourdomain.com` in their browsers, then `www.yourdomain.com` is your domain name. Actually, that's not the whole truth, but it's good enough of a definition for now. I'll revisit domain names in Chapter 2.

Only one person or organization can own a particular domain name. The only way to enforce this rule is to put someone in charge of managing domain names. The organizations that manage domain names are called *domain registrars*, or *registrars*, for short.

Registrars maintain records about a domain and charge an annual fee for the service. Domain records contain information such as the person or the organization who owns the domain, the contact information of the person who is responsible for the domain, information about the computers in the domain, and ways to find those computers on the Internet.

Typically, you open an account at a registrar's web site. Then you choose a domain name that hasn't been snapped up by someone else yet. After supplying some personal information and a credit-card number, the domain name is officially yours.

After you publish your web site, you must come back to your registrar's web site to point the domain name to your web site.

Building Web Pages

The first step in building web pages is to decide what goes on them. Web pages typically contain some text and a few images. The text on your web pages is called *copy*. You have to write the copy, find suitable images to go with it, and transform this content into formatted web pages.

Web pages have their own language called *Hypertext Markup Language* (*HTML*). HTML text looks more or less like English text typed by a typist of questionable skill—English words are interspersed with angular brackets, colons, exclamation marks, and other keyboard characters. It's not exceptionally hard to learn. If you master HTML, you will have complete control over the look and feel of your web pages, which is why professional designers like to hand-code all their pages in a text editor.

If you don't want to abandon your present career in favor of web design, you would do well to buy a site-design tool such as Microsoft Expression Web or Adobe GoLive. Designing sites with tools such as these is a lot easier than going the Notepad route.

However, these tools usually have a learning curve. If you think you can design a complete web site in one Saturday afternoon with these tools while watching TV with your kids, you're in for a rude awakening.

Still, building a web site with these tools is not impossible. If you persist with them, you will eventually have a web site, even if it does nothing more than sit on your computer's hard disk.

Finding Space on the Web

A site that sits on your C: drive may be a source of pride and joy for *you,* but it's of little use to others if they can't view it. To make the site available to everyone, you have to move it to the hard drive of a specialized computer on the Web. These computers are called *web servers.*

Unless you have plenty of money and an overpowering desire to install and maintain web servers, the job is best left to professionals. People who maintain web servers for a living are called *hosting service providers (HSPs).*

SPEAKING THE LANGUAGE

Web Hosting

- **Domain name**: The name your web site is known by. My web site is `www.acxede.net`. For all practical purposes, `acxede.net` is my domain name. I'll revisit domain names in greater detail in Chapter 2.

- **Domain-name registration**: The process of reserving a domain name. Once you register a domain name, nobody else can get it.

- **Domain registrars**: Authorized organizations that reserve domain names on your behalf and manage the necessary records for an annual fee.

- **Server**: A computer that fulfills requests for data or service. For example, a file server serves files and documents, and a database server answers queries about the data stored on it. Technically speaking, a computer can't fulfill requests; a software program running on it does. The software program is also called a server.

- **Web server**: A computer dedicated to serving web pages. As stated previously, a computer can't serve web pages by itself; it needs a special software program to do so. The software program is also called a web server.

- **Web storage space**: The amount of disk space available to you on your web server for storing your pages, pictures, and other documents.

- **Bandwidth**: The total amount of data that can be sent to and from your web server in a given period—usually a month. Whenever someone requests a web page, the web server sends back the HTML page along with the images and other types of information associated with it. These transfers consume bandwidth.

- **Internet service provider (ISP)**: The company that connects your computer to the Internet. If you have a DSL connection, your phone company is usually your ISP. If you have a cable connection, your cable company is your ISP.

- **Hosting service provider (HSP)**: The company that connects your web server (and, therefore, your web site) to the Internet. In a way, an HSP is also an ISP. Calling it an HSP helps you distinguish between the Internet connection to your computer and the Internet connection to your web server.

- **Mail server**: A computer dedicated to processing e-mail for a domain. The computer runs a software application that is also called a mail server.

- **E-mail account**: A unique e-mail address in a domain. For example, info@acxede.net and webmaster@acxede.net are both e-mail accounts.

- **Mail forwarding**: Automatically redirecting e-mail from one e-mail address to another e-mail address. Many small businesses set up multiple mailboxes, such as sales@somedomain.com and support@somedomain.com, and then forward all mail to one e-mail address, such as john@somedomain.com. It helps them appear larger than they really are.

- **Hosting plan**: A package of services that usually includes a web server, domain-name management tools, a mail server, a certain number of e-mail accounts, a fixed amount of bandwidth, some storage space, and an online application to manage the account. HSPs charge a monthly fee for the package.

HSPs offer *hosting plans*, which are preconfigured bundles of their services. A typical hosting plan includes the following:

- An allotted amount of space on the web server's hard disk

- A fixed amount of bandwidth, which is the amount of data that can flow to and from your web site

- A certain number of mailboxes with e-mail addresses that can be customized, such as you@yourdomain.com

- An assortment of features, typically known by three- and four-letter acronyms such as ASP, PHP, ODBC, and SQL, which determine what you can do with your web server

- A number of grand-sounding but meaningless features, such as 99.99998% up-time, to fluff up the plan

Hosting plans have more options to choose from than cell-phone plans. To make an informed choice, you need the ability to decide whether 2 GB of extra bandwidth and three fewer e-mail addresses will compensate for 1 GB of extra disk space and an additional $1.95 a month. Even geeks can't make such decisions easily. In fact, eeny, meeny, miny, moe might be the best way to choose a hosting plan.

Setting Up E-mail Accounts

Strictly speaking, setting up e-mail accounts has nothing to do with your web site. But you will invariably have links on your web pages for visitors to contact you via e-mail. For these links to work, you must have working e-mail accounts. And you might as well set them up before your web site goes live.

Your HSP usually includes a mail server in your hosting plan and gives you an administrator's account on it. You have to sign in to that account on the HSP's web site to create e-mail accounts in your domain and set up rules for processing your e-mail.

Publishing Your Site

Once you find a home for your site on the Web, you have to transfer the site from your C: drive to the web server using a program called an *FTP client*. Most operating systems, including Windows, have FTP clients built right in. Browsers can act as FTP clients too. However, these free options are usually difficult to use. Almost always, you are better off buying a commercial FTP client instead. Your HSP gives you an FTP account, which you can use to connect to your web server from your FTP client.

FTP clients are whiners. From time to time, they come up with novel excuses for not transferring your files as instructed. But it's not really their fault. File transfer across the Internet is not always reliable, especially if your files are really large. Fortunately, if you retry failed transfers, they usually succeed.

Pointing Your Domain Name to Your Web Site

Even though you have registered a domain name, built your web pages, and copied them to your web server, you're still not done. People who type www.yourdomain.com in their browsers still can't reach your web site. For that to happen, you must set up a pointer in your domain registration records that establishes a relationship between your domain name and your web server.

Your HSP will supply you with a couple of numbers that seem to have too many decimal points. These strange numbers are called *IP addresses*. You must sign in to your account with your domain registrar and enter these IP addresses in your domain records. These entries link your domain name to your web server and your mail server. They are called *name server* entries.

Now you're done.

But don't be in a hurry to type your domain name in your browser. You have to pace up and down, like an expectant father, for about 24 hours before the link actually begins to work. This whole process is not always smooth. Many things can go wrong. When they do, you usually get error messages that, like the sections of the penal code, are expressed only in numbers, such as 403.9, 404, and 500.13. Troubleshooting these errors is often quite tedious, which is why the pizza-eating, Coke-guzzling guys charge an arm and a leg to fix them.

Thankfully, There's an Easier Way

As you can see, building web sites with your bare hands is quite a convoluted process in which you must perform the following tasks:

- Sign up for two new accounts—one with your registrar and one with your HSP.

- Manage four sets of user IDs and passwords—one for your registrar's web site, one for your HSP's web site, one for your FTP account, and one for your mail-server administration account.

- Install and learn two software programs—your web site design tool and your FTP client.

- Log in to these accounts several times and in the correct sequence to tweak settings.

Why can't there be a service that does all this for you with a single registration? Ideally, such a service would

- Register a domain name for you

- Open a hosting account

- Set up a mail server

- Include a site design tool

- Feature an FTP client, or even better, allow you to build your web site directly on your web server

- Set up domain pointers for your web site in your domain records

- Provide tools for managing your web site after you build it

As a matter of fact, there is such a service—Microsoft Office Live.

What Is Office Live?

The name *Microsoft Office Live* has a familiar ring to it. It sounds like an edition of the Microsoft Office of Word, Excel, and PowerPoint fame. It's not.

Let me repeat that.

Office Live has absolutely nothing to do with Microsoft Office. It's actually a bundle of services for taking your small business online.

■**Note** The marketing folks at Microsoft often come up with confusing names for their products. Then they add to the confusion by changing the already confusing names. And they repeat this process several times.

My teacher at Harvard Extension School, David S. Platt, came up with a term for this phenomenon— MIcrosoft Nomenclature Foul Up (MINFU). He even tried to get it added to Oxford English Dictionary, but the good folks at OED declined politely, citing lack of common usage.

Office Live comes in three flavors: Office Live Basics, Office Live Essentials, and Office Live Premium, which happen to be marketing terms for Free Web Site, Cheap Web Site, and Not-So-Cheap Web Site, respectively.

Office Live Basics

As its name suggests (for once, thank goodness!), Office Live Basics is the entry-level edition of Office Live. It is a web-presence package complete with domain-name registration, web-site hosting, simple site-building tools, domain-branded e-mail accounts, and assorted bells and whistles. And it is free.

You read that right. *Free.* No strings attached.

Whenever the provider of an online service touts a free offering, the first question that should come to mind is "Who is paying for it?" At the top of the list of suspects are, of course, advertisers. And Office Live is indeed supported by revenue from advertisements. The advertisements, however, do not appear on the public face of a web site built with Office Live, as you can see in Figure 1-1.

Figure 1-1. *Look, Ma! No ads! Advertisements don't appear on the public face of Office Live sites.*

Only the site's administrative interface (see Figure 1-2) and e-mail pages carry advertisements. Owners and administrators are the only people who can see these pages; visitors to the site can't.

■Note There was a time when you had to pay $25 to get an e-mail address. But now, thanks to the change in the revenue model, e-mail is largely free. I believe that reliable, good-quality hosting will go the same route. Someone had to take the first step in that direction, and Microsoft has taken it with Office Live.

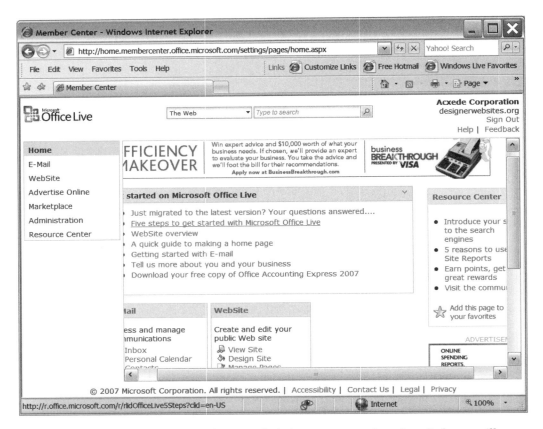

Figure 1-2. *Advertisements appear only in a web site's management interface. Only you will see them.*

SPEAKING THE LANGUAGE

Web Sites and Web Applications

- **Public web site**: What *web site* generally means. Public web sites are visible to anyone on the Web.

- **Intranet**: A web site for the use of people within an organization. It houses information that you would not normally share with outsiders. Retirement-plan and health-insurance documents, internal memos, announcements, and company-wide telephone directories are examples of information you can expect to find on intranets.

- **Extranet**: A web site for sharing information with clients, partners, associates, and other stakeholders outside the organization, but not with the general public. An extranet site could deliver custom monthly reports to clients and make billing information available to them online. This kind of information is obviously private, and it is usually protected by passwords.

- **Application server**: A software program that processes business rules and provides business logic to other software programs. Application servers can be run on web server computers to generate web pages on the fly. Blogs and forums are examples of web-based applications that use application servers. In fact, Office Live itself is an application that runs on an application server called ASP.NET.

- **Microsoft Office SharePoint Server**: Microsoft's platform for building intranets and extranets. SharePoint Server is quite a sophisticated application, and it requires an elaborate setup, so it is mostly used by larger organizations. Office Live's "applications" are built with SharePoint technology. Microsoft is attempting to bring SharePoint technology within the grasp of smaller organizations with Office Live Essentials and Office Live Premium.

- **Site statistics or traffic reports**: A detailed account of visits and visitors to your site. Site statistics can tell you a lot about how visitors use your site. Based on the reports, you can make an educated guess about what visitors like on your site and what turns them away. You can use such information to improve your site. Office Live has site statistics built in. They are called Site Reports.

For a free package, Office Live includes quite a few features:

- Registration and annual renewal of one domain name

- Twenty-five domain-branded e-mail accounts (i.e., you@yourdomain.com), 2 GB of storage space per account, antivirus software, and a configurable spam filter

- 500 MB of disk storage space

- 10 GB bandwidth

- Web Designer, a built-in site-design and web-page-creation tool

- Detailed web site traffic reports

- adManager, a tool for purchasing and managing keywords for Windows Live Search

- Free technical support by e-mail

To build a web site with Office Live Basics, you must use Web Designer; you can't use any other tool. Web Designer is geared toward novice users and is therefore very easy to use. Figure 1-3 shows what Web Designer looks like. I'll walk you through it in Chapters 9 and 10.

If you don't know HTML or don't want to bother learning it, Office Live Basics is perfect for you. However, the ease of use comes at the cost of flexibility. If you know HTML, you won't be able to put your skills to use by building your site with a tool such as Microsoft Expression Web or Adobe GoLive. And if you already have a web site, you might have to scrap it and build a new one from scratch with Office Live's Web Designer.

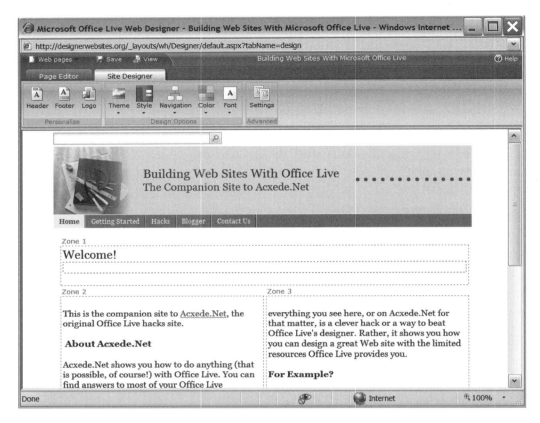

Figure 1-3. *You can build web pages with Office Live's Web Designer even if you don't know HTML.*

Note Only Office Live Basics subscribers are limited to using Web Designer. If you're an Office Live Essentials or an Office Live Premium subscriber, you can use a design tool of your choice instead. However, you can only use existing sites from other hosting providers if they are plain HTML sites. If your site is built with a dynamic page-generation technology such as Active Server Pages (ASP) or PHP Hypertext Preprocessor (PHP), you won't be able to reuse your pages; you will have to start over.

The domain-branded e-mail accounts that come with Office Live Basics are glorified Hotmail accounts, although they have the look and feel of the new Windows Live Hotmail. They are web-mail accounts. You can't use e-mail clients such as Microsoft Outlook or Microsoft Outlook Express with them, nor can you forward mail automatically to another e-mail address—something that people who have multiple e-mail addresses like to do.

■**Note** *Windows Live Hotmail* is yet another MINFU. A few years ago, Microsoft rechristened Hotmail to MSN Mail, but people still called it Hotmail. When Microsoft unveiled the *Live* platform, MSN Mail's name was changed to *Windows Live Mail*. This confused people to no end. Predictably, the service was re-rechristened to Windows Live Hotmail.

Office Live lists Microsoft Office Accounting Express 2007 as a feature of Office Live subscriptions. It is a surprisingly complete accounting package. But just about anyone can download it free of charge, even without an Office Live subscription. The same is true for adManager, a tool for creating your own keyword-based ads for Live Search, Microsoft's new search engine.

Subscribers get free technical support for any aspect of their Office Live Basics account, but only via e-mail. While it can't beat phone support, it is not a bad deal for a free service. And the folks there actually reply to your questions—at the time of this writing, at least. You usually get a reply within just a couple of hours.

Office Live Basics is an appropriate package for individuals and small businesses in need of simple web sites with a few pages and domain-branded e-mail addresses. If you don't have a web site, if you're unhappy with your current web site, or if you're still making do with Hotmail addresses, take a look at Office Live Basics. It is a rare opportunity to get something for nothing.

Office Live Essentials

Office Live Essentials is Office Live Basics' big brother. But it is not free. A subscription to Office Live Essentials sets you back $19.95 per month. In exchange, you get everything you get with an Office Live Basics subscription, along with several additional features and a few feature upgrades.

Office Live Essentials' features include the following:

- Registration and annual renewal of one domain name

- Fifty domain-branded e-mail accounts (such as you@yourdomain.com), 2 GB of storage space per account, antivirus software, and a configurable spam filter

- 1 GB of disk storage space

- 15 GB bandwidth

- Web Designer, a built-in site-design and web-page-creation tool, as well as the ability to use a tool of your choice, such as Microsoft Expression Web or, if you're feeling especially masochistic, Notepad

- Detailed web-site traffic reports

- Office Live Business Contact Manager, a rudimentary customer relationship management (CRM) package

- Microsoft SharePoint-based workspaces for ten users with 500 MB of total storage space for the workspaces

- adManager, a tool for purchasing and managing keywords for Windows Live Search

- Toll-free phone support

FAQ

Can I Switch Between Web Designer and a Tool of My Choice?

Yes and no. If you're an Office Live Essentials or an Office Live Premium subscriber, you can switch between design tools, but the site you build with Web Designer won't be compatible with other tools. In other words, if you switch tools, you must abandon your current site and start building it again with the new tool.

However, all bets are off if you're an Office Live Basics subscriber—Web Designer is your only option.

Office Live Essentials doesn't provide precanned applications, such as shopping carts and community builders; you'll have to write your own code for them, if you can, using a scripting language. This is harder to do than you might think, because Office Live doesn't permit you to place any server-side code in your pages.

FAQ

What's Server-Side Code?

A typical application running on your desktop has one or more windows, or *screens*, as some people like to call them. Because the application runs entirely on your computer, it knows how to pass information from one window to the next. It also knows how to store, or *cache*, the information for reference further down the road. Programmers refer to this as *maintaining state*. Desktop applications, therefore, are often called *stateful* applications.

With web applications, however, the story is entirely different. Each web page you see in your browser is the result of an independent request to the web server. One web page doesn't know anything about the next. Web pages in their simplest form don't maintain state. As a result, they are *stateless*.

Stateless applications can only solve the simplest of problems. To build advanced features into your web applications, you would somehow need to make them stateful. In other words, you would need some kind of mechanism that would help you store information between page requests.

Such a mechanism does exist. It's called a *session*. When you point your browser at a stateful web application, it toils with your browser to simulate an environment that appears stateful to you. However, to simulate a stateful environment, the web server must be able to execute programming code. Such code is called *server-side code*. Most web applications that you take for granted—online stores, chat rooms, blogs, and bulletin boards, to name a few—need server-side code.

Server-side code basically gets processed on the server, and then the results of that processing are sent to your web browser (the client) to be displayed, whereas client-side code is sent from the server to the client unprocessed, and then processed and displayed all on the client. The advantage with server-side code is that pages can be made a lot more dynamic (i.e., things can be updated depending on different conditions, and different information can be shown) than with client-side code alone.

The main disadvantage of server-side code is complexity. Writing server-side code requires extensive training in computer programming. It is not a skill set Office Live subscribers are likely to possess. Trying to write server-side code without adequate training can produce disastrous results. Therefore, Office Live doesn't allow server-side code.

Office Live Essentials' subscription includes domain-branded e-mail addresses for 50 users—an upgrade over the 25 for Basics. And you may use Microsoft Outlook as your e-mail client. But Essentials' most significant improvement over Basics is *Office Live Business Contact Manager*, a rudimentary CRM application. Business Contact Manager is a derivative of the *Business Contact Manager* application in the Small Business edition of Microsoft Office. You can use it to synchronize mail and customer information with Microsoft Outlook. If you decide on Outlook as your e-mail client, then you'll get the added advantage of being able to manage multiple e-mail accounts from one place.

To justify the $19.95 monthly tab, Office Live Essentials includes Microsoft SharePoint-based *workspaces* for ten users. Workspaces are configurable storage locations for storing and sharing information. You can think of workspaces as temporary web sites that you can create on the fly. You can then grant access to your workspaces to specific people. In effect, Office Live Essentials workspaces enable you to create simple intranet.

Office Live Essentials offers better technical support too. In addition to e-mail-based support, you can call a toll-free number to get your questions answered right away.

Office Live Premium

Office Live Premium is the proverbial Cadillac of the Office Live lineup. Its subscription lightens your wallet (or rather loads up your credit card, to be precise) by $39.95 every month. In exchange, you get everything you get with an Office Live Essentials subscription, along with even more additional features and feature upgrades.

A subscription to Office Live Premium includes the following:

- Registration and annual renewal of one domain name

- Fifty domain-branded e-mail accounts (such as you@yourdomain.com), 2 GB of storage space per account, antivirus software, and a configurable spam filter

- 2 GB of disk storage space

- 20 GB bandwidth

- Web Designer, a built-in site-design and web-page-creation tool, as well as the ability to use a tool of your choice instead, such as Adobe GoLive, Microsoft FrontPage, Microsoft Expression Web, or Notepad

- Detailed web site reports

- Office Live Business Contact Manager, a rudimentary CRM package

- Online "applications" for managing employee, customer, and project data

- Microsoft SharePoint-based workspaces for 20 users and 1 GB of total storage space for the workspaces

- adManager, a tool for purchasing and managing keywords for Windows Live Search

- Toll-free phone support

Office Live Premium ramps up storage space and the number of accounts as compared to Office Live Essentials, but the crown jewel is its collaborative functionality—*applications* and *sites*.

Like the workspaces in Office Live Essentials, Office Live Premium's applications and sites have their roots in Microsoft's SharePoint technology. Applications are views of custom data lists. They are not programs, as the word *application* commonly implies. So you can't use these applications to file your taxes or to keep your accounts. The Expense application in Office Live Premium, for example, is just a list of your expenses with a custom view. You can't transfer the expenses to Intuit QuickBooks, like a real application could do. Microsoft has precanned approximately 30 such applications for various purposes, such as listing employees, managing contacts, tracking company assets, and monitoring the progress of a project.

A site, in Office Live Premium's lingo, is a container to group and hold applications. You can create a Customer site, for example, by grouping customer lists and customer projects together. You can then give selective access to the site to your colleagues or even to customers. All those who have access to the site can share the data and documents on the site, which is a much better alternative than e-mailing documents and notes back and forth.

You can use sites creatively. If you have a meeting with a client, you can create a "Meeting Workspace" site that has the meeting agenda, related documents, and reference materials. Or you can create a "Team Site" to exchange documents and information with members of your team. You can, in effect, create intranets and extranets at will.

However, Office Live Premium is appropriate only for those businesses that have the need for people to share a lot of information and documents in collaborative projects. If you're a one-man plumbing service, you may not need collaborative features. But if you're tired of e-mailing documents back and forth, sending copies of the same information to lots of different people, figuring out which of the 200 copies of the same document is the latest, or repeatedly collating information that you must extract from communications from the same set of people, Office Live Premium will make perfect sense to you.

You can quickly compare the features of Office Live's three versions by scanning Table 1-1.

Table 1-1. *Feature Summary of Microsoft Office Live Editions*

Feature	Office Live Basics	Office Live Essentials	Office Live Premium
Public Web Site			
Domain-name registration	Included	Included	Included
Storage space	500 MB	1 GB	2 GB
Ability to buy additional storage space	Yes	Yes	Yes
Built-in Web Designer tool	Included	Included	Included
Ability to customize web sites with other tools	No	Yes	Yes
E-mail and Communication			
Custom-domain mailboxes	25	50	50
Windows Mobile/Smartphone access	Yes	Yes	Yes
Web mail access	Yes	Yes	Yes
Outlook synchronization and integration	No	Yes	Yes
Windows Live Messenger	Included	Included	Included
Support			
Free support via e-mail	Yes	Yes	Yes
Free support via toll-free phone number	No	Yes	Yes
E-commerce			
Ability to advertise online with adManager	Yes	Yes	Yes
Ability to sell on eBay with Office Accounting Express 2007	Yes	Yes	Yes
SharePoint-Based Business Applications			
Workspaces	Not included	Included	Included
Business Contact Manager	Not included	Included	Included
Document Manager	Not included	Not included	Included
Project Manager	Not included	Not included	Included
Time Manager	Not included	Not included	Included
Company Administration	Not included	Not included	Included
Ability to install custom/third-party applications	No	No	Yes
Workspaces/application storage space		500 MB	1 GB
Ability to buy additional space	No	Yes	Yes
Number of workspace user accounts		10	20
Ability to buy additional user accounts	No	Yes	Yes
Fees and Charges (*)			
Monthly service charge	None	$19.95	$39.95
Additional domain names (per year)	$8.95	$8.95	$8.95
Additional bandwidth (24 GB/per month)	$1.95	$1.95	$1.95
Additional storage space (500 MB/per month)	$4.95	$4.95	$4.95

* The charges, of course, are subject to change.

FAQ

What Happened to Office Live Collaboration Beta?

During Office Live's beta days, it also had three editions: Office Live Basics Beta, Office Live Essentials Beta, and Office Live Collaboration Beta. But they were somewhat different from their present-day counterparts.

Office Live Basics Beta was the entry-level package even then. Its features were more or less comparable to those of Office Live Basics. Office Live Essentials Beta, on the other hand, had more in common with the present-day Office Live Premium; it was then the high-end edition. Office Live Collaboration Beta was the odd one. It did not include domain registration or a public web site. It only had the SharePoint-based collaborative features of Office Live Essentials Beta.

At some point, Microsoft decided that Office Live Collaboration didn't make sense. Rightly so, if you ask me. But now Microsoft has a problem on its hands—what to do with the Office Live Collaboration Beta accounts. Microsoft chose to leave those accounts in the beta program. Their future is somewhat unclear.

If you're one of the Office Live Collaboration Beta subscribers, you have my sympathies.

What Office Live Is Not

Although Office Live packs plenty of wallop, even in its free version, it's not a suitable platform for some types of web sites. You can't build the following types of web sites with it:

- Online storefronts (Yes, you can sell on eBay using Microsoft Office Accounting Express 2007, but that's not the same thing as selling on your own web site.)

- Blogs

- Communities

- Bulletin boards

- Streaming audio and video

- Complex web sites that require server-side code

It's important to understand that you don't get these features even if you subscribe to Office Live's most expensive edition, Office Live Premium. The Office Live platform is just not appropriate for such applications.

However, these deficiencies shouldn't deter you from considering Office Live for your web site. Many small businesses only need calling-card web sites—that is, sites that provide information about their businesses, products, and services. Office Live is the perfect package for such sites.

Before you dismiss Office Live, ask yourself whether your site really needs a blog or a community. A blog with a daily entry during its first week of existence—but nothing after that—is very common on the Web. Do your clients really need to know your opinions? Would they *want* to read your opinions? Would these features really add value to your web site? A blog for the sake of simply having a blog makes little sense.

A little soul-searching may lead you to conclude that these features are not the must-haves you once thought them to be. Office Live may be the right platform for you after all.

Summary

Office Live is Microsoft's new web-presence platform for individuals and small businesses. It is a complete package that you can manage with a single account. You can build a simple but attractive web site with Office Live without spending a penny. Or you can use it to build sophisticated, collaborative online environments for a low monthly fee.

In this chapter, I gave you an overview of Office Live's features. Here are the important points that you should remember:

- Building a simple web site is not impossibly hard, but you need a good understanding of how the Web works, familiarity with several site-building tools, and a few online accounts to manage it all.

- Office Live attempts to simplify your life by providing everything you need to build a web site under a single account.

- Office Live comes in three versions—Basics, Essentials, and Premium. Basics is the free version and is appropriate for simple web sites. Essentials and Premium require a monthly subscription. These versions are appropriate for those who need collaborative intranets or extranets in addition to a simple web site.

- All editions of Office Live include a built-in design tool called Web Designer. It's great for building simple but attractive web sites without spending a penny.

- Office Live Essentials and Office Live Premium include tools for collaborating online with Microsoft's SharePoint technology, but they both require a monthly subscription.

- Office Live is not the right platform for building advanced web applications, such as online stores and communities, which require server-side programming. But if your requirements fall within the realm of its capabilities, Office Live is an irresistible deal.

In the next chapter, I'll go through the requirements for opening a new Office Live account and help you prepare to sign up for one.

CHAPTER 2

■ ■ ■

Getting Ready to Sign Up

Whenever you sign up for a new account online, you're expected to provide personal information such as your name, your mailing address, and your e-mail address. Office Live wants all this information from you too. But that's not all. Office Live requires you to be ready with three critical bits of information when you sign up for an account:

- A domain name for your web site

- A Windows Live ID for signing into your Office Live account

- A credit card

You can't sign up for Office Live unless you have all three. In this chapter, I'll give you a brief idea about why each of them is required.

Understanding Domain Names

Just as every telephone connection has a unique telephone number, every computer on the Internet has a unique Internet Protocol (IP) address. Your web server has an IP address too. Whenever someone wants to request a web page from your web server, that person's computer has to "call" your web server at its IP address.

As I mentioned in Chapter 1, an IP address looks like a large number with too many decimal points—three, to be precise. 216.246.42.123 is my web server's IP address, for instance. I could tell people to go visit my web site at 216.246.42.123, if I really, truly wanted to, but I don't, because people aren't good at memorizing long numbers. They would rather memorize names. So I tell them that my web site is located at www.acxede.net instead.

The Need for Domain Names

My web server's full name is www.acxede.net. Actually, its name is just www, but since a few million other people also have web servers named www, there is no way to distinguish my web server from, say, Microsoft's web server, which is also named www. Because a computer's name is an alternative to its IP address, it must be unique too.

That's where the acxede.net part comes in. It's called a *domain name*. Think of it as my web server's family name. Once I suffix my web server's name, www, with my domain name, acxede.net, it becomes unique across the Internet. Now my web server is www.acxede.net, and Microsoft's web server is www.microsoft.com. Thus, a domain name enables us to identify every computer on the Internet by a unique name.

FAQ

Do All Web Addresses Start with www?

No. www is simply the name of the server a web site sits on. In the Web's early days, everyone called their web servers www by convention, and it became the de facto standard. I could have named my web server *Joe* if I wanted to. My site's web address would then have been joe.acxede.net.

However, many people think that all web addresses have the prefix www. So if I printed the web address joe.acxede.net on my business cards, many would still type it in their browser's address bar as www.joe.acxede.net. Since I don't have a web site on a server named www.joe, they would get a "Page not found" error.

Naming web servers is one endeavor where it pays to conform.

Domain Names and Registrars

The name www.acxede.net will remain unique so long as nobody else uses the domain name acxede.net. Unfortunately, you can't leave domain names to an honor system—crooks would love to own a web server named www.citibank.com or www.bankofamerica.com. Therefore, some sort of policing is necessary to maintain law and order in cyberspace.

The cyber-police who ensure that only one person or organization gets any given domain name are called *domain registrars*, or *registrars* for short. When I decided to register the acxede.net domain name, I contacted a registrar that I found on the Web. A representative asked me for some personal information and my credit-card number and officially gave the ownership of the acxede.net domain to me. For a charge that goes on my credit card every year, the registrar will make sure that nobody else is able to steal my domain name.

Parts of a Domain Name

Acxede.net has two parts separated by a dot: acxede and net. Acxede is called the *domain*, and net is called the *top-level domain* (*TLD*). The most common TLDs are com, net, and org. Although these TLDs are used mostly in the United States, they are considered to be generic TLDs because in theory, they can be used anywhere in the world.

However, other countries have adopted two-letter country-code TLDs instead. For example, the TLD used in Germany is *de*, and the one used in India is *in*. If I were to register my domain acxede in India, it would be called acxede.in.

■**Note** Even the United States has a country-code TLD, us. However, most Americans prefer com or net TLDs.

Most computers you come across will have three-part names, such as www.acxede.net. However, a three-part name is not mandatory. You can have any number of parts separated by dots. Once you acquire a domain name, you can subdivide it into as many divisions as you want.

If this book makes me rich beyond belief, I may decide to divide my company into eastern and western divisions, and have a separate web site for each. I can then create *subdomains* called east.acxede.net and west.acxede.net and call web servers in those subdomains www.east.acxede.net and www.west.acxede.net, respectively.

In the United Kingdom, authorities have adopted such a system. The TLD, uk, is divided into several subdomains. For example, the subdomain for commercial enterprises is co.uk, and that for educational institutions is ac.uk. If I were to register my domain in the United Kingdom, I would register it as acxede.co.uk, and my web server would be www.acxede.co.uk.

Translating Domain Names to IP Addresses

While people prefer names to numbers, the reverse is true for computers. People-friendly names, such as www.acxede.net, which you type into your browser, must be translated into computer-friendly addresses, such as 216.246.42.123, which web servers understand.

With the help of specialized software called the Domain Name System (DNS), computer names are automatically translated on the Internet into their IP addresses. Whenever you type www.acxede.net into your browser, DNS software running on your computer looks up the IP address of the computer whose name is www.acxede.net and establishes a connection to it using its IP address.

The DNS software on your computer doesn't store all possible computer names and their IP addresses locally. This cross-reference is, in fact, distributed across the Internet. Each domain has a special server called a *domain name server* that stores the names of all computers and their IP addresses in that domain.

Large organizations that maintain their own Internet infrastructure have their own domain name servers. If you host your domain with a hosting service provider, the HSP will maintain the domain name server on your behalf.

FAQ

How Does a Web Page Appear in My Browser When I Enter Its Address?

Let's say you type http://www.acxede.net/default.aspx into your browser. This string is the web address of the page default.aspx, which resides on a web server named www.acxede.net.

Some people refer to a web address as a URL, which stands for Uniform Resource Locator. No matter what you call it, it still points to the location of default.aspx on the Web. Your browser splits this string into three parts: the protocol, the hostname, and the resource name.

The first part, http://, is called the *protocol*. You can think of a protocol as a method of delivery. Just as an item you buy online can be shipped to you via United States Postal Service (USPS), FedEx, or some other shipping method, a file you request from a server on the Internet can be sent to you via one of the available protocols. The World Wide Web uses the *http* protocol.

The last part, default.aspx, is called the *resource name*. It is the name of a resource, such as a web page, a file, or an image, that resides on the web server.

The part in the middle, www.acxede.com, is the *hostname* or the name of the web server on which the resource resides.

Your computer must open a connection to the computer www.acxede.net in order to download the web page. To open the connection, your computer must know www.acxede.net's IP address. Let's say it doesn't know the IP address. It now has to ask a domain name server for help.

The domain name server closest to your computer belongs to your ISP, which connects your computer to the Internet. Your computer establishes a connection to it. If computers could talk, here's how their conversation would go:

Your Computer: Hi! Do you know www.acxede.net's IP address?

Your ISP's name server: Actually, I don't, but I can ask the name server of the .net TLD. I know its IP address. Hold on for a moment.

Your ISP's name server then puts your computer on hold and establishes a connection with .net TLD's domain name server on the other line.

Your ISP's name server: Hi! Do you know www.acxede.net's IP address?

.net TLD's domain name server: I'm really busy right now. There are too many domains in .net TLD, and I'm having a tough time keeping track of everyone's IP address. But here's the IP address of acxede.net's domain name server: 66.55.44.22. You can ask him.

Your ISP's name server: Thanks!

Your ISP's name server then disconnects from .net TLD's name server and establishes a connection with acxede.net's domain server using the IP address it just received.

Your ISP's name server: Hi! Do you know www.acxede.net's IP address?

Acxede.net's name server: Of course I do! It's one of our servers. Its IP address is 216.246.42.123.

Your ISP's name server: Okay, thanks!

It disconnects from acxede.net's domain name server and starts talking to your computer again.

Your ISP's name server: Okay, here it is: 216.246.42.123.

Your computer: Thanks!

Using the IP address it just received, your computer establishes a connection with www.acxede.net and requests the file default.aspx (the home page) from it via the http protocol. www.acxede.net obliges, and the page loads in your browser.

"Hey! Wait a minute!" you might say. "How did the ISP's name server know the IP address of .net TLD's name server?"

The answer is rather anticlimactic. IP addresses of TLD's name servers are built into the DNS. All domain name servers know them. But that still leaves one question unanswered: how does .net TLD's name server know the IP address of the acxede.net domain's name server?

The answer is: courtesy of acxede.net's domain registration records with its registrar. Every domain's registration records include the IP addresses of its name servers. These records are part of the DNS, and TLD's name servers can access them.

This is, of course, a simplified version of what goes on behind the scenes, but it captures the essence of the process.

Office Live and Your Domain

When you open a new Office Live account, you can choose how you want Office Live to work with your domain. You have two options:

- Register a new domain name through Office Live during sign-up.

- Register a domain name with another registrar and change the name servers in your domain records to Office Live's name servers—a process known as *domain redirection*.

Registering a New Domain Name Through Office Live

Office Live seeks to take the bite out of this whole business of registrars, hosting providers, and name servers. When you open a new account and opt to register a new domain, Office Live automatically registers your domain, establishes your hosting account, and sets the name servers in your domain registration records. Best of all, Microsoft foots the bill for the registration.

Office Live has its own hosting facilities and name servers, but Microsoft is not a registrar. So Office Live has teamed up with a registrar called Melbourne IT.

■**Note** Microsoft officially became an accredited domain name registrar on October 31, 2006. But just as James Bond doesn't go on a killing spree simply because he has a license to kill, Microsoft hasn't started registering domain names even though it is licensed to do so. Melbourne IT is still the registrar for all Office Live domain registrations, although that may change in the future.

Melbourne IT is the sole registrar for new domains registered with Office Live; you can't choose any other registrar. After registration, Office Live is in charge of your domain records. You must route changes to your domain records through Office Live's customer service.

FAQ
Who Really Owns My Domain Name—Office Live or Me?
You do. Although an Office Live account deprives you of the flexibility of making changes to your domain records, Microsoft compensates you for your sacrifice by paying your registration charges.
Still, you own the domain and if, for any reason, you wish to part ways with Office Live, you can certainly do so.

This scheme of things is quite restrictive for those who are accustomed to managing their own domain records. For the rest, it's wonderfully simple.

Choosing a Domain Name

Finding a name you like that is still up for grabs is more difficult than you might imagine. Rest assured that any name with three letters or less is already taken. So is almost any word in the dictionary. Office Live makes matters worse for you because it only hosts web sites with `.com`, `.net`, or `.org` extensions. This narrows your choices considerably.

■**Note** If you live in the United Kingdom, Japan, or the European Union, Office Live will let you register domain names with `.co.uk`, `.jp`, and `.eu` extensions, respectively.

After a cursory search for a domain name, you will quickly arrive at that famous conclusion: *all the good ones are taken!* Unfortunately, you can't proceed with opening your Office Live account without a domain name.

TIPS FROM THE TRENCHES

How to Pick a Good Domain Name

Finding a domain name that's catchy, memorable, and relevant to your business is not easy. Chances are you'll have to settle for a name that you aren't exactly nuts about. Here are a few tips on making the best of the situation:

- The name of your business is obviously the best domain name you can get. But more often than not, it won't be available. You can increase the odds in your favor by adding words before or after your business name. A few years ago, I wanted the name `websites.com`. It was already taken, but `designerwebsites.com` was available.

- If you're starting a new business, you may want to settle on a domain name before deciding on a name for your new venture.

- Include keywords in your domain name—for example, `designerwebsites.com` rather than `rahulsbusiness.com`. Someone who wants a web site designed isn't likely to search for *rahul's business*. Chances of the person searching for *web site designers* or something similar are much greater. Besides, search engines are more likely to place your web site higher in search results if your domain name contains keywords.

- Although easier said than done, look for a short domain name. Short names are easier to remember.

- Try to register a domain name with a `.com` extension. People remember it more easily than `.net` or `.org` extensions.

Several online tools are available to help you brainstorm for a domain name. The "Hands-On Lab" sidebar on the next page steps you through searching for a domain name with one such tool.

HANDS-ON LAB

Brainstorm for a Domain Name Online

A good place to look for domain names is www.domainsbot.com. To find a domain name using the tools at this web site, follow these steps:

1. Point your browser at www.domainsbot.com. You should see the web page shown in the following figure.

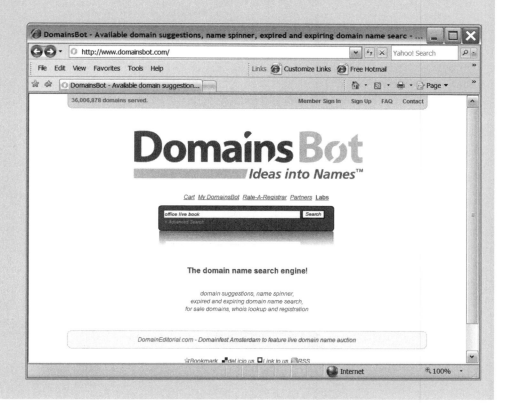

2. Enter a keyword or a phrase related to your web site's topic. You can enter the name of your business or a short phrase that describes your web site. In this example, I have entered the phrase *office live book*, because I want a companion site for this book. As you type the phrase, DomainsBot gets to work. A couple of seconds after you're done, you should see a pop-up box like the one shown in the following figure.

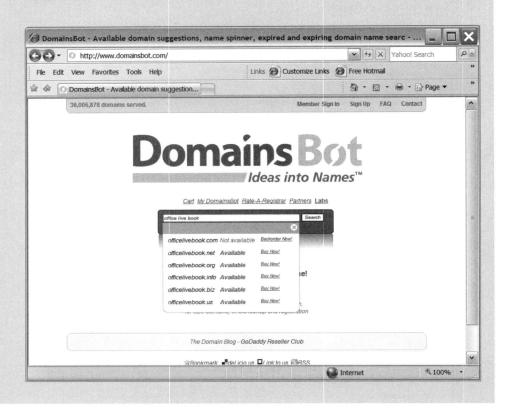

3. The pop-up box shows a list of available names based on the phrase you entered. If you don't like any of them, click the Search button. You should see a web page like the one in the following figure.

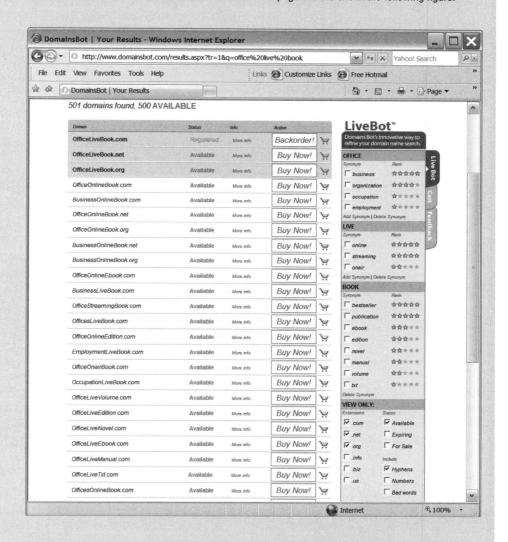

4. This page displays creative reiterations of the phrase you entered in the search box on the previous page. Check or uncheck boxes in the LiveBot panel to the right to expand or narrow down choices that DomainsBot presents to you.

DomainsBot can serve up better choices if you add synonyms to your keywords using the Add Synonym links in the LiveBot panel.

Finding the perfect domain name for your web site is usually a long process. Don't expect to get it done in a few minutes. In fact, you may spend a good bit of time muttering four-letter words under your breath (or questioning the pedigree of people who have snapped up domain names you would give your left hand for) before you find a domain name that's good—or, at least, good enough—for your purposes.

Domain Registration and Privacy

Along with name server information, your domain records contain your contact information, which is available to anyone who wants it. During the Internet's early days, this information helped solve traffic problems, because anyone could get in touch with you regarding your domain and your servers.

These days, it's more of a nuisance than a good thing. It's a gold mine for spammers. Registering a domain instantly qualifies you to receive offers for everything that is illegal, immoral, or carries a life sentence. To address this issue, many registrars offer private domain registration for a fee.

When you register a private domain, your domain registration records contain your registrar's contact information. Therefore, anyone trying to contact you ends up sending a message to your registrar. If the message is relevant to your domain, the registrar forwards it to you. If it's spam, the registrar discards it.

Although you have to pay your registrar a few additional dollars every year for the privilege of receiving spam on your behalf, private registrations are hugely popular. Unfortunately, Melbourne IT doesn't offer private registrations to Office Live domains.

■**Caution** Offers for cheap narcotics aren't the only kind of spam you can expect. You'll also receive offers from competing registrars for transferring your domain registration to them. Their wording is often misleading, and their tone can be anywhere from a polite request to a veiled threat.

You can safely shred such letters or delete such e-mails. Microsoft pays for your domain registration, and the renewal is automatic. You don't have to lift a finger to manage your domain.

Redirecting a Domain to Your Office Live Account

If you already own the domain name of your dreams, you can redirect it to your Office Live account instead of choosing a new one. Domain redirection spares you the agony of finding a new domain name, but you have to pay the annual registration fees yourself; Microsoft won't foot the bill.

If you redirect an existing domain to Office Live, you'll receive instructions on changing domain name servers in your domain's registration records while signing up.

FAQ

Can I Transfer My Domain to Office Live Instead of Redirecting It?

Transferring a domain means firing your current registrar and entrusting your domain's registration records to another registrar. Many people want to transfer their domains to Melbourne IT in order to avoid paying domain registration fees.

Unfortunately, Office Live doesn't allow domain transfers. Microsoft is not trying to save money by refusing transfers; it simply doesn't want unnecessary headaches.

Transferring domains is a tricky process. You have to monitor the transfer closely and fix problems if they arise during the process. If something goes wrong during the transfer, your domain will go into a state of suspended animation. Nobody can visit your web site, and you won't be able send or receive e-mail. During Office Live's early days, domain transfers were allowed. Many people initiated transfers of their domains but didn't follow up on them. As a result, their domains remained in a limbo for long periods of time. This frustrated quite a few people and generated plenty of undesirable publicity for Office Live, so Microsoft stopped accepting domain transfers for Office Live accounts.

TIPS FROM THE TRENCHES

Write Down Your Domain Name

Write down the domain name you'll use for your Office Live account here:

    Domain name for your new Office Live web site: _____

    Here's why.

    Brainstorming for a domain name can take a long time. Most people consider dozens of names before finally choosing one. It is not uncommon to choose a domain name late one night and forget which one you chose the next morning.

    A friend of mine signed up for Office Live with a new domain name and couldn't remember it a couple of days later. The good folks in Office Live's customer service department had to look it up based on his name and credit-card number, and it took a couple of days.

Understanding Windows Live IDs

Next, you must choose a single sign-on credential, called *Windows Live ID*, to sign in to your Office Live account.

A single sign-on credential is a single user ID/password combination that allows you to access several computer or online accounts. Windows Live ID is Microsoft's single sign-on credential. With a Windows Live ID, you can sign in to any of Microsoft's web sites, and a few other web sites such as www.mcafee.com, which participate in Microsoft Passport Network.

Why Do You Need Single Sign-On Credentials?

Generally speaking, you have to create sign-on credentials on every web site that requires you to sign or log in. Each web site has different rules for user IDs and passwords. Everyone knows what a nightmare it is keeping track of several user IDs and passwords.

The Windows Live ID authentication system seeks to solve this problem. The system has two components: an account information database and an authentication service. You create sign-on credentials with the Windows Live ID web site, which become a part of Windows Live ID's account information database. Then you can use your Windows Live ID to sign on to any web site that uses Windows Live ID's authentication service.

All Microsoft web sites use Windows Live ID for authentication. Therefore, you can use a Windows Live ID to sign on to any of them. For instance, I use my Windows Live ID to manage my Office Live Basics web site, my Microsoft Partner Program membership, my Microsoft Office Online account, my Microsoft Learning subscription, and my Windows Live Hotmail account.

A single ID to access all your accounts makes a lot of sense. In fact, Windows Live IDs are not new. They've been around for years, way back when they were called Passport IDs (another case of MINFU). The network of web sites that used Passport IDs for authenticating users was called the Passport Network. Microsoft's vision was to create a single sign-on credential for all web commerce. With that goal in mind, Microsoft tried, for many years, to enlist other web sites to adopt Passport authentication, but with little success. User information is an important asset for businesses, and few were willing to let Microsoft manage it, despite Microsoft's good intentions.

Like most authentication systems, Windows Live ID requires you to have an ID and a password. The ID is typically your e-mail address, so be advised that you need to pick one in order to create a Windows Live ID.

■**Note** You can create a Windows Live ID without an e-mail address. It's called a Limited Account. But I will restrict this discussion to the more established convention of using e-mail addresses as user IDs.

Choosing a Windows Live ID for Your Office Live Account

Even if you already have a Windows Live ID, Office Live will ask you to create a new one for your account when you sign up. The ID must be an e-mail address in the domain you associate with your Office Live account.

FAQ

I Already Have a Windows Live ID. Why Do I Need a New One for Office Live?

You can have as many Windows Live IDs as you want, but each must have a unique e-mail address.

During Office Live's beta days, you could use any Windows Live ID, but if the e-mail address used for that Windows Live ID was not in your domain, you couldn't access your mailbox from Office Live.

This behavior is quite normal. To give you an example, if your e-mail address is you@yourofficelivedomain.com, your mail server will be hosted by Office Live and you will be able to see your mailbox from within Office Live. But if your e-mail address is you@yahoo.com, there's no way for Office Live's mail system to access your mailbox at Yahoo!.

Many users found this quite confusing, and the Office Live forums were flooded with "Where is my mailbox?" messages. To avoid these problems, you must now create a new Windows Live ID in the domain you plan to host with Office Live.

The domain name associated with my Office Live account, for example, is acxede.org. Therefore, the e-mail address I choose as the Windows Live ID for my account must be from the domain acxede.org—something like rahul@acxede.org.

You don't have to create a Windows Live ID right away. And the e-mail account with that address need not exist. You simply have to pick an e-mail address that you will use as your Windows Live ID when you sign up for Office Live. Office Live will create the e-mail account for you automatically during the sign-up process.

■**Note** Additional users of your Office Live account can use just about any e-mail address, as long as they register it with the Windows Live ID authentication system. I'll discuss additional user accounts in Chapter 5.

TIPS FROM THE TRENCHES

Write Down Your Windows Live ID

Write down the e-mail address you'll use for your Windows Live ID here:

E-mail address for your new Windows Live ID: _____

Here's why.

You'll need this ID for logging in to your Office Live account. Office Live associates this ID with the owner of an Office Live account. If you forget it, you will have to prove your identity to Office Live's support people before you can coax them into giving it to you again.

Understanding Credit Cards

Just kidding. You'll be relieved to know that I'm not going to explain what a credit card is and how to go about reading out your credit-card number when asked. I trust you already know.

But what you may not know is that Office Live requires you to provide credit-card information even if you try to subscribe to Office Live Basics—the free version. Rest assured that Office Live Basics is indeed a free service—you don't have to pay a dime for it. Your credit card will never be charged.

This never-charge policy has one exception. Immediately after you sign up, Microsoft checks whether your credit card is active by requesting a temporary authorization for a $1 charge. If you check your credit-card transactions online, you may see the $1 charge for a few days, but it is refunded by the time your credit-card company generates your monthly statement.

FAQ

Why on Earth Does Microsoft Need My Credit-Card Number to Sign Me Up for a Free Service?

While it sounds suspiciously like a mail-in rebate scam, there are several good reasons for this seemingly ridiculous requirement:

- Minors usually don't have credit cards. Requiring a valid credit card helps prevent them from opening hosting accounts (it's illegal for them to do so.)

- Law enforcement agencies can trace the owner of a credit card far more easily than the owner of a domain, if need be.

- Scam artists often set up hundreds of similar web sites to lure unsuspecting victims. The "one sign-up per credit card" policy prevents them from doing so.

- Microsoft can limit the number of Office Live Basics accounts (and therefore, free domains) a person can get from Office Live. Microsoft pays a few dollars a year to Melbourne IT for your "free" domain. That's good enough of a reason to prevent you from registering 5,000 domains just because they don't cost you anything.

- You might get hooked on Office Live and upgrade to a paid version one day. Or you might want to add additional services to your account. Having a credit card on file makes it easier for Microsoft to separate you from your money later.

Therefore, you can open only one Office Live Basics account with one credit card. If you try to open a second one, Office Live will tell you to use a different credit card or upgrade to a paid subscription.

TIPS FROM THE TRENCHES

Save with a Prepaid Subscription Card from Best Buy

Microsoft has teamed up with Best Buy to sell prepaid subscription cards for Office Live. If you plan to subscribe to Office Live Basics, a prepaid card is unnecessary. But if you're planning to get one of the paid versions, you can save on monthly charges for two months.

A prepaid card gives you three months of service for the price of one. It's really meant for people who aren't savvy enough to sign up for the service and design a web site by themselves. Best Buy's Geek Squad will set up the site and provide hand-holding on request—for an outrageous fee, of course. But Best Buy will sell you a prepaid card even if you don't want to engage the Geek Squad.

After the three-month period is over, you can provide your credit-card number to continue your service.

Summary

In this chapter, I explained what domain names and Windows Live IDs are and why you need them, along with a credit card, to sign up for Office Live. Here are a few points to remember from this chapter:

- Every computer on the Web has a unique IP address. IP addresses are difficult for people to remember, so each computer has a name as well.

- A domain name helps keep computer names unique. DNS software translates domain names to IP addresses and vice versa. Domain names must be registered with a registrar.

- Finding a domain name that you both like and is still up for grabs is quite difficult, but some online tools can make your quest easier.

- If you already own the domain name of your dreams, you can use it with Office Live. If not, you can register a new one during sign-up.

- A Windows Live ID is a single sign-on credential that you can use for identifying yourself to Office Live. The ID must be an e-mail address in the domain you associate with your Office Live account.

- You must provide a credit-card number during sign-up. If you sign up for Office Live Basics, the free edition, Microsoft will merely keep your credit card on file but never charge it.

In the next chapter, I'll help you sign up for Office Live.

CHAPTER 3

■ ■ ■

Signing Up

After all the legwork you did in Chapter 2, signing up for Office Live should be a snap. I'll walk you through the process in this chapter.

Registration is quite straightforward. You can wrap it up in under ten minutes, but plan to complete it in a single sitting. If you stroll out for a cup of coffee halfway through it, the web page shown in Figure 3-1 may greet you when you return. You'll then have to go back to square one and start the process all over again.

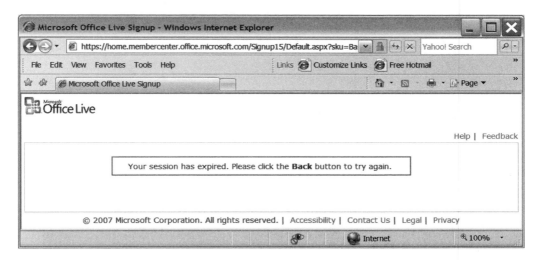

Figure 3-1. *Plan on completing the sign-up in one sitting.*

Opening an Account

To open a new Office Live account, follow these steps:

1. Point your browser at Office Live's home page, `www.officelive.com`. You'll see the web page shown in Figure 3-2.

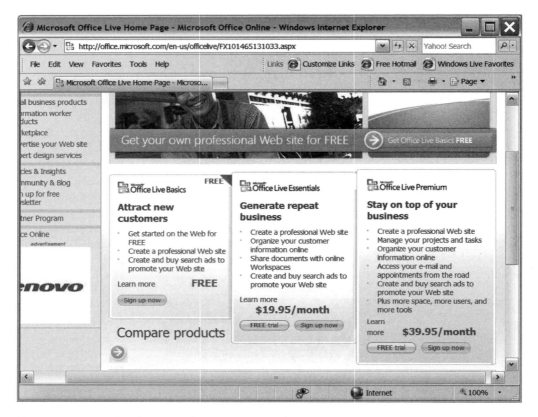

Figure 3-2. *Sign up for the service here on Office Live's home page.*

■**Note** Figure 3-2 shows how the page appears to users in the United States at the time of this writing. This page can and will change over time. It may also be different depending on the country you live in; Office Live's home page in the United Kingdom, for instance, is at www.officelive.co.uk. The page you reach may look different, but you'll find the links to sign up for all three versions of Office Live somewhere on the page—the overall process won't change, so don't worry.

2. Click the Sign up now button under the version you'd like to sign up for. You'll see the Microsoft Office Live Signup web page shown in Figure 3-3. There are several forms on this page that you must fill out in sequence. When the page loads, the first form, Register a new domain name, is expanded, and the others are collapsed. After you fill out a form, it collapses, an Edit link appears in its header, and the page scrolls down to expand the next form. You can always go back and correct the information you've already entered in a form by clicking on the Edit link in its header.

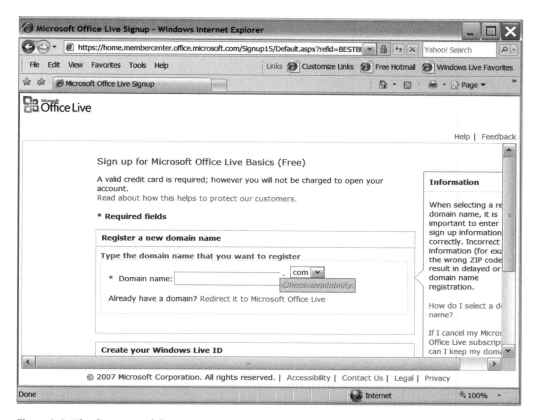

Figure 3-3. *The first step of the sign-up process is entering the domain name you'd like to associate with your account.*

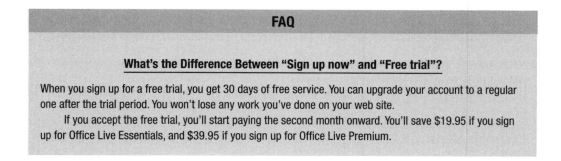

FAQ

What's the Difference Between "Sign up now" and "Free trial"?

When you sign up for a free trial, you get 30 days of free service. You can upgrade your account to a regular one after the trial period. You won't lose any work you've done on your web site.

If you accept the free trial, you'll start paying the second month onward. You'll save $19.95 if you sign up for Office Live Essentials, and $39.95 if you sign up for Office Live Premium.

3. If you'd like to register a new domain name, enter it in the Domain name box and click the Check availability button beside it. If you already own the domain name that you want to redirect to your new Office Live web site, click the Redirect it to Microsoft Office Live link under the box. The Redirect an existing domain name form shown in Figure 3-4 replaces the Register a new domain name form in your browser.

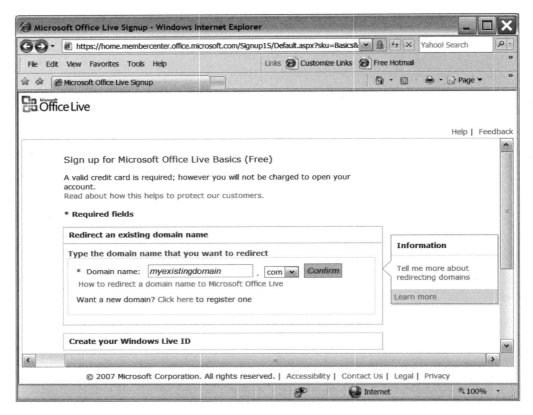

Figure 3-4. *If you already own a domain name, you can associate it with your Office Live account instead of signing up for a new one.*

4. Enter your domain name in the box and click the Confirm button. Whether you asked to register a new domain or redirect one you already own, you'll see the confirmation request shown in Figure 3-5.

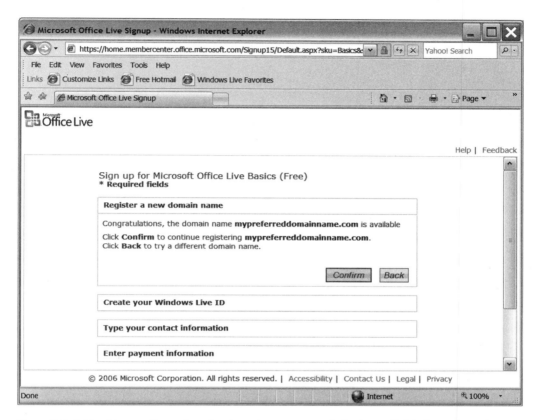

Figure 3-5. *Office Live confirms that the domain name you desire is available for registration or redirection.*

5. Click Confirm. The page scrolls down automatically to reveal the Create your Windows Live ID and Type password reset information forms in Figure 3-6, where you must create a Windows Live ID to manage your Office Live account.

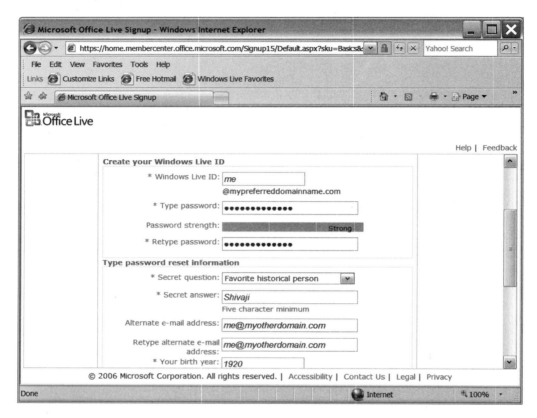

Figure 3-6. *On this page, you create a Windows Live ID to manage your Office Live account.*

As I mentioned in Chapter 2, your Windows Live ID must be an e-mail address in the domain associated with your Office Live account. That's why you can't change the domain name component of the Windows Live ID in the form shown in Figure 3-6.

Your password must be between 6 and 16 characters long, and it can't contain any part of your e-mail address. As you enter it, the strength indicator below the Type password box tells you whether your password is weak, of medium strength, or strong.

TIPS FROM THE TRENCHES

Choosing Strong Passwords

It's *extremely* important to choose a strong password.

    Do choose a password that

- Has a minimum of eight characters

- Includes both uppercase and lowercase letters

- Includes a number

- Includes a special character, such as an underscore or the ampersand (&) symbol

    The best way to come up with a password is to choose the first character of each word in a phrase or a sentence because it's easy to remember. Think of a sentence—sometimes called a *passphrase*—such as *We visited Labrador & Newfoundland in August 2005*. Your password, then, could be *WvL&NiA2*.

    Do not choose a password that

- Includes names or people or places

- Includes words in the dictionary

- Is the word *password* itself

- Includes personal information such as your name, date of birth, or pet's name

- Includes keyboard patterns such as *qwerty* or *asdfg*

    The idea behind strong passwords is to make it difficult for crackers or automated password-cracking programs to guess your password or find it by brute force.

6. Complete the password reset information on the Type password reset information form and then click OK. You'll arrive at the Type your contact information form shown in Figure 3-7.

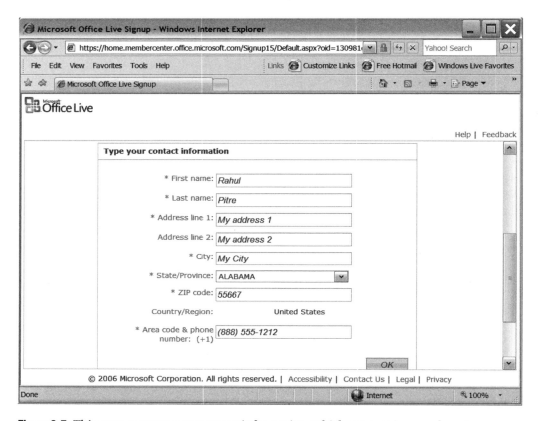

Figure 3-7. *This page requests your contact information, which appears in your domain registration records.*

If you register your domain through Office Live, the information you enter on this form also appears in your domain registration records with Melbourne IT.

7. Fill in your contact information, and click OK. The registration wizard will take you to the `Enter payment information` form shown in Figure 3-8.

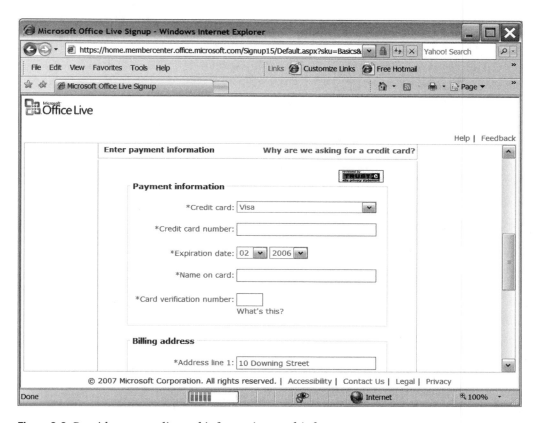

Figure 3-8. *Provide your credit-card information on this form.*

If you're signing up for Office Live Basics, your credit card will simply stay on file; it will never be charged.

8. Enter your credit-card information, and click OK. You'll arrive at the Business information form shown in Figure 3-9.

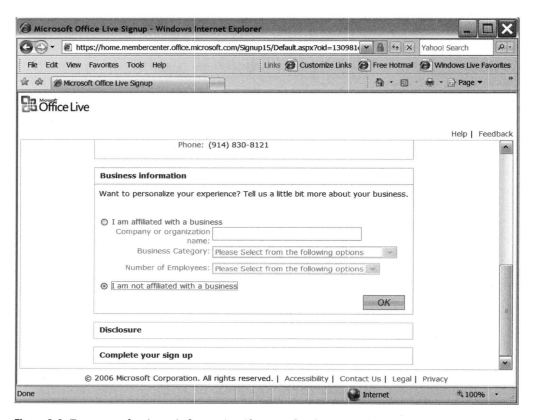

Figure 3-9. *Enter your business information if you wish. It's optional.*

9. Enter information about your business on this form, if you wish. If you enter an organization name, it will appear in your domain registration records. If you're not sure, click the I am not affiliated with a business radio button, and then click OK. You'll see the Disclosure form shown in Figure 3-10.

■**Note** Microsoft probably uses your business information to decide which advertisements to show you!

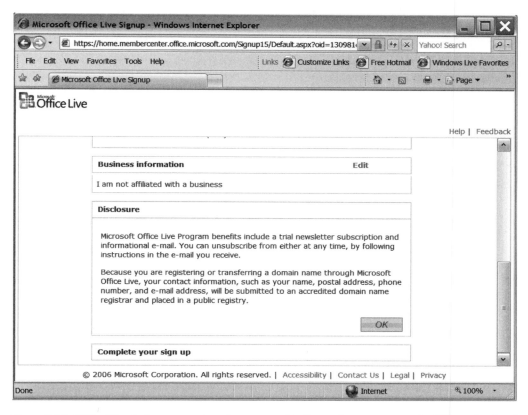

Figure 3-10. *Office Live informs you that the personal information you entered will be submitted to the domain registrar and that it will then be publicly available.*

10. Read the disclosure statement, and then click OK. You'll see the Sign up confirmation form shown in Figure 3-11.

Note The disclosure text may change from time to time.

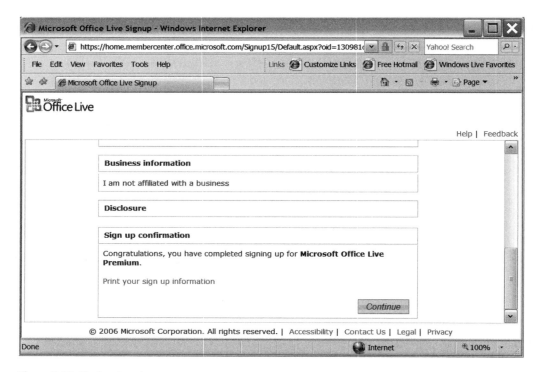

Figure 3-11. *You're done!*

11. That's it. You're done. Congratulations! You're now the proud owner of a spanking new Office Live account. Click the `Print your sign up information` link to print a copy of your registration for your records.

12. Click `Continue`, and you'll arrive at the `Member Center` page shown in Figure 3-12.

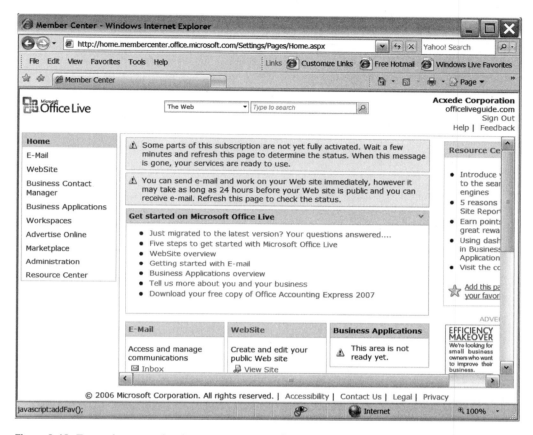

Figure 3-12. *Every time you sign in to your account from now on, this* Member Center *page will be the first page you'll see.*

A message at the top of the Member Center page draws your attention to the fact that Office Live takes a few minutes to activate your account.

13. Go get that cup of coffee I made you defer at the beginning of this chapter. When you get back, refresh the web page by hitting the F5 key on your keyboard. You'll see a new version of the page as shown in Figure 3-13.

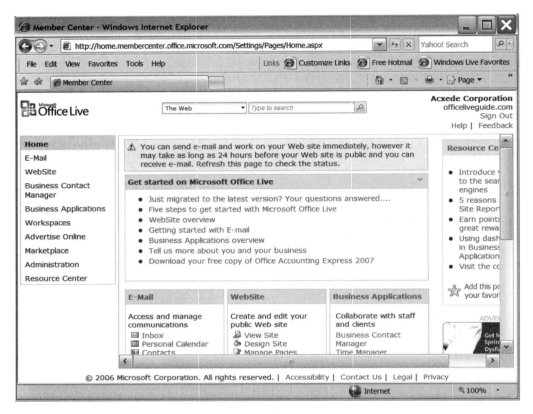

Figure 3-13. *The activation-related message disappears from the* Member Center *page. Your account is now ready for use.*

Your account is now set up and you're ready to go. If you've just registered a new domain during sign-up, Office Live will make name server entries in your domain records. These entries take roughly 24 hours to propagate across the Internet to other name servers. That's why you'll see a little warning message, as shown at the top of Figure 3-13. It's nothing to worry about.

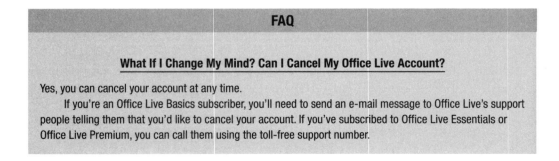

FAQ

What If I Change My Mind? Can I Cancel My Office Live Account?

Yes, you can cancel your account at any time.

If you're an Office Live Basics subscriber, you'll need to send an e-mail message to Office Live's support people telling them that you'd like to cancel your account. If you've subscribed to Office Live Essentials or Office Live Premium, you can call them using the toll-free support number.

What Happens to My Domain Name If I Cancel My Service?

The domain name is yours. You keep it.

Office Live informs Melbourne IT that your Office Live account is closed. From then on, you get an account with Melbourne IT as with any other registrar.

When you register a domain through Office Live, Microsoft pays Melbourne IT the annual registration fees for the first year. However, remember that the domain name belongs to you, not to Microsoft. If you cancel your Office Live account before the year is up, Melbourne IT won't refund the fees to Microsoft. As a result, you get free registration for the rest of the year. Once the year is up, you must pay the registration fees to Melbourne IT directly or transfer the domain to another registrar.

But don't try to beat the system and get free registration by opening and canceling an Office Live account. A domain transfer can take a long time.

Can I Upgrade My Office Live Subscription to a Higher Edition?

Yes, you can. You can upgrade Basics to Essentials or Premium. You can upgrade Essentials to Premium as well.

When you upgrade, the new features will be added to your account. Contents of your current account are preserved, so you don't have to build your web site all over again if you upgrade.

Can I Downgrade My Office Live Subscription to a Lower Edition?

Yes, you can. You can downgrade Premium to Essentials or Basics. You can downgrade Essentials to Basics as well.

When you downgrade, you'll lose features not available in the new edition you've subscribed to. Be sure to download all data from your account before you downgrade.

Summary

In this chapter, I helped you sign up for Office Live. You now own a piece of real estate on the Web. Here are some points to keep in mind:

- It's important to choose a strong password. A good trick for coming up with a good, strong password is to think of a *passphrase* and use the first character of each word to build your password.

- You may upgrade or downgrade your subscription, or even cancel it if you aren't happy.

- After you sign up, it may take a day or so before you can start using your new e-mail account.

- Your web site may not respond to www.yourdomain.com for roughly 24 hours.

- You can upgrade or downgrade your Office Live subscription anytime. If you downgrade, you'll lose data associated with features that your new subscription doesn't have.

In the next chapter, I'll give you a tour of your new home on the Web.

CHAPTER 4

A Quick Tour of Office Live

Your Office Live account comes with a *management console*—or *dashboard*, as some people like to call it—which you use to build your web site as well as to manage your account. Office Live calls its dashboard Member Center. If you want to take charge of your account, you must know Member Center like the back of your hand.

Like any unfamiliar dashboard, Member Center can overwhelm you a little in the beginning. In this chapter, I'll help you overcome the jitters. As you read through it, you'll take the first steps toward mastering your account's dashboard.

When Office Live activates your account, it builds a starter web site for you automatically. I'll end this chapter with a sneak preview of your starter web site.

Signing In to Member Center

You'll find a link to the Sign In page on Office Live's home page. Follow these steps to sign in to your account:

1. Point your browser at www.officelive.com. Office Live's home page, shown in Figure 4-1, will appear.

∎**Note** Figure 4-1 shows the page that visitors in the United States see at the time of this writing. You might see a different home page in the future, but you'll find the Sign in link somewhere on that page.

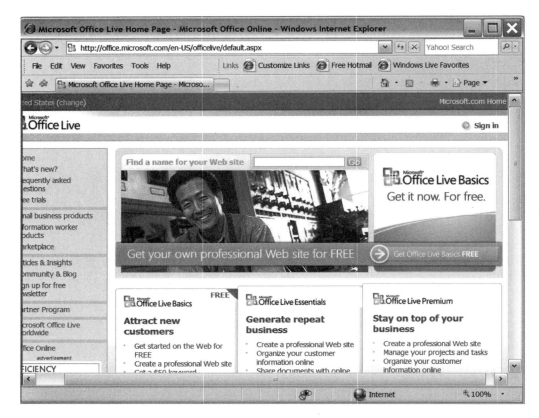

Figure 4-1. *Office Live's home page. Signing in to your account from this page will take you to your site's mangement console automatically.*

2. Click the Sign in link in the top right-hand corner to get to the Sign In page shown in Figure 4-2.

3. Enter the Windows Live ID and password you used to sign up for Office Live.

4. The two check boxes under the password box can make signing in easier in the future. Check the Remember me on this computer box if you want Office Live to remember your Windows Live ID. Check the Remember my password box below it if you want Office Live to remember your password as well. It's okay to check these boxes as long as you're doing so on your own computer and nobody else has access to it.

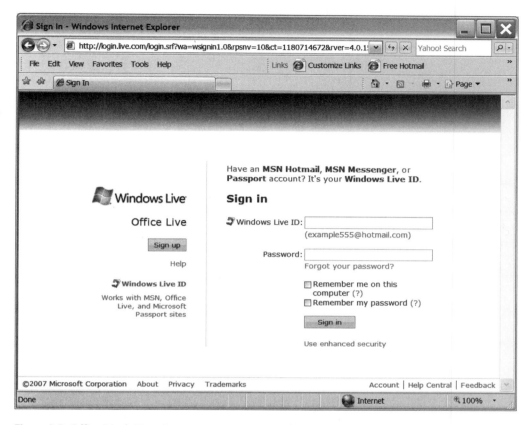

Figure 4-2. *Office Live's* Sign In *page*

■**Caution** Once you check both the Remember me on this computer and Remember my password boxes, anybody who has access to your computer account will have access to your Office Live account as well. Personally, I prefer to enter my credentials every time to avoid potential problems.

---

5. Note the link below the Sign in button, which reads Use enhanced security. If you click this link, Office Live will send your credentials for authentication over the Web in an encrypted format, just as online stores and financial institutions do. But unlike those sites, the subsequent pages won't be encrypted.

6. After signing in successfully, you'll see the Member Center page shown in Figure 4-3.

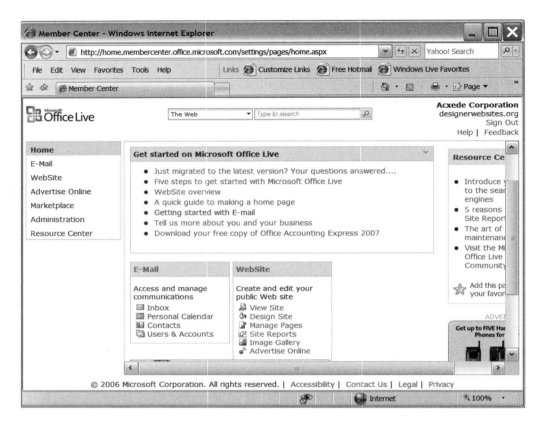

Figure 4-3. Member Center *is the management console for your Office Live account.*

FAQ

If Everyone Signs In from Office Live's Home Page, How Does Office Live Know Which Web Site Is Mine?

Although you start at the same `Sign in` link as a quarter-million other people (and counting), the Windows Live ID you registered while signing up for an account is unique. Office Live associates it with your domain and subsequently uses this association to take you to `Member Center` when you sign in.

But What If I Have Two Web Sites with Office Live?

That's not a problem. In fact, you can have any number of web sites hosted with Office Live. If you do, you will see a nice little domain picker after signing in, as shown in the following figure.

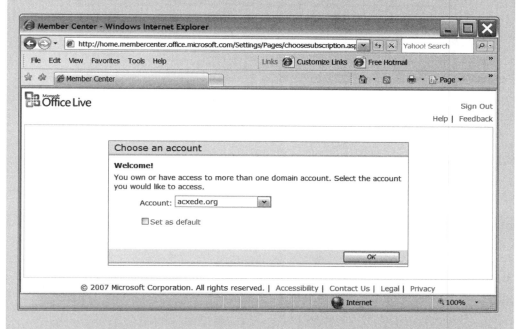

You can use the domain picker to select the web site you want to work on. If you use one of the sites more than the others, you can even set it to be your default web site.

Layout of Member Center Pages

The Member Center page is your dashboard's home page. Like most pages in the dashboard, it's divided roughly into four sections: the header, the left navigation pane, the content area, and the footer (see Figure 4-4).

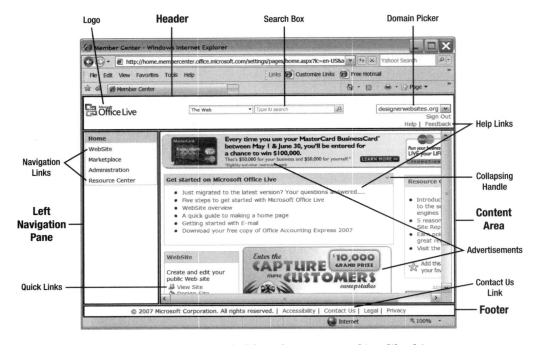

Figure 4-4. *Most pages in your account's dashboard are structured just like this page.*

Header

At the left margin of the header is the Office Live logo. You can click on it from anywhere within Office Live to return to Member Center. On most Office Live pages, you'll find bread-crumb navigation to the current page below the logo. The Member Center page is an exception, though, so you can't see the bread crumbs in Figure 4-4.

At the center of the header is the search box. You can search either the Web or the Office Live Help page for the term you type in the search box.

The text at the top-right margin of the header reminds you who you are, which is quite handy if you suffer from a sudden bout of amnesia. Below your name is a link to sign out of Member Center.

■**Tip** If you're accessing your site from a public-access computer, such as one at an Internet café, it's a good idea to click on the Sign Out link after you're done instead of just closing the browser window.

Clicking on the adjacent Help link ought to display context-sensitive help. But don't count on it—Help links on some pages simply open up the default help page.

The last link to the right is the Feedback link. It's for sharing your joy or frustrations about Office Live with Microsoft. I'm not sure whether anyone reads your submissions. You certainly don't get replies.

Left Navigation Pane

The left navigation pane is home to the page's navigation menu. The current page you're on is highlighted. Throughout this book, I'll ask you to click on links in the left *navigation pane*. This is where you'll find those links. Of course, each page has its own left navigation pane with its own links.

Links in Member Center's left navigation pane correspond to the main tasks you'll perform with Office Live. If you click on the Administration link, for instance, you'll see the Administration page shown in Figure 4-5. Judging by the links in its left navigation pane, it appears to be the home page for all administrative functions. Note that you can see the promised bread-crumb navigation under the Office Live logo in Figure 4-5.

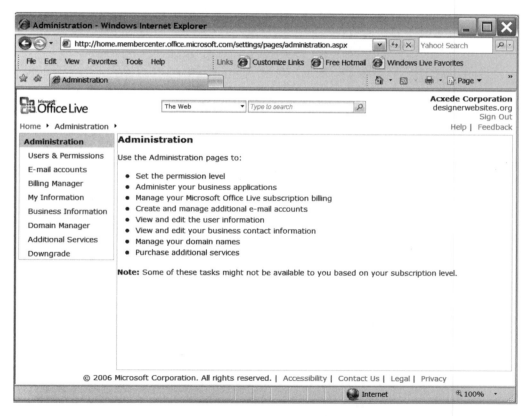

Figure 4-5. *The Administration page is the gateway to all of Office Live's administrative functions.*

You can access every page in Office Live's administrative interface by drilling down on the links in left navigation panes of successive pages. On some pages, links to a few frequently used pages appear as quick links in the content area.

Content Area

The remainder of the Member Center page is mostly the content area. A good deal of it is covered with advertisements, which enable you to enjoy Office Live without spending a penny. But don't worry—these advertisements appear only when you're signed in to Member Center. People visiting your web site won't see them; only you have to put up with them while editing your site.

Help links disguised under headings such as Get Started on Microsoft Office Live and Resource Center fill up most of the space not taken up by advertisements. You'll soon come to ignore these links just as you ignore the advertisements.

Tip Click on the downward-pointing arrow at the top right-hand corner of the Get Started on Microsoft Office Live box to collapse it. Even if you sign out, Office Live will remember the setting and keep the box collapsed the next time you sign in. You can collapse any box with the downward-pointing arrow on any page of the Office Live web site.

When you collapse a box, the downward-pointing arrow is replaced by an upward-pointing one. Click it to expand the box again.

The two remaining boxes in Member Center's content area provide quick links to e-mail and web-site-related functions. You can also get to these links via the links in the left navigation panel. However, it's not easy to find them that way because they're often buried deep in the navigation hierarchy. Therefore, you'll often find yourself using these quick links instead.

Footer

At the bottom of the page is the footer, which houses links to the fine print. You'll find the need to click on those links only if you're contemplating suing Microsoft (or if, god forbid, Microsoft is contemplating suing you!). Hidden among the fine print links is the Contact Us link. It looks fairly standard and innocuous, but you would do well to stuff its location in the quick-reference section of your brain. The link leads you to the E-mail Support form. If you're an Office Live Basics subscriber, the only way you can ask for technical support from Office Live is by filling out this form.

Member Center from 30,000 Feet

Member Center's left navigation pane is its nerve center. Depending on your subscription level, you'll see a different set of links in it. Each link leads you to a section where you can manage a distinct aspect of your Office Live account. If you're an Office Live Basics subscriber, you'll see the following links:

- E-mail

- WebSite

- Advertise Online

- Marketplace

- Administration

- Resource Center

I'll take you on a quick tour of the sections that each of these links leads to.

Note If you subscribe to a higher version, you'll see three additional links: Business Contact Manager, Business Applications, and Workspaces. These links lead you to sections of Member Center that are relevant to intranets and extranets but not to building web sites. I won't address these sections in this book.

Taking Charge of Your E-mail

Click on the E-mail link in Member Center's left navigation pane. Office Live will serve up the E-Mail page shown in Figure 4-6.

From the E-Mail page, you can

- Read and send mail

- Manage your personal calendar

- Manage your contact list

- Share your calendar

- Create and manage e-mail accounts in your domain

- Download Windows Live Messenger

Note As you can see, the E-Mail page is quite similar to the Member Center page, except that the quick links for managing your web site are replaced by those for Windows Live Messenger. In fact, the only useful link on this page that you don't find on the Member Center page is one for sharing your calendar.

You can share your calendar from the calendar's menu, though, so this page is rather redundant at present. However, the quick links on the Member Center page may change in the future as new features are added to Office Live.

You'll learn everything about managing Office Live Mail in Chapter 5.

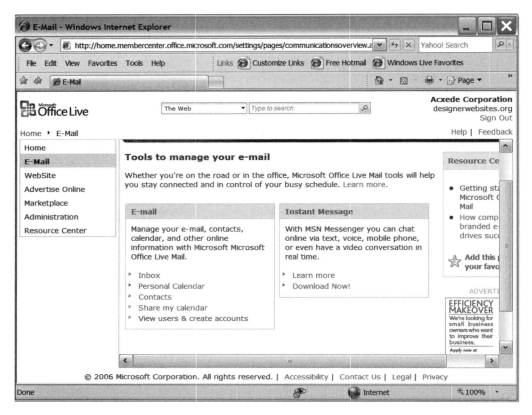

Figure 4-6. *The* E-Mail *page is home to tools for managing e-mail accounts in your domain.*

Tip   You'll need to sign in to Office Live only for managing e-mail accounts in your domain. Office Live mailboxes are glorified Hotmail (later renamed to Windows Live Mail and now called Windows Live Hotmail because of yet another MINFU) mailboxes. If you simply want to check your e-mail, you can check it at www.hotmail.com or http://mail.live.com after signing in with the Windows Live ID you use with your Office Live account.

Building and Maintaining Your Public Web Site

Click on the WebSite link in the left navigation pane of the Member Center page. You'll arrive at the Page Manager web page, as shown in Figure 4-7. This page is your web site's administrative dashboard. You'll navigate through it every time you edit your web site. You'll encounter Page Manager often in the next few chapters.

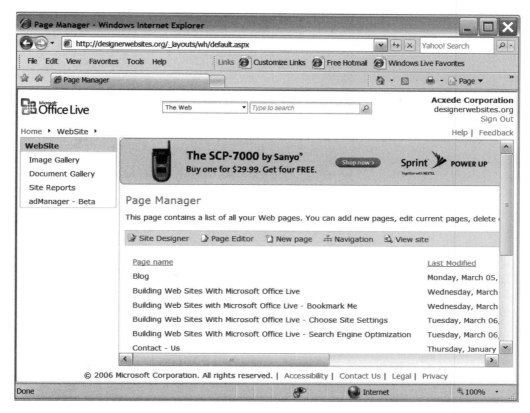

Figure 4-7. Page Manager *has links to tools for building, editing, and managing your public web site.*

From the Page Manager page, you can

- Add new web pages to your web site

- Edit or delete existing web pages

- Configure your web site's navigation

- Set and edit site-wide defaults such as fonts, colors, and width

- Restore the web site from backup if disaster strikes

- Authorize others to work on your web site

- Upload and manage images that appear on your site

- Upload and manage downloadable documents

- View traffic statistics reports

If you've subscribed to Office Live primarily for building a public web site, you can expect to spend a great deal of time on this page. I'll walk you through the nitty-gritty of building your web site in Chapters 7, 8, 9, and 10.

Advertising Online

Click on the Advertise Online link in the left navigation pane of Member Center to arrive at the adManager page shown in Figure 4-8.

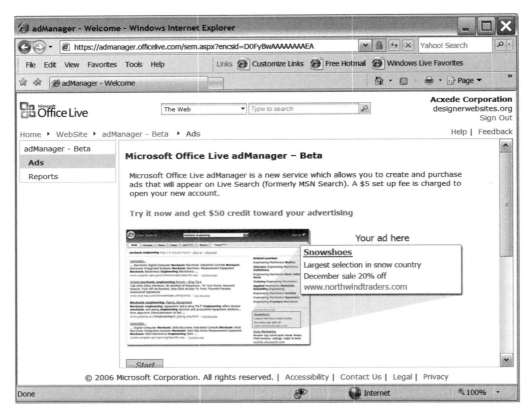

Figure 4-8. adManager *has tools for advertising your products or web site on Windows Live Search's results pages.*

FAQ

What Is adManager?

The name *adManager* might suggest to you that the tool will help you manage ad placements on your site (and help you make some money, as with Google's AdSense). Not so. Quite the contrary, in fact. It helps you place your keyword ads on Windows Live Search results. When people search the Web using Windows Live Search, the advertisements you "buy" will be displayed on the search result pages.

Let's say you sell baseball equipment. You can purchase the keyword *baseball* and a placement for it on the results page. When someone searches for *baseball* using Windows Live Search, your advertisement will show up above or to the right of the search results in the form of Sponsored Sites, as shown in the figure, assuming of course that you've coughed up more money than other baseball equipment vendors who have purchased the keyword *baseball*.

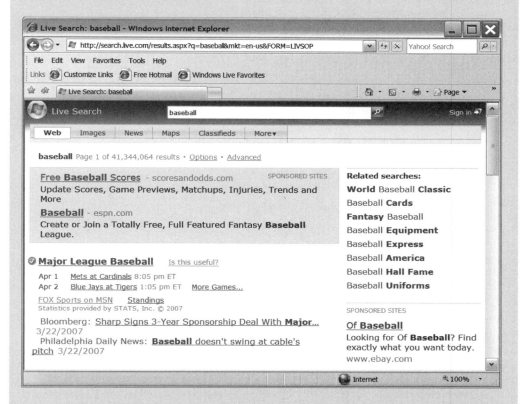

Now, what does adManager have to do with your Office Live account? Quite frankly, absolutely nothing! You can subscribe to adManager even without an Office Live account. The reason you'll find the adManager link in Member Center is that Microsoft hopes you'll start using Office Live as your primary gateway for all web-related tasks.

From the adManager page, you can

- Sign up for an adManager account

- Buy keywords and placement

- View reports on how your ads were actually displayed

■Note You'll notice that the Office Live navigation isn't very streamlined. Many differently worded links seem to point to the same web page. The navigation refers to the adManager page with links named Advertise Online, adManager - Beta, adManager, and a few other names I may not have noticed yet.

But remember that Office Live is still evolving. Microsoft wants you to make it your gateway to your online presence. Expect more products and services to be added to Office Live in the future. As the feature set evolves, expect the navigation to get less confusing and more intuitive.

Buying Additional Products and Services

Click on the Marketplace link in the left navigation pane of the Member Center page to come to the Additional Products & Services page shown in Figure 4-9.

From this page, you can add two kinds of add-ons to your Office Live account:

- Add-ons you can buy directly from Microsoft, such as additional storage, user accounts, or bandwidth

- Add-ons you can buy from third parties for enhancing your web site

---

FAQ

Why Would I Need Third-Party Add-Ons?

A subscription to Office Live Basics is just a teaser. Microsoft hopes you'll be sufficiently hooked and will adopt Office Live as a platform for all your intranet, extranet, and online application needs.

To get an idea of what third-party add-ons are, consider the Business Contact Manager application that comes with Office Live Essentials and Office Live Premium. It's a *horizontal* offering, which means customers in any line of business can use it. A third-party vendor may build *vertical* customizations of the contact manager, which are geared toward specific industries. The Additional Products & Services page is the place where the vendor can put its products up for sale.

Microsoft is, in fact, encouraging vendors to build such solutions on the Office Live platform in an attempt to popularize the platform. Presently, most vendors are developing SharePoint-based add-ons, which you can use only with the intranet/extranet features of Office Live Essentials and Office Live Premium. In the future, however, you may be able to buy modules to enhance your public web site as well—for instance, someone may build a module for selling products using PayPal.

In the meantime, if you must spend your budget by year-end, you can splurge on buying more storage space, bandwidth, and e-mail accounts from Microsoft.[1]

---

1. And while I'm on the subject of budgets, you might want to buy a copy of this book for each of your employees, clients, and friends!

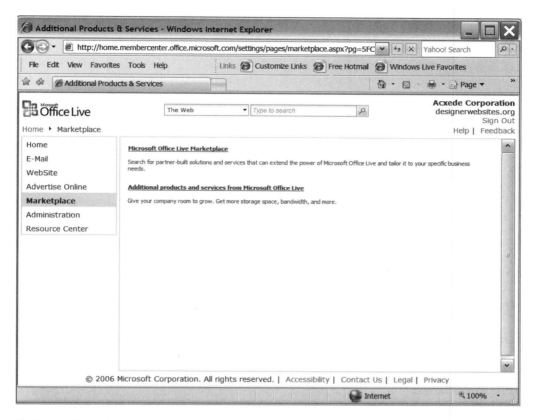

Figure 4-9. *From the* Additional Products & Services *page, you can buy add-ons to your Office Live account. You may be able to buy custom add-ons from third parties in the future.*

Taking Charge of Your Office Live Account

Click on the Administration link in Member Center's left navigation pane. Office Live serves up the Administration page shown in Figure 4-10.

From this page, you can

- Create and manage user accounts for your Office Live service

- Create and manage mailboxes in your domain

- Manage your account information, contact information, and billing information

- Buy and manage additional domain names for your account

- Buy account add-ons, such as additional storage space and additional user accounts from Microsoft

- Downgrade your subscription if you currently subscribe to Office Live Essentials or Office Live Premium

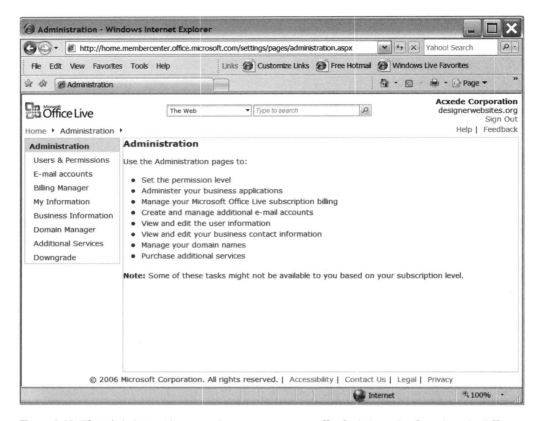

Figure 4-10. *The* Administration *page is your gateway to all administrative functions in Office Live. You manage your account and web site from here.*

■Note Strangely, there is no Upgrade link on this page to upgrade from Office Live Basics to Office Live Essentials or Office Live Premium. Instead, you'll find it on the Additional Services page. To get there, click on its eponymous link in the left navigation pane.

Apart from Page Manager, you'll probably visit the Administration page most often. I'll explore it in more detail in Chapter 5.

Seeking Help

Click on the Resource Center link in Member Center's left navigation pane. You'll arrive at the Resource Center page shown in Figure 4-11, which has links to a wide variety of help topics.

Figure 4-11. *The* `Resource Center` *page is home to Office Live's online help system.*

Office Live's help is a mixed bag. Some help topics are quite informative, while others merely state the obvious. However, that need not be a concern for you. Since you've bought this book, you won't need to click on any of those links!

You can look up help topics in a couple of other ways. You can click on the `Help` link in the header, or you can use the search box at the top of your dashboard.

The Public Web Site

Now that you're well acquainted with your account's management console, it's time to explore its public face—your web site.

Office Live builds a starter site for you when it activates your account. To see your starter site, point your browser at `www.yourdomain.com`. You'll see a page very similar to the one shown in Figure 4-12. This is how your web site would appear to a visitor if he were to pay a visit right after you open your account.

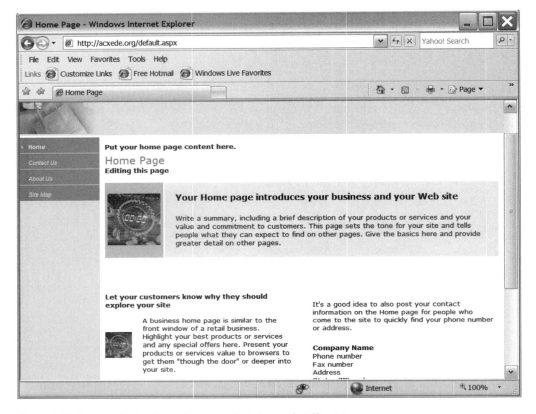

Figure 4-12. *Your web site, brought to you by Microsoft Office Live*

The starter site has four web pages, each with instructions on editing it. In Part 2 of this book, you'll use these pages to experiment with Office Live's features. Then you'll discard them and build new ones that you'll be proud of.

Depending on your disposition, you might either be thankful for the starter site or be utterly horrified by it. No matter what your reaction is, the site is visible to the world, although it's still unfinished.

What if you want to prevent people from viewing your starter site? Is there a way to hide it while it's under construction?

The answer, unfortunately, is *no*!

The best way to get rid of your starter site is to build the real one quickly.

■**Tip** You may want to admire your handiwork while you're building your site with the Page Manager. A quick way to do so is to click the View site icon. It's the last icon on the blue toolbar in the content area of the Page Manager page in Figure 4-7. Your site will open in a new browser window.

Summary

In this chapter, I gave you a view of your Office Live account from the proverbial 30,000 feet. Here are the most important points you should remember:

- Every Office Live account comes with a management console and a public web site.

- Only you, the account owner, can access the management console, which Office Live calls Member Center.

- Anyone who types www.yourdomain.com in his browser will see your public web site. Office Live automatically creates a starter site for you when it activates your account.

- Member Center is your gateway to managing your account and building your web site. Pretty much everything you can do with Office Live begins at a link on this page.

- The starter site is nothing to write home about, so you'll probably want to redesign it. There's no way to hide the starter site during redesign. The only way to deal with this problem is to complete the redesign as quickly as you can.

You're now ready to look at Office Live from lower altitudes. As Julie Andrews mentioned in *The Sound of Music*, the very beginning is a very good place to start. Learning to manage your Office Live account, adding and authorizing users, and creating e-mail accounts are perhaps the first steps you should take toward mastering the Office Live environment. I'll address these tasks in Chapter 5.

CHAPTER 5

■■■

Managing Your Account

An Office Live account is not like a free e-mail account that you can forget about after opening. From time to time, you may have to change your credit-card information, buy additional storage space, set up associates to design or edit your web site on your behalf, or create e-mail accounts for your employees. Office Live lumps all such administrative tasks under a separate administration section.

In this chapter, I'll show you how to manage your Office Live account from its administration section. Specifically, you'll learn how to

- Add additional users to your Office Live account and manage their user accounts

- Assign administrative roles to users

- Manage e-mail accounts in your domain

- Keep your billing information up-to-date and manage bills from Office Live

- Manage your personal and business contact information

- Buy additional domain names for your web site

- Subscribe to additional services from Office Live

- Upgrade or downgrade your service

Office Live's Administration Page

To go to the Administration section, click Administration in the left navigation pane on the Member Center page. The Administration page, as shown in Figure 5-1, should appear.

The Administration page is your gateway to all administrative tasks in Office Live. You can perform these tasks by clicking on the links in its left navigation pane. As the note at the bottom of the content area points out, some of the links may be irrelevant to your subscription. If you're an Office Live Basics subscriber, for instance, the Downgrade link is of no significance to you because you're already as far down as you can be in Office Live's hierarchy.

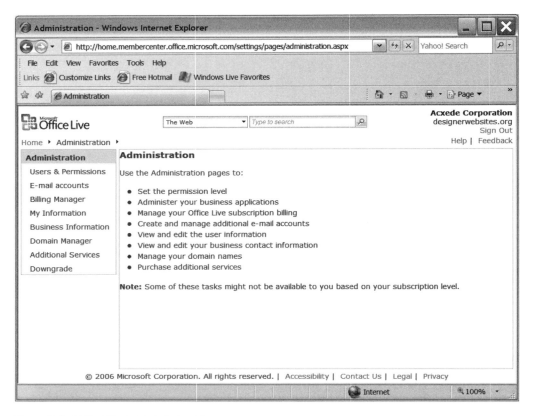

Figure 5-1. *Office Live's* Administration *page*

Users and Roles

If you're the only person who'll work on your web site, your subscriber account is the only one you'll need. But if you plan to get a hand from friends, family members, or employees in updating your web site, then you must create user accounts for them.

■**Note**   Why does the heading of this section read "Users and Roles" when the link in the left pane on the Administration page reads Users & Permissions? A role is just a set of permissions that allows you to perform some tasks on the web site and prevents you from performing some others. As you move around Office Live, you'll see the term *role* on some pages and the term *permission* on some others. They both mean the same thing. It's easier, however, to write "If you are an administrator" than to write "If you have an administrator's permissions," so I've used *role* more often in this chapter than *permissions*.

A user is someone who can help you design your web site or edit its content. Depending on her role, she may have the rights to add and delete user accounts as well. An Office Live user can have one of three roles: owner, administrator, or editor.

The Owner Role

Every Office Live account has only one owner. When you sign up for Office Live, you automatically become the owner, and your subscriber account is assigned the *owner* role. Owners have special privileges. They have unrestricted access to all account maintenance and web-site management functions. They are the only users who have access to domain registration records and billing information.

The Administrator Role

Administrators are a notch below owners in what they can do. They can't edit account information, domain registration records, or billing preferences, but other than that, they have all the powers of the owner.

The Editor Role

Editors can only work on web sites. They can add pages to or delete pages from web sites. They can add or change text on web pages. They can work with images and documents too, but that's it. Editors can't do anything else that administrators or owners can.

User Accounts

A user needs an account to sign in to Office Live. As you read in Chapter 2, each account requires a Windows Live ID. Recall that Windows Live IDs are simply valid e-mail addresses registered with the Windows Live authentication system.

While creating new user accounts, you merely have to supply a valid e-mail address that belongs to the proposed user. If the owner of the e-mail address has already registered it as a Windows Live ID, then he can start working with your web site right after you create an account for him. If he hasn't, he must go through Windows Live ID's registration process and accept its terms of use just as you did while signing up.

TIPS FROM THE TRENCHES

Follow the Principle of Least Privilege

When assigning roles to users, follow the Principle of Least Privilege, which states that users should have access only to the resources they need to do their job.

If a user will only be editing your web site, assign him the editor role; don't make him an administrator even if he happens to be your trusted lieutenant.

The idea is to prevent accidental disasters. Ideally, you should be the only administrator of your account. If you must delegate responsibility, don't create more than one additional administrator.

Managing Users and Roles

Managing users and roles comprises

- Creating new users and assigning them roles

- Changing the roles of existing users

- Deleting users

To perform these tasks, go to the `Administration` page and click the `Users & Permissions` link in the left navigation pane. You should see the `Users & Permissions` page as shown in Figure 5-2.

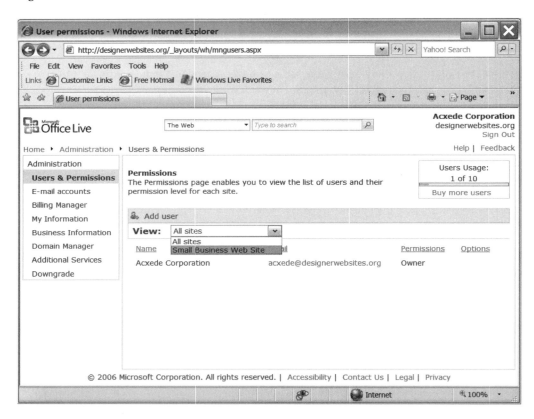

Figure 5-2. *Office Live's* Users & Permissions *page*

When you first visit this page, your subscriber account is the only one listed. Notice that it has `Owner` permissions.

The `View` drop-down list just above the user information tells you which web site the users underneath belong to. You might question the necessity of this drop-down list, but there's a perfectly reasonable explanation for it. If you're an Office Live Basics subscriber, your public web site is the only web site you can have. But if you've signed up for Office Live Essentials or

Office Live Premium, you can create Microsoft SharePoint-based intranet or extranet sites as well. Although few people think of intranets and extranets as web sites, they are from Office Live's point of view. Naturally, each web site can have its own unique set of users.

The default selection in the View drop-down is All Sites. As an Office Live Basics subscriber, you don't have to bother changing it because you only have one site. However, with the other two subscriptions, you must select the appropriate site in this drop-down. Otherwise, you'll end up either adding a user to all your sites or deleting him from all your sites.

Adding Users

To add a new user to your web site, follow these steps:

1. Click on the Add user icon in the blue toolbar a third of the way down in the content area. (The toolbar is the blue rectangle with a little icon of a person in it. It doesn't look like it's clickable, but it is, trust me.) A Webpage Dialog, like the one shown in Figure 5-3, pops up.

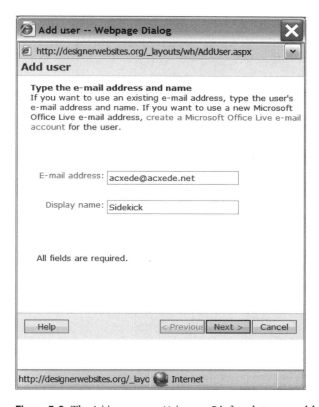

Figure 5-3. *The* Add user -- Webpage Dialog *lets you add a new user.*

2. Enter the e-mail address of your web site's new user in the E-mail address box. Enter the name you want to identify her by in the Display name box. This is how her name will appear in the list of users you saw in Figure 5-2.

■**Note** If you're an Office Live Basics subscriber, the e-mail address you enter must be a valid e-mail address. If it's from your domain, you must create it before you can create a user account for its owner. Refer to the "Managing E-mail Accounts" section for instructions on creating e-mail accounts in your domain. But you don't have to put up with the inconvenience if you're an Office Live Essentials or Office Live Premium subscriber. In that case, if the e-mail address you enter is from your domain but you haven't created it yet, then Office Live will create it for you behind the scenes. Moral of the story: money talks.

   3. Click Next. The Webpage Dialog changes, as shown in Figure 5-4.

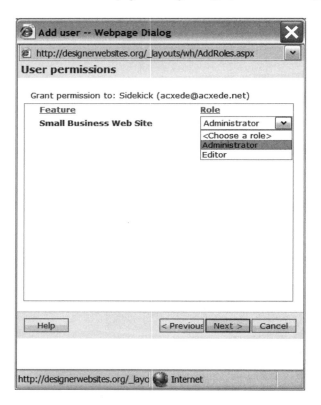

Figure 5-4. *This new* Add user -- Webpage Dialog *lets you set user permissions.*

   4. Choose either Administrator or Editor as the role for the user. Notice that the header of the dialog is User permissions, but the title of the drop-down is Role. As I mentioned earlier, the two terms are used interchangeably throughout Office Live.

   5. Click Next. The Webpage Dialog will change, as shown in Figure 5-5.

Figure 5-5. *This* Add user -- Webpage Dialog *lets you invite the user.*

6. Since you're granting someone access to your web site, it's a good idea to let her know about it. Enter an invitation and click Send. Office Live sends a welcome e-mail to the new user. The e-mail has instructions on registering the e-mail address as a Windows Live ID.

7. The Webpage Dialog changes to show you a summary of what you just did and to confirm that an invitational e-mail has been sent to the new user. Click Finish.

The Webpage Dialog goes away, and the Users & Permissions web page refreshes itself. After the refresh, the user you just added appears in the list of users.

TIPS FROM THE TRENCHES

Don't Create Unnecessary User Accounts

Although you use a person's e-mail address as his Windows Live ID when you make him a user of your Office Live account, remember that an e-mail address and a Windows Live ID are two different entities. You'll probably want to create e-mail addresses for all your employees or associates. But all of them don't need to be users of your Office Live account.

Create user accounts only for people who'll be assisting you with your Office Live account or your web site.

Editing User Information

You may have noticed that the information you entered about your users while creating their accounts is rather skimpy. A user's profile is limited to an e-mail address, a display name, and a role. And as it turns out, two of these three items are non-editable.

You can't change a user's Windows Live ID. If a user decides to get a new Windows Live ID or a new e-mail address, you must delete his Office Live user account and create a new one for him with his new Windows Live ID.

The display name is really a feature of the Windows Live ID. Although you entered one while creating the account, the user can change it any time from his Windows Live ID account. So that's another item you can't edit.

That leaves the role. You'll be happy to know that you can change it at will. To edit a user's role, take these steps:

1. Click the Edit link next to the user's name on the Users & Permissions page. The Edit user information -- Webpage Dialog, like the one shown in Figure 5-6, pops up.

Figure 5-6. *The* Edit user information -- Webpage Dialog *lets you edit the user's role.*

2. Choose the desired role in the Role drop-down list. Click Save.

The Edit user information -- Webpage Dialog disappears, and the Users & Permissions page refreshes itself. After the refresh, the Permissions column of the user account you just edited shows the updated permissions.

Deleting Users

To prevent a user from accessing a web site, you must revoke her access to it. A user may have access to multiple web sites. You can prevent a user from accessing some sites while still allowing her to access others. So the phrase `Delete user` is somewhat misleading. Deleting a user doesn't mean getting rid of her account altogether. It just means removing her access permissions from one or more web sites.

To delete a user, follow these steps:

1. Click the `Delete` link next to the user's name on the `Users & Permissions` web page. The `Delete user -- Webpage Dialog`, like the one shown in Figure 5-7, should pop up. It shows a list of all the sites the user can access.

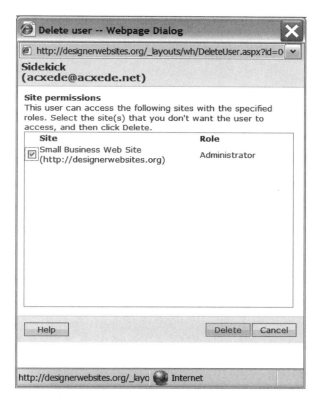

Figure 5-7. *The* `Delete user -- Webpage Dialog` *lets you delete a user from the site.*

2. Check the boxes next to the sites you want to prevent this user from accessing.

3. Click `Delete`. The `Webpage Dialog` will refresh to confirm that the user has been deleted from the selected sites.

4. Click `Close`.

The `Delete user -- Webpage Dialog` disappears, and the `Users & Permissions` web page refreshes itself. After the refresh, the user you just deleted disappears from the list of users.

Managing E-mail Accounts

To manage e-mail accounts, go to the `Administration` page and click the `E-mail accounts` link in the left navigation pane. You should see the `E-Mail` page shown in Figure 5-8. It shows a list of all e-mail accounts in your domain.

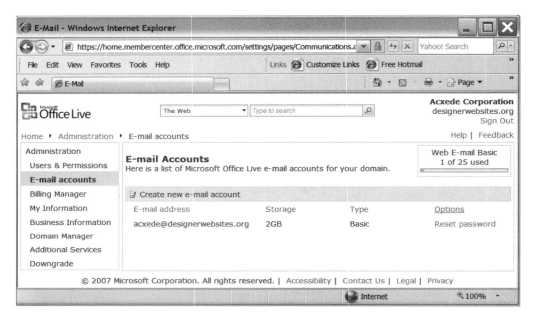

Figure 5-8. *As the owner, your e-mail address appears here when you first visit this e-mail account-management page.*

The e-mail address you used for your subscriber account appears in the list. A little meter in the top right-hand corner of the page's content area shows the number of e-mail addresses your subscription entitles you to and how many of them you've used already.

The `Options` column has links for manipulating the corresponding e-mail address's account information. As you can see in Figure 5-8, you can only reset the password for the account owner's e-mail address; you can't delete the address itself. However, you can delete any other e-mail address from your domain.

Creating an E-mail Account in Your Domain

To create a new e-mail account, take the following steps:

1. Click on the `Create new e-mail account` icon in the blue toolbar that spans across the top of the web page, as shown in Figure 5-8. The `Create new e-mail account -- Webpage Dialog`, as shown in Figure 5-9, pops up.

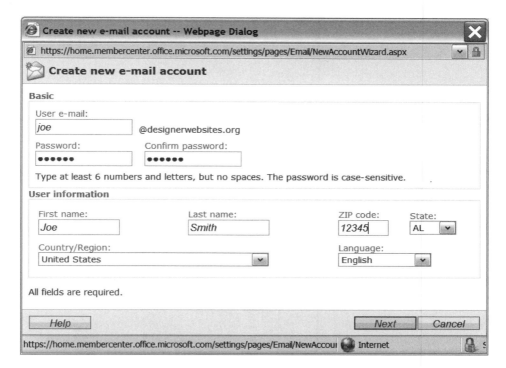

Figure 5-9. `Create new e-mail account -- Webpage Dialog` *allows you to create a new e-mail account in your domain.*

2. Notice that you can enter only the portion of the e-mail address before the @ symbol. Office Live automatically populates the domain name component of the address. You must supply all requested information. If you don't, Office Live will prompt you for it. Fill out the form and then click `Next`.

3. After a brief delay, you should see the `Webpage Dialog` shown in Figure 5-10.

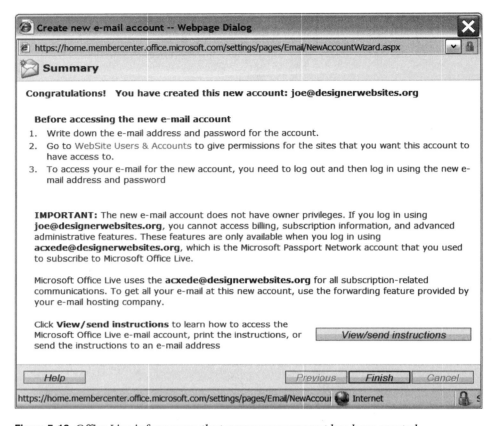

Figure 5-10. *Office Live informs you that a new user account has been created.*

4. It's helpful to send new users their new account information. To do so, click the View/send instructions button. The web page shown in Figure 5-11 opens up. It has instructions on using the new e-mail account. To send these instructions to the new user, type his or her e-mail address in the unnamed text box at the bottom of the page, right next to the Send button.

■Note Don't type the e-mail address you just created in the box. Use this box only if the owner of the new e-mail address has *another* e-mail address. He would then be able to receive your message in his other mailbox.

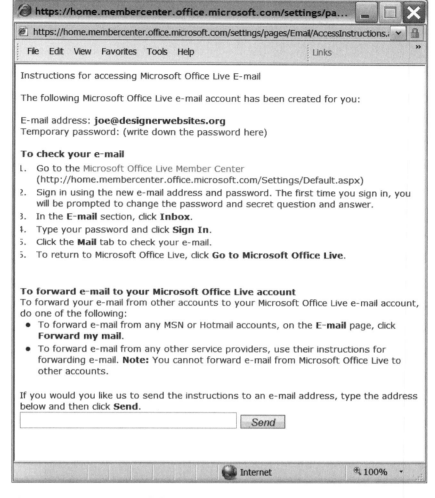

Figure 5-11. *You can e-mail these instructions on how to use Office Live e-mail to the owner of the e-mail address you just created.*

5. Click Send. Office Live dispatches the e-mail and notifies you that the message was sent. The notification comes in the form of a miniscule change to the text of the web page, so you may not even notice it. However, you'll know that the message was sent when the page flickers a bit. When it does, banish the web page from your monitor by closing the browser window. You should see the e-mail page in your browser, as shown in Figure 5-12.

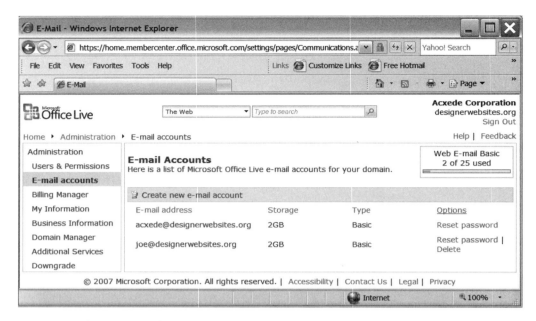

Figure 5-12. *The new e-mail account appears in the list.*

6. Note that the new e-mail account has a Delete link in the Options column, unlike the owner's e-mail account, which you can't delete.

Resetting the Password for an E-mail Account

Sometimes people forget their passwords and turn to you for help. At other times, you may want to prevent a person from accessing his e-mail for various reasons—because he left your employment, for example. Such are the joys of being a webmaster.

You can reset the password for an e-mail account from the E-Mail page shown in Figure 5-12. Follow these steps to reset a password:

1. Click on the Reset password link next to the correct e-mail address. The Reset account password -- Webpage Dialog, shown in Figure 5-13, pops up.

Figure 5-13. *Resetting the password of an e-mail account*

2. Enter a new password, and then retype it in the Confirm password box.

3. Click OK. You should see a Webpage Dialog confirming the change, as shown in Figure 5-14.

Figure 5-14. *This* Webpage Dialog *confirms that you've resent the password; additional steps may be necessary before the change takes effect.*

Don't be alarmed at the security warning you see. It's only trying to tell you that although you changed the password on the e-mail account, the user can still use other identifying information on the account, such as the secret question and the alternate e-mail address, to retrieve the password. You don't have to worry about this if you've changed the password simply because the owner forgot it. However, if you changed it because you wish to prevent the owner of the account from accessing mail at this address, you must change the identifying information as well.

The Windows Live authentication system (called Passport Account Services in its previous incarnation) maintains the identifying information. To change it, click on the Go to Passport Account Services link at the bottom of the Webpage Dialog, log in to the e-mail account with the new password you just created, and change the identifying information.

Deleting an E-mail Account

You may delete any e-mail account from your domain, except the owner's. To delete one, follow these steps:

1. Click the Delete link next to the e-mail account under the Options column on the E-Mail page shown in Figure 5-12. The Delete account -- Webpage Dialog, shown in Figure 5-15, pops up.

Figure 5-15. *Remember that once you delete an e-mail account, it can't be re-created for 30 days.*

2. Read the warning very carefully. Once you delete an e-mail account, you can't create it again for 30 days. If you're sure you want to proceed with the deletion, click the Delete button at the bottom. You should see the confirmation page, as shown in Figure 5-16.

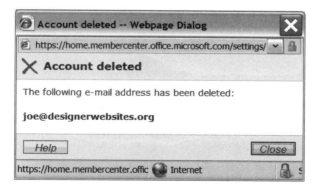

Figure 5-16. *Sayonara! The e-mail address has been deleted.*

TIPS FROM THE TRENCHES

Change Passwords of E-mail Accounts Instead of Deleting Them

If you don't want to delete an e-mail account altogether, but merely want to stop its owner from accessing it, reset its password and identifying information.

Let's say Joe, your marketing honcho, resigns. You'll naturally want to prevent Joe from accessing his mailbox any longer. But deleting his e-mail account will get rid of all the mail in his mailbox as well. When you change the password on Joe's e-mail account, *you* will still be able to read and send mail from it, but Joe won't be able to access it.

Updating Your Billing Information

Office Live's Billing Manager is its account management interface. To access it, go to the `Administration` page and click on `Billing Manager` in the left navigation pane. A new browser window, like the one in Figure 5-17, opens up.

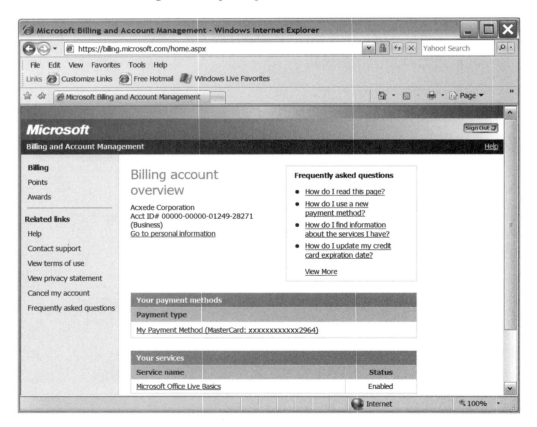

Figure 5-17. *The* `Microsoft Billing and Account Management` *page lets you control your billing.*

FAQ

The Billing Page Doesn't Seem to Be on the Office Live Site. Is Everything OK?

Yes. In fact, as you made your way from feature to feature in the previous chapter, you may have noticed that some of the web pages shown there weren't from Office Live's web site either but rather from the Windows Live, Microsoft, Windows Live Hotmail, Office Online, Microsoft Passport, and even Xbox 360 sites. You'll see many more as you make your way through this chapter as well.

The page in Figure 5-17, for instance, isn't on Office Live's web site, but don't be alarmed. Nothing insidious is going on here. This confusion arises from the fact that Microsoft, from time to time, repackages old services in new cartons, or uses existing services in new offerings. Windows Live ID, for example, has been around for a while under various names, while the rewards program started its life as an incentive for Xbox customers.

Web pages from these underlying services show up from time to time in their original attire, especially when you're performing administrative tasks. As Office Live matures as a product, you can expect at least some of these idiosyncrasies to go away.

When you go from the Office Live web site to the web site where the Billing and Account Management page resides, your Windows Live account takes care of signing you in to that site automatically. But sometimes, a glitch can occur in the behind-the-scenes sign-in process. If that happens, you'll see a Sign In page like the one shown in Figure 5-18. Go ahead and enter your password. Office Live will take you to the Billing and Account Management page, which you should have arrived at to begin with.

The Billing Manager helps you track two pieces of information:

- Your payment methods

- All Microsoft services you subscribe to with this Windows Live ID

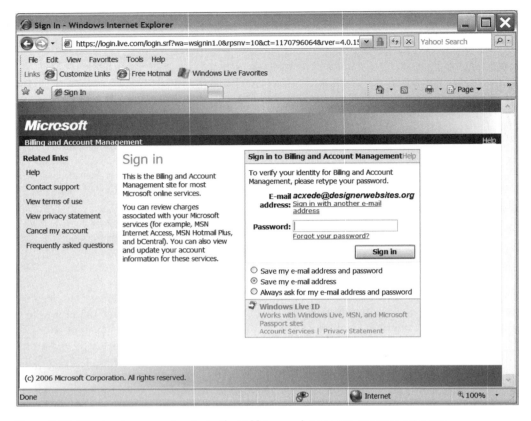

Figure 5-18. *Here's where you sign in to the* Billing and Account Management *page.*

Payment Methods

Even if you signed up for Office Live Basics, you still had to provide your credit-card number. Microsoft will charge this credit card if you buy additional services such as extra storage space or an additional domain name. It will also charge your card if you upgrade your subscription to Office Live Essentials or Office Live Premium.

All credit cards that you have used in the past to settle this account are listed under the Your payment methods section. To change credit-card information or to see online copies of your invoices, click a credit card's link.

Your Service Subscriptions

As I mentioned in Chapter 2, you can use your Windows Live ID not only to buy Office Live subscriptions, but to buy other services from Microsoft as well. The Your services section lists all the services that you've bought from Microsoft with this Windows Live ID. Click one of them to view the account details for that service.

Updating Your Contact Information and Preferences

The My Information page is home to your contact information and your preferences for using the Office Live web site. To access it, go to the Administration page, and click on My Information in the left navigation pane. You'll see a page like the one shown in Figure 5-19.

Contact Information

To edit your contact information and site preferences in Office Live, click the Edit link, edit the information, and click Save.

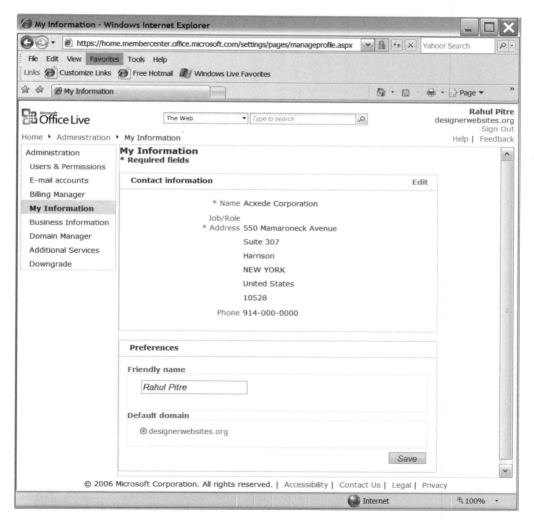

Figure 5-19. *Accessing your contact information in Office Live*

Preferences

You can only set two preferences—not exactly an overwhelming number of choices at present, but that may change in the future. The first preference setting is the Friendly name for your account. This name appears on the top-right corner of your administration pages instead of your first name and last name.

The second preference setting is the Default domain. You may have noticed that when you sign on to Office Live, you don't need to provide a domain name; Office Live automatically figures out the domain you have access to and takes you there. But if you happen to be a user of multiple Office Live sites, Office Live must find out which of them you intend to work with. It does so by showing you a page such as the one shown in Figure 5-20, right after you log in.

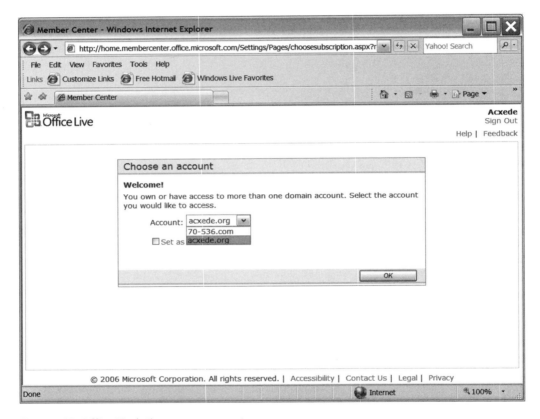

Figure 5-20. *Office Live's* Choose an account *prompt*

You can avoid this prompt by selecting one of the domains that appears in the Default domain box under Preferences. To set your preferences, follow these steps:

1. Enter a friendly name, if you wish.

2. Select one of the domains that appear under the Default domain box. (If you have access to only one domain, that option will be selected automatically.)

3. Click Save.

Updating Your Business Information

The Business Information page, naturally, gathers your business information. Microsoft uses this information to help "improve your service," which is probably a euphemism for "tell us which advertisements to show on Member Center pages." If you subscribe to the philosophy of providing information on the web only when absolutely essential, you can leave this section blank.[1] If you prefer to provide the information, go to the Administration page and click on the Business Information link in its left navigation panel. The Business Information page should open up. It asks you to fill in the following information:

- Your business address and phone numbers

- The time zone you live in

- The contact information of the person in charge of sales in your organization

Fill in the information you won't be embarrassed to see on the front page of *The New York Times*, and click Save.

Managing Domain Names

A domain manager is usually an application that lets you manage your domain settings. If you've ever managed a domain with a registrar such as Network Solutions or GoDaddy.com, you may have used a domain manager application to change name servers for your domain or to create subdomains. If you expect to do the same with Office Live's Domain Manager, you're in for a big disappointment.

Office Live's Domain Manager is simply a tool that lets you buy additional domain names and point them to your web site. You don't have access to any of your domain's management features.

FAQ

Why Would You Need Additional Domain Names?

Additional domain names are quite common. If your domain is yourdomain.com, you wouldn't want your competitor to snap up the names yourdomain.net or yourdomain.org. Even worse, you wouldn't want someone to start an adult site at yourdomain.net or yourdomain.org. These are good reasons to register yourdomain.net and yourdomain.org along with yourdomain.com.

Even though you own three domain names, you don't need three web sites. You can build a web site for yourdomain.com and simply redirect visitors to the other two domains to it by setting up domain pointers. When you buy an additional domain name through Office Live, the redirection is set up automatically.

---

1. I haven't bothered to enter any of my business information, and I am yet to face dire consequences as a result.

To access Domain Manager and purchase additional domain names, go to the Administration page and click on the Domain Manager link in the left navigation pane. The Domain Manager page, as shown in Figure 5-21, appears.

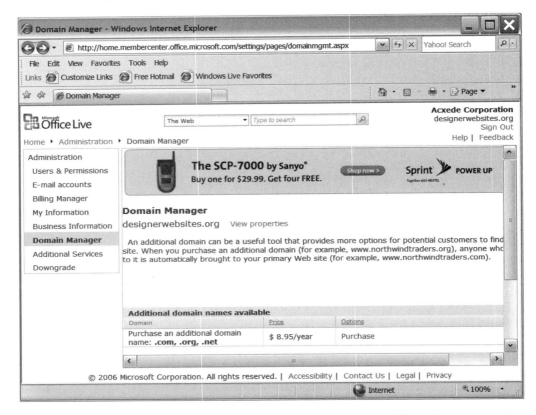

Figure 5-21. *With Office Live's Domain Manager, you can buy additional domain names to point at your web site.*

To purchase additional domains, click on the Purchase link toward the middle of the page. You'll then get to the same set of pages that you worked your way through when you registered your primary domain while signing up for Office Live.

After you purchase the additional domain name, it will appear below your primary domain name on the Domain Manager page. Click on the View properties link next to any of the domain names to see the contact information for that domain.

■**Note** Anyone can look up the contact information for your domain by accessing the Whois database maintained by InterNIC at www.internic.net/whois.html.

It's in your interest to keep your domain contact information current. All domain-related communication from your registrar is sent to you at the e-mail or postal address in your domain contact information. If you move your office to a new address or decide to change your e-mail address, make sure you go to My Information and update the contact information.

Buying Additional Services

Advertising and higher-end subscriptions are not the only ways Microsoft makes money with Office Live. It also sells you additional services for your Office Live account. Office Live Basics subscribers can buy additional services too. That's another reason why Microsoft needs your credit-card information even if you sign up for Office Live Basics.

Depending on your subscription level, Office Live gives you a particular fixed amount of disk storage, a fixed number of e-mail boxes, and a fixed number of web site user accounts. If you exceed those limits, you can buy additional storage space or accounts from the Additional Services page.

To buy one or more of these services or to upgrade your subscription level, click on the Additional Services link in the left pane of the Administration web page and follow the instructions on the page that appears in your browser window.

Downgrading Your Subscription Level

Office Live Essentials and Office Live Premium subscriptions are meant for people who want to build intranet and extranet sites for collaborating among employees, customers, vendors, and business associates. While intranets and extranets may sound exotic to many small-business owners, they aren't suitable for everyone. You, too, may come to the conclusion that you can't make much use of those facilities. If you do, you may want to downgrade your sub-scription to Office Live Basics and save some money every month.

To downgrade your subscription, click on the Downgrade link in the left pane of the Administration web page and follow the instructions on the page that appears in your browser window.

If you're a Microsoft Live Basics subscriber, you're already at the bottom of Office Live subscriber food chain. You can't downgrade any further. But if you try to do so anyway, Office Live will remind you that you can't.

Summary

The Administration page on your web site helps you manage your Office Live account. In this chapter, I introduced you to the administrative chores you have to do as a site owner. Here are the important points you should remember about managing your Office Live account:

- Some administrative tasks you perform on the `Administration` page, such as creating user accounts and e-mail accounts, are related to the operation of your site. Some others, such as managing your billing information and updating your contact information, have more to do with your account relationship with Microsoft.

- Some of the pages that you encounter while working on your account may be on other Microsoft sites and not on the Office Live site. You may suspect a phishing scam when that happens. That's not the case, and there's no need for alarm.

- You can create additional user accounts for people who will help you manage your web site and Office Live account. They can be *editors* or *administrators*.

- Editors can only help you maintain your web site. They don't have administrative rights.

- In addition to maintaining your web site, administrators can perform a few, but not all, administrative tasks. They can't change your billing information, for example.

- You can beef up your Office Live subscription with additional user accounts, e-mail accounts, and disk space. You must pay additional charges for these features.

- You can buy additional domain names, which you can point at your web site.

- You can upgrade or downgrade your Office Live subscription.

By now, you should know your way around your Office Live account quite well. I'll change gears in the next part of the book and start addressing the main reason you probably bought this book: building your web site.

PART 2

■ ■ ■

Building Your Site

CHAPTER 6

■ ■ ■

A Crash Course in Web Design

Recently, I asked my eight-year-old daughter whom she would call a good driver. "Mommy," she said. "She's a better driver. You keep changing lanes. It makes me dizzy." I considered strangling her.

"I mean, how would a person have to drive for you to call him a good driver?"

"Oh! Let me think," she said. She thought for a moment and came up with this list of good driving habits:

- Stop when traffic lights turn red.

- Obey speed limits.

- Stop for pedestrians and animals.

- Don't honk unnecessarily.[1]

- Be nice to fellow drivers.

While this is an eight-year-old's idea of good driving habits, many adults could stay out of mandatory defensive-driving classes by following her simple rules.

Designing web sites is no different. An advanced degree in communications, graphic arts, or computer science can no doubt be of immense help, but simply following a few basic principles can take you a long way toward creating a good web site.

Although opinions about what makes web sites "good" vary greatly, they usually converge on some combination of awe-inspiring animations, dazzling audio-visual effects, and clever programming tricks.

Nonsense.

Good web sites are those whose visitors can find desired information quickly, easily, and intuitively. This chapter is about creating such user-friendly sites.

A single chapter is too short to cover the entire subject of web design. To stay focused, I'll spare you the history of the Internet, the origin of the World Wide Web, and the Web's astounding progress in the last decade. I'll hold back on the nuances of creating complex graphics, and I'll spare you tutorials on HTML, CSS, XML, SQL, Ajax, PHP, ASP.NET, and a few other incomprehensible acronyms. Instead, I'll jump straight to a few guidelines that anyone who wants to build a user-friendly web site would do well to follow. A site built on these guidelines won't pose a clear and present threat to Amazon.com, but it will make your customers happy and your friends jealous.

---

1. Not applicable to New Yorkers.

Build Your Site with a Clear Purpose

If you're contemplating building a web site, the first question you should ask yourself is "Why do I want one?" If your answer is "Because everyone else has one" or "It doesn't hurt to have one," you're not ready for a web site. You should take a step back, put on your thinking cap, and ponder the question.

After sufficient thought and a good amount of coffee (or Scotch), you should be able to come to the conclusion that you want to build a web site for one or more of the following reasons:

- To build a better awareness of your products or services

- To save operating costs

- To generate revenue by selling online

- To communicate more efficiently with your partners and affiliates

- To support your customers better

Whatever your objective might be, the key is not to deviate from it. If you lose sight of your objective, your site will quickly morph into a mishmash of random, unrelated pages. If, for instance, you're building a site to put up your sales brochures, stick to sales brochures. If your objective is customer support, limit your site to product information, online manuals, knowledge bases, support tickets, contact forms, and the like. Resist the temptation to add a blog, advertisements, Google Search, forums, picture galleries, background music, and other items irrelevant to your objective—at least in the first pass.

Take an Iterative Approach

To help keep your objective in focus, an iterative approach is often the best. Keep it simple at the beginning. Restrict your site to only a few pages, such as Home, About Us, Products & Services, Contact Us, and an additional page or two that'll focus on your objective. This is all you'll need to get your site off the ground. Spend a good amount of time and energy on getting these few pages right. Don't be too ambitious and plan a grand site with 500 pages.

Beware of Copying Cute Features from Other Sites

Almost every web site you visit will have a feature you like. Don't replicate every one of them on your site. Most cute features are cute only when viewed in isolation. When you cram 50 cute features on a single site, the result is usually quite hideous.

Add Pages Judiciously

When you're tempted to add a new page to your site, consider carefully whether it fulfills one of your objectives. If it does, go ahead and add it. If it doesn't, discard it ruthlessly. If you follow this simple guideline, you'll end up building a focused site over time.

Write Good Copy

Our challenge is to interactively foster low-risk, high-yield sources to allow us to efficiently facilitate excellent paradigms in order to solve business problems. We have committed to proactively simplify excellent methods of empowerment so that we may completely network resource-leveling catalysts for change, because that is what the customer expects.

Impressive copy, right? Wait 'til I tell you where I got it from: the Mission Statement Generator at `www.dilbert.com`.

You might have come across web sites that have page after page of such profound yet meaningless gobbledygook. Such copy serves little purpose. The text on your web pages need not *sound* intelligent, but it must *communicate* intelligently. You should strive to provide information by writing clear and concise copy.

Writing good copy is arguably the most difficult aspect of building a web site. That's why so many sites are stuffed with animated GIFs, sound effects, and other useless features that are a snap to add. But when all is said and done, an informative, well-written web site with no pictures is vastly superior to a site with terrific artwork and lousy information.

TIPS FROM THE TRENCHES

Writing Good Copy

Writing for the Web is a different skill from the day-to-day writing you're used to. However, you don't have to take continuing-education classes to acquire it. Whenever you write copy for a web page, keep these basic principles in mind:

- Write short sentences, but don't go overboard doing it. Very short sentences stir up childhood memories of Dr. Seuss books.

- Keep your paragraphs short. Present information as bulleted lists whenever possible. The column on the left in the following figure has the same text as the column on the right, but the column on the right is easier to read because it contains several short paragraphs instead of one large blob of text.

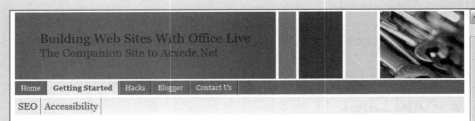

Getting Started

 ★

This is the companion site to Acxede.Net, the original Office Live hacks site. Acxede.Net shows you how to do anything (that is possible, of course!) with Office Live. You can find answers to most of your Office Live questions on the Forums at Acxede.Net. This site implements the techniques shown at Acxede.Net. The site is built with the new version of Office Live Basics. But as long as you are not using FrontPage, everything here will apply to your site even if you subscribe to Essentials or Premium. Although a few hacks are inevitable, not everything you see here, or on Acxede.Net for that matter, is a clever hack or a way to beat Office Live's designer. Rather, it shows you how you can design a great Web site with the limited resources Office Live provides you.

This is the companion site to Acxede.Net, the original Office Live hacks site.

About Acxede.Net

Acxede.Net shows you how to do anything (that is possible, of course!) with Office Live. You can find answers to most of your Office Live questions on the Forums at Acxede.Net.

About This Web Site

This site implements the techniques shown at Acxede.Net.

The site is built with the new version of Office Live Basics. But as long as you are not using FrontPage, everything here will apply to your site even if you subscribe to Essentials or Premium.

Is Everything Here a Hack of Some Sort?

Although a few hacks are inevitable, not everything you see here, or on Acxede.Net for that matter, is a clever hack or a way to beat Office Live's designer. Rather, it shows you how you can design a great Web site with the limited resources Office Live provides you.

- Use simple, easily understandable language. Avoid marketese or jargon.

- Keep your readers in mind while writing copy. Professors of philosophy and teenagers have very different vocabularies.

- Keep your pages short. Avoid more than five or six paragraphs on a page.

- Spell-check! Almost every word processor has a built-in spell-checker. Use it.

- Check your grammar. However, don't depend on your word processor's grammar-checker. The advice it offers is dubious at best and often outright ridiculous.

- Maintain a uniform tone of voice for the content on all pages. Don't be friendly on some pages and dour on others.

- Don't use big, meaningless words just because you think they sound impressive. Say what you want to say directly.

A great resource for learning to write well is *The Elements of Style, Fourth Edition* by William Strunk Jr. and E.B. White (Allyn & Bacon, 1999). It distills everything your English teachers hammered into your head over the years into 100 pages. You can find a *free* online version at `www.bartleby.com/141/`.

Be Consistent

Consistency imparts a sense of continuity and familiarity as visitors move around your site. Consistency of a web site has two aspects: internal consistency and overall consistency.

Internal Consistency

A web site is internally consistent if all its pages appear similar, the same logo and navigation style appear on all its pages, all its content has a similar tone, and its visual elements such as fonts and colors are common to all pages.

Overall Consistency

Overall consistency has to do with conforming to the generally accepted (and expected) norms of the web as a medium. Take navigation, for example. People expect to find primary navigation on a web site at the top or to the left. Nothing prevents you from putting it at the bottom, but if you do, it confuses a visitor to no end.

Or take shopping carts. When people are ready to check items out from an online store, they expect to see a picture of a shopping cart or the words *Cart* or *Shopping Cart* toward the top right-hand corner of the web page they're on (see Figure 6-1). If you put your cart in the bottom left-hand corner and call it a *Basket*, a *Bag*, or a *Bin*, you're still well within your legal rights but just a little poorer, perhaps, because potential customers won't be able to fathom how to buy items from your store.

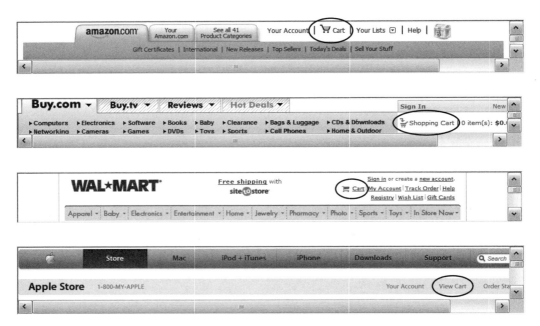

Figure 6-1. *Notice that the shopping-cart links on these popular online stores are toward the top-right corner of the page and are called* carts—*not* bags *or anything else.*

Many web sites with such unexpected elements may fall in the "cool" or "awesome" category, but they thoroughly confound users. It's a good idea to follow established conventions instead.

TIPS FROM THE TRENCHES

Building Consistent Web Sites

Office Live's architecture forces a great deal of consistency on you. You must use the same header and footers on all pages, for instance, and you must use the same navigation scheme across all pages. Still, you'll be adding plenty of your own content to your web site. Follow these tips to keep it consistent:

- If you call something a *widget* on one page, don't call it a *thingamajig* or a *whatchamacallit* on another. The words may be synonyms, but the change in terminology confuses users.

- Add features uniformly across pages. If you decide to provide a link to print or bookmark a page, provide it on all pages. Make sure the link appears at the same location on all pages as well.

- Use the same fonts and colors on all your pages.

- Standardize image sizes. If you have four pictures of products on a page, make them the same size. If each is of a different size, the page will look nothing short of ugly.

- If the content on your pages appears to "jump around" rather than refresh itself as you move from page to page, you need to check the formatting of pages that cause the jumps.

- Visit other, more established web sites in your field and note what they have in common in terms of content and visual elements. This is what visitors to your site will expect. Strive to provide it on your web site as well.

After you're done building your web site, have a few friends and family members surf it and comment on it. You'll be surprised at what they can come up with.

Choose Pleasing Fonts and Backgrounds

When you start building your site with Office Live, the first thing that usually comes to mind is images. However, if you want your site to stand out, you should be focusing on the text instead.

Employ a Consistent Font Scheme

A common problem with many do-it-yourself sites is that each page has a different font. Viewing such sites is like reading a document that has different font face, size, and color on every page. This disparity is usually the result of cutting and pasting from a word processor at different times and probably on different computers. To give a uniform feel to your site, be consistent with your fonts. It's all right to choose a different font for headers and titles, but use the same font face/size convention across the site.

Let's say you come up with this font scheme:

- **Headers**: Trebuchet MS, size 14, bold

- **Subheaders**: Verdana, size 12

- **Text**: Verdana, size 10

Now use the same scheme on *all* your pages. The idea is not to limit your font choices; you can make as elaborate a scheme as you like, but make sure that you use it consistently across the entire site.

Pick Easy-to-Read Fonts

Would you read a newspaper printed in a thick gothic font? A script font, perhaps? Most people wouldn't. Then why put the visitors to your web site through the same ordeal?

Choose sans-serif fonts such as Verdana or Arial. They don't have the little "wings" that serif fonts have (see Figure 6-2). Therefore, they're easier on the eyes when reading large amounts of text, and they don't smudge words when the text is in bold or italics. If you hate sans-serif fonts with a passion, choose a serif font such as Georgia or Times New Roman.

Serif   Sans-serif

Figure 6-2. *The font on the left is Georgia, a serif font, and the font on the right is Verdana, a sans-serif font.*

FAQ

Why Only Verdana or Georgia?

Most fonts made their way to computer screens from printed publications. Many of them look fantastic in print but awful on screen because the quality of letters on screen is limited to the number of available pixels. Often the quality worsens when you make letters bold or italicize them.

When Microsoft rolled out Windows 95, it introduced a brand-new font: Verdana. Microsoft designed Verdana from the ground up specifically to look good onscreen. When you use Verdana, the letters in a word don't touch each other, even if you bold or italicize them. And they look equally good in print.

Verdana is a sans-serif font. Not everyone is fond of sans-serif fonts; some prefer serif fonts. To cater to their taste, Microsoft also had a serif font designed close on the heels of Verdana: Georgia. Like Verdana, Georgia looks great both on and off screen.

Stay with Normal Fonts

Bold and italic letters are used for emphasis; use them precisely for that purpose on your site. Don't make entire pages bold or italic, and don't type an entire page in uppercase letters either; your readers may think you're shouting at them. In Figure 6-3, notice that you can't read the paragraph headers in the left-hand column very well because the font isn't suited for computer monitors.

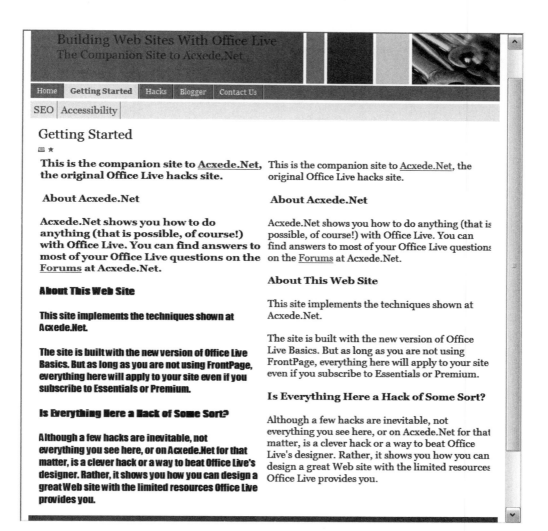

Figure 6-3. *The right-hand column has the same text as the left-hand column but is easier to read.*

Opt for Light Backgrounds and Dark Text

Black or dark gray (not light gray!) letters on a white background is the best foreground-background color combination you can have for a site, irrespective of the site's color scheme. It makes your pages easier to read. Almost all print publications employ the combination, and so should your web site.

If black-on-white is too drab a combination for you, by all means use a colored background. But ensure that the letters and the background have just the right contrast—dark-colored letters on pastel backgrounds work better than light-colored letters on dark backgrounds.

Avoid Scrolling or Blinking Text

With the notable exceptions of stock traders on trading floors and news anchors on television, people are used to reading text that stays put. Avoid scrolling text. Similarly, the only places where people expect to see blinking text are at traffic lights and on digital clocks. Avoid it as well.

Align Text to the Left Margin

Unless you're used to reading Arabic, your eye is trained to read from left to right. That's why text in books is aligned to the left margin. If each line begins at a different place, as is the case with centered or right-aligned text, the text is very difficult to read. Microsoft Word has popularized the "align justify" option, which is equally irritating to the eye. On your web site, stick to "align left" (assuming, of course, that the text on your web site is written in English). Figure 6-4 demonstrates text that is aligned to the left; your eyes don't have to adjust with every line.

Figure 6-4. *The right-hand column has the same text as the left-hand column but is easier to read because all the lines start at the same left margin.*

Keep User Accessibility in Mind

An accessible web site is one that people with disabilities can surf without difficulty. On an accessible web site, people with low vision can make the font size bigger, for instance, and blind people can use screen readers to get to all the content that people with 20/20 vision can. While navigating accessible web sites, people who have trouble using a mouse can use the keyboard instead, and deaf people don't have to miss out on audio content because it's also available in transcript form.

There are many examples of accessible content in the conventional media. Television broadcasts and films on DVD are closed-captioned, for example, and books come in large print or braille editions. As the Web becomes the primary source of information for an increasing number of people, expecting web sites to be accessible is not unreasonable. Yet, few web sites can truly claim that distinction.

There are several reasons why accessibility is given scant attention while building web sites. Some designers believe that it will restrict their creativity. Others think it's too complex and too expensive. Still others don't know what's involved in creating accessible web sites to begin with. In the end, people rationalize that the effort is not worth the trouble because few disabled people, if any, will visit the site.

Building accessible web sites is no black art. Like most other aspects of building web sites, it only amounts to following a few guidelines and best practices. If you follow the tips in the "Tips from the Trenches" sidebar, you'll end up incorporating many best practices into your site design that will make visiting your site a pleasant experience not only for people with disabilities, but for everyone.

With Office Live, you don't have control over all aspects of a web page. Office Live generates part of the page, and you then add content to it. You should keep accessibility guidelines in mind while adding content.

TIPS FROM THE TRENCHES

Building Accessible Web Sites

The main tenet of accessible design is simplicity. Follow these simple tips to make the content of your pages accessible:

- Don't render blocks of text as images; screen readers and text browsers can't read text in images.

- Don't use image-based navigation or use images as buttons. Image-based navigation is extremely difficult to use with screen readers and text browsers.

- Maintain high contrast between the foreground and background of your pages. Black letters on a white background is usually the best combination. Avoid red-and-green color combinations; color-blind people may find them difficult to decipher.

- Don't use too small a font. If possible, use relative font sizes, which users can make bigger or smaller using buttons on their browsers. Avoid font sizes smaller than 10 pixels, if you must specify the size in pixels. If your grandmother can't read the text on a web page, it's too small.

- Don't use animated or blinking text. Not only does it annoy users, but it also makes some people dizzy.

A great way to check your web pages for accessibility is using the accessibility checker at www.wave.webaim.org. When you see the results, you'll notice that some of the problems are a result of HTML that Office Live generates. There's nothing you can do about it, but fix all issues that you have control over.

Make Your Site Search-Engine-Friendly

If you're taking the trouble to create a web site, it's safe to assume that you expect people to come and visit it. Unless you give them your site's URL, most people will find your site through search engines. Naturally, search engine optimization (SEO) should be high on your list of priorities.

SPEAKING THE LANGUAGE

Search Engine Optimization (SEO)

- **Keyword(s)**: A term or a phrase a user wants to search for using a search engine. If you go to Google's search page and type "Office Live," then *Office* and *Live* are the keywords for your search operation. Also called *search terms* or *query terms*.

- **Search engine**: An application that helps users find information using keywords. Search engines use automated programs called robots or spiders to scour the Web for information. The information is stored in massive databases, which users can search by entering keywords on a web page. Google is an example of a search engine.

- **Directory**: An application similar to a search engine except that people collect information manually instead of by employing spiders. The information is subsequently categorized and stored in a database with a manually generated description. Users can search the database by entering keywords on a web page, just like they can on search engines. Although search engines and directories are two different things, people often refer to both as *search engines*. I'll follow suit.

- **Search algorithm**: A set of rules used by search engines to come up with possible matches for keywords a user enters on a search page.

- **Search results (aka listings)**: A list of possible matches in a search engine's database for the keywords a user enters on a search page.

- **Rank (aka position)**: The position of a specific listing in the search results relative to other listings.

- **PageRank**: PageRank is Google's proprietary scheme of ranking search results. This is a Google-specific term. The *Page* in *PageRank* refers to Larry Page, Google's founder, and not to a web page.

- **Metatag**: A hidden HTML tag that describes a document or a feature of a document. Search engines look for metatags when they attempt to match a user's search term with the page content to determine a match.

- **Link popularity**: One of the parameters supposedly used by search engines to determine the rank of a web page in search results. The theory is that more links to your pages is a reflection of their greater popularity. As a result, pages with higher link popularity have a better rank among listings in search results.

- **Search engine optimization**: The process of optimizing web pages so as to help search engines make better sense of them and consequently index them correctly so that they show up in the results of relevant searches.

Making rational decisions about SEO isn't easy. There's no dearth of advice about submitting your site to search engines and "improving" your site's position in search results. The advice comes in all shapes and forms, from lengthy do-it-yourself instructions to paid SEO services that will do everything for you at the click of a mouse (and, of course, in exchange for your credit-card number). Some simply submit your site to hundreds of search engines. Others also "monitor" your site's position on an ongoing basis. Still others offer to "optimize" your site's position in the search results. The entire process is shrouded in mystery, which makes discerning fact from fiction difficult, if not impossible. To make a rational decision, you need some straight talk on SEO.

■**Caution** Before you subscribe to an SEO service, consider this question: if every person in the world pays ten bucks a month to monitor and improve his site's search-result positioning, whose site will really show up at the top? My guess is as good as yours.

Optimizing your site for search engines is a worthy goal, but attempting to manipulate search engines to push your site higher in search results is a complete waste of time. Search engines use different algorithms to list search results. They take into account a combination of several factors before coming up with a result set. Therefore, there's no standard way of improving the search result ranking of your site across the board.

Besides, users typically scroll across only a page or two of search results. If your site is not among the top 25 or so, it doesn't really matter whether it's at the original position of 16,383 or at the improved position of 5,234. Users are unlikely to find it anyway. Therefore, trying to "improve" your site's position in search results is generally a meaningless exercise.

FAQ

Should I Submit My Web Site to As Many Search Engines As Possible?

Quick, name all the search engines you know in 10 seconds! How many did you come up with? Chances are, not more than you can count on one hand. The average person probably uses one on a regular basis and a couple more intermittently, if at all. In fact, roughly 97% of all search-engine traffic flows through the top-five search engines: Google, Yahoo!, MSN, AOL, and Ask. Therefore, submitting your site to 50 or 100 search engines isn't likely to produce any gains in the traffic to your site. The incremental gain from submitting your site to each additional search engine after the first 5 is close to 0.

Once I Optimize My Site, Will It Appear At the Top of Google's Search Results?

Search results depend largely on the exact phrase the user keys in and its context as understood by the search engine. No amount of optimization will change that. Try this exercise: go to www.yahoo.com and enter the phrase Acxede.Net. You'll see this site listed right at the top. Now try entering Acxede. You'll see the entry for Acxede, which is me, on PC Mechanic's site, where I write a weekly business column. Why? Because your search phrase is simply *acxede*, a word repeated several times on that page.

Try another search. Enter `Will`. Your top 20 results will include, among others, will planning, *Will and Grace*, Will County (Illinois), and Will Smith. I don't see any good reason why Will's Bookstore should trump them all, if your search phrase happens to be just *Will*.

Will Lots of Metatags Improve My Site's Rank?

Metatags are perhaps the most misunderstood entities in the search-engine optimization process. People who believe metatags can cure all ills, including baldness and cellulite, add hundreds of metatags to their pages. Those many metatags do you little good.

Try this: bring up any product at `www.amazon.com` in your web browser. Click on the `View` menu and then click on `Source` (assuming you're using Internet Explorer; if not, do whatever it takes to view the page source in your browser). Search for the word *meta*. How many metatags did you find? Probably no more than two or three. If Amazon.com can make do with a couple of metatags, and everyone can find their pages, there's no reason why you should adorn your pages with hundreds of them.

Will My Site's Link Popularity Score Increase If I Pay Other Sites to Host My Links?

A link popularity score is a measure of how many other sites link to yours. If more sites link to your site, it is assumed that your site must be of interest to others and therefore worthy of a higher rank than sites that don't boast as many external links. Other sites might want to link to yours for two reasons:

- People who run those sites like your content, product, or service and think it's worthwhile sharing it with their readers.

- You pay them to link to your site.

Search engines attach more importance to links in the first category, for obvious reasons. Paying someone to increase your link popularity score is likely to serve little purpose.

People who attempt to manipulate search engines claim to have developed techniques to outsmart the search engines. The fact is, the search engines have always kept a step ahead of the rank manipulators by updating their technology frequently, and for good reason. After all, as a user, would you use a search engine if all the results you saw were doctored, easily manipulated, and probably meaningless to your search?

TIPS FROM THE TRENCHES

Optimizing Your Site for Search Engines

A few simple measures can go a long way toward optimizing your web site for search engines:

- **Give a meaningful title to each page**: Every web page has a title that appears in the browser's title bar when someone brings up the page in a browser. It also doubles as the text of a bookmark should a visitor decide to bookmark it. If you don't give a page a title, Office Live will fill something in for you. Don't depend on Office Live's wisdom. Think of a title yourself.

- **Write copy that's relevant to the topic of the page**: Think of terms your users are likely to search for and weave them into your page's text. See the "Expert's Voice: Jakob Nielsen" sidebar.

- **Don't go overboard with metatags**: Although Office Live lets you enter description and keyword metatags on every page, don't overdo it. Add a short description and only a few keywords that are relevant to the context and the text on that page.

- **Attempt to increase the link popularity score of your pages**: Have your site, services, or products reviewed or mentioned on other web sites.[2]

Submit your site to the top three search engines. Then sit back and let the search engines do their job. Don't attempt to manipulate the rankings. Above all, be patient. Don't expect page ranks to shoot up overnight.

Search engines are designed to find the most appropriate sites based on a user's query. By all means, make your pages search-engine-friendly. But don't waste your time trying to outsmart the bright people who write search algorithms. A better and more fruitful approach would be to concentrate on building a good web site and leave the search-result positioning to search engines.

EXPERT'S VOICE: JAKOB NIELSEN[3]

Use Old Words When Writing for Findability

Familiar words spring to mind when users create their search queries. If your writing favors made-up terms over legacy words, users won't find your site.

"Speak the user's language" has been a primary usability guideline for more than 20 years. The fact that the Web is a linguistic environment further increases the importance of using the right vocabulary.

How New Words Ruin Your Search Rankings

Many forces pressure Web writers to diminish a website's value by filling it with words that are unlikely to appear in search queries. Here are some guidelines for writing to ensure that users will find your site:

- **Supplement made-up words with known words.** It's tempting to coin new terms because you can own the positioning if the term catches on. But, more likely, people will continue to use their old terminology. It's long been a usability guideline to avoid made-up words in navigation menus, because users scan them for words they know. In full-text content, you can include new words for effect, but make sure to supplement them with legacy words — that is, words that your customers know and use in everyday business practice.

---

2. Start with my web site, Acxede.Net!

3. Reprinted with permission from Jakob Nielsen's AlertBox, "Use Old Words When Writing for Findability," www.useit.com/alertbox/search-keywords.html, August 28, 2006.

- **Play down marketese and internal vocabulary.** Call a spade a spade, not a digging implement. Certainly not an excavation solution. Many marketers like to embellish products to make them seem grander than traditional fare. But customers define their needs in known terms, so be sure to use them, even if you don't think they're exciting. The very fact that a word is unexciting indicates that it's frequently used. People search for terms like "cheap airline tickets," not "value-priced travel experience." Often, a boring keyword is a known keyword.

- **Supplement brand names with generic terms.** If people know and already like your brand enough to search for it, wonderful: you're halfway home. This is particularly true if you're a B2B site, where a main goal is to simply survive the sales funnel's initial discovery and research stages and make it to the shortlist. You should of course include your brand name when describing your products so that fans can find you. But don't abandon the other 95% of prospects who are searching for their problem and don't know the name of your solution. In the funnel's early stages, people tend to use non-branded search terms, because they haven't yet decided which companies to put on the shortlist. This is exactly the time when you have the potential to influence them.

- **Avoid "politically correct" terminology.** When writing about accessibility, for example, talk about blind users or low-vision users, not visually challenged users. First, nobody searches for a made-up phrase like "visually challenged." Second, "blind" and "low-vision" are more precise: they refer to two separate groups of people. Each group uses different assistive technologies and has a different experience of your website. They therefore have distinct usability needs.

If you fill your pages with fancy new words, you'll lose the most powerful tool in Internet marketing: the ability for users to find you in search. Making the search listings is a crucial first step, but it's not the only step: users must also click your entry, and your site must have a good conversion rate.

We know from eyetracking studies that users often scan right past high-ranking listings when the headlines don't make sense. And we know from hundreds of usability studies that users abandon websites with product pages that are confusing or fail to answer their questions. These two problems definitely also deserve the attention of your writers and your usability studies.

There's more to website success than simply being found, but it is the first step. Use old words and you'll be that step ahead of the competition and their useless new words.

Inspire Confidence

Publishing information on the Web is quite easy these days. Anyone can do it easily with free services such as Office Live, and that's precisely what many people do.

Now you can't trust everything that you come across on the Web. You may not hesitate in giving your credit-card information at Amazon.com, for instance, but when it comes to providing the same information at a web site you've never heard of, you're likely to think twice—especially if the site gives you the creeps. The same is true of people visiting your web site. If you want them to take your site seriously, you must make it as credible as you can.

Many people don't buy anything from or fill out forms at a site that doesn't list a physical address and a telephone number, for instance. The presence of contact information on a web site inspires confidence in visitors. It tells them that the site is not a fly-by-night operation. When they see a phone number listed on the site, it tells them that they can actually pick up the phone and speak to a person should there be a problem. A toll-free number is naturally worth a few more credibility points. A physical address tells visitors that when push comes to shove, it's possible to go bang on the door at that address to get issues resolved.

The look and feel of a web site matters too. If a site projects a professional image, it inspires confidence. If, on the other hand, it sports unprofessional language or factual errors that even laymen can identify, it's hard to pay much credence to it.

Shopping carts present another case in point. A secured shopping cart or checkout form radiates trust, but a security-certificate warning instantly causes alarm bells to ring.

A visitor will find your site trustworthy if it puts her at ease while she surfs around. Do all the little things you can to allay her fears.

TIPS FROM THE TRENCHES

Building Credible Web Sites

No magic potion can add instant credibility to a web site with a single dose; attention to detail across the board is what makes it credible. Follow these tips to build a more credible web site:

- **Create a user-friendly site**: Well-organized and high-quality information creates a feeling of trust and comfort in your visitors.

- **Keep the content on your site current**: Outdated information and broken links indicate that the site is being neglected. It makes users weary of dealing with you.

- **Ensure that the information on your site is factually correct**: Incorrect information indicates a lack of authority.

- **Verify that the text on your site is grammatically correct and free of spelling errors**: Poorly constructed sentences and obvious spelling mistakes make visitors wonder about the people behind a site.

- **Provide alternate ways of contacting you**: Provide a physical address, not a PO Box. List your phone and fax numbers. A toll-free number, if you have one, can do wonders to your image. The idea is to emphasize that a respectable organization and trustworthy people are behind your site.

- **Provide an e-mail address or, better, a contact form on your site for users to contact you**: Make sure that the e-mail address you use is in the same domain as your web site. If your web site is www.yourdomain.com, your e-mail address should be you@yourddomain.com or info@yourdomain.com, not you@msn.com or you@yahoo.com. Office Live provides such custom-domain e-mail addresses. Use them.

- **When visitors to your site contact you, answer promptly**: An unreasonable delay in replying sows a seed of doubt in people's minds.

- **Unless you're creating a community portal, don't sport advertisements on your site**: Contrary to what you're led to believe, hosting online advertisements is not a lucrative business. Income from it, if any, is hardly worth losing the credibility of your site. Besides, advertisements on business or personal sites are an instant turnoff to many people.

Like many virtues, credibility is tough to acquire and easy to lose. Work hard at acquiring it by paying attention to all the small things on your site that put a visitor at ease.

Pay Heed to Your Common Sense

The human mind has a limitless propensity for mindless design decisions. So remember this: *if something feels silly to you while building your site, then it probably is.*[4] This is perhaps the most profound design advice you can get.

TIPS FROM THE TRENCHES

Use Common Sense While Building Your Web Pages

The following checklist is just a small sample of what *not* to do on your web site:

- **Don't include site map if you have only three pages of content**: This principle apples to site search too.

- **Don't include a "Search the Web with Google" search box**: This is unnecessary on any site except Google's own. Those who want to search the Web are extremely unlikely to come to your site to search something on Google.

- **Don't display a photo of yourself**: Only celebrities, insurance agents, and realtors need their photograph on their home pages. If your business card doesn't have your photograph on it, neither should your home page.

- **Don't display advertisements on your site unless you're building a community site—a feat quite difficult to accomplish with Office Live**: Displaying Google AdSense advertisements on web sites has gathered a cult following these days. Advertisements are fine, and even desirable, on content portals. On identity web sites, they are utterly unnecessary. The only act of comparable foolishness that I can think of is putting up billboards in your living room—for 25 cents a month, payable to you only if you can prove your guests read them!

- **Don't add page counters to your pages just because they're free**: Whether 39,472 people have viewed a page or just three is generally of no concern to your visitors. They serve no purpose other than making your site look amateurish.

I highly recommend reading *Don't Make Me Think: A Common Sense Approach to Web Usability, Second Edition* by Steve Krug (New Riders Press, 2005). It's short, funny, and informative.

Summary

In this chapter, I presented a few simple guidelines for building better web sites. The list is obviously not exhaustive; there's much more to web design than what this chapter covers. Reading this chapter a few times certainly won't make you a professional web designer, but it will put you on the right track toward fooling people into thinking you're one.

---

4. Pitre's First Law of Web Design. Okay, I made that up.

Here's a list of items you should remember while designing your site:

- Build your site with a clear purpose.
- Write good, clear copy that's appropriate for your audience.
- Use style elements and terminology consistently across the site.
- Use fonts and colors that are easy on the eye.
- Don't forget to make your site accessible to disabled people.
- Make your site friendly to search engines.
- Inspire confidence in your visitors.
- Listen to your common sense while building your site.

The next four chapters will show you how to put all these principles to practice using Office Live's site-building tools. Once you build your first simple site and publish it online, you can keep on improving it one feature at a time. Building good web sites isn't a skill that you can acquire overnight; it takes time and a lot of practice.

CHAPTER 7

Planning Your Site

Whenever you start building anything, it's nice to have a blueprint to go by—especially if you want the end result to look something like what you had in mind when you started out. This is true of web sites too. In this chapter, I'll help you plan your site with Office Live's features, capabilities, and limitations in mind.

Planning a small web site with Office Live isn't as complicated as planning a huge commercial web site that uses a slew of tools and technologies. In fact, your plan will consist of only two steps. You'll

1. Make a rough sketch or a blueprint of your site, right down to the page level

2. Create a staging area on your computer to organize the text, images, and documents that will ultimately go on your web site

Making a Blueprint of Your Web Site

Many great designs are conceived on the backs of dinner napkins. In my experience, however, dinner napkins aren't exactly suitable for sketching outlines of web sites. Pull out an A4-size paper from your printer's tray, grab a pencil, and let's get started:

1. Draw an oval at the center of the paper, and write *Visitor* in it.

2. Put yourself in your visitors' shoes and think about what questions they may have when they visit your web site. Write each question in a box, and connect each box to the visitor's oval in your sketch.

   At the end of your exercise, you should have a sketch something like the one shown in Figure 7-1, which shows questions I thought of for the web site of an imaginary business that sells and services widgets. To make the example manageable, I didn't write down every question I could think of, but you should be sure to write down every question that comes to your mind.

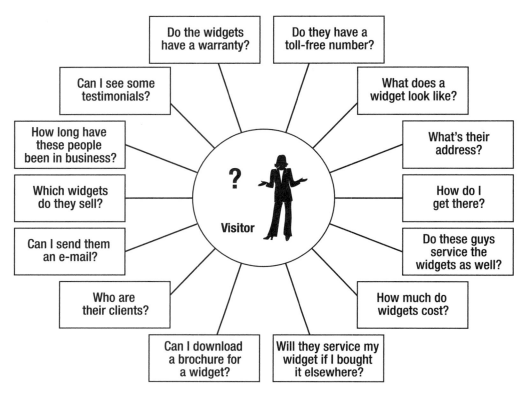

Figure 7-1. *Visitors come to your web site to look for answers. Your sketch begins with a list of questions they might have.*

3. Group the questions in Figure 7-1 into broad categories. For example, I could divide the questions in my sketch into four categories:

   - Contact info

   - About the business

   - Products

   - Service

   Write the category names side-by-side on a new piece of paper. Summarize each question in one word or a short phrase, and write the word under the appropriate category. For instance, I could summarize the question "How do I get there?" as *Directions* and write it under the category *Contact Info*. When you've done so with all your questions, you should have a sketch similar to the one in Figure 7-2.

Contact Info	About the Business	Products	Service
Address	Business Description	Widgets	Services
E-mail	Clients	Pictures	Prices
Directions	Testimonials	Brochures	Warranty
Phone		Prices	Terms
		Warranty	

Figure 7-2. *You can arrange the list of questions you came up with logically into a number of categories.*

4. The categories become the navigation links on your web site. Each navigation link leads to a web page that serves as the main page of that section. For instance, the Products link leads to a page called Products, which displays some generic information about products and leads to individual product pages.

   Each of the words or phrases under the category heading potentially becomes a web page. I say *potentially* because some words or phrases won't require an entire page to themselves. For example, I could consolidate the words *Address*, *Phone*, and *Directions* under *Contact Information* into a single page called Address page. On the other hand, I may not be able to fit all the widgets I sell on a single page under *Products*, so I may need a separate page for each widget that shows its picture, price, warranty, and a link to its downloadable brochure.

5. Repeat the process of consolidation for every item in your version of Figure 7-2. When you're done, you should have something similar to the sketch in Figure 7-3.

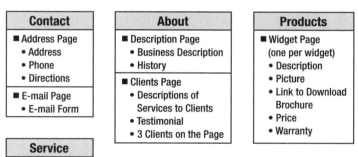

Contact	About	Products

■ Address Page
  • Address
  • Phone
  • Directions
■ E-mail Page
  • E-mail Form
	■ Description Page
	  • Business Description
	  • History
	■ Clients Page
	  • Descriptions of
	    Services to Clients
	  • Testimonial
	  • 3 Clients on the Page
		■ Widget Page
		  (one per widget)
		  • Description
		  • Picture
		  • Link to Download
		    Brochure
		  • Price
		  • Warranty

Service

■ Service Page
   (one per service)
   • Description
   • Price
   • Terms
   • Warranty

NOTES:
• Can I add a paypal button to buy a product?
• 'Contact' page required? (Replace with address page?)
• 'About' page required? (Replace with description page?)

Figure 7-3. *By refining your categories and redistributing the content, you arrive at a sketch such as this one. This is your web site's blueprint.*

This is the blueprint of your site. It shows

- The main navigation links on your site

- The individual pages under each link

- The rough content on each page

You may have noticed that the structure in Figure 7-3 has two levels. The category pages are at the first or the top level, and the pages in each category are at the level below or the second level. There's a very good reason for this relatively flat structure: Office Live's Web Designer can accommodate only two levels of hierarchy. If you plan a site that's five levels deep, you won't be able to build it with Office Live's Web Designer.

6. As you work through the list, you may have questions or hunches about your pages. In my example, for instance, I'm not sure whether I need a separate *Contact* page and another called *Address* page, because they overlap in scope. Therefore, I may decide to move all the information from the *Address* page to the *Contact* page and get rid of the *Address* page altogether. I have made a note of it on my sketch in Figure 7-3. You should note such details on your sketch too. You'll refer to these notes when you actually build the pages.

This blueprint gives you a bird's-eye view of your web site, but it's not cast in stone yet. You might, and probably will, need to improve upon it as you go along. It's a good starting point nevertheless.

■**Note** Coming up with a blueprint seems deceptively simple in this chapter's example. When you sit down to plan your real-world web site, you may find this exercise to be much more complex. Don't get frustrated if you can't get it done in a few minutes. The process takes a good bit of time, and you may not be able to finish it in a single sitting. Don't give up, and don't continue without a plan. A rough map is absolutely essential before you start building your site. Trying to build a web site without a plan is like building a house without a blueprint. Both are likely to be equally disastrous.

Creating a Staging Area on Your Computer

Now that your site's blueprint is ready, you can start thinking about what goes on each of your pages. I suggest creating a one-page document in Microsoft Word for each web page in your sketch.

However, before you start creating documents, you need to know how to name them and where to store them. I recommend creating a folder structure on your computer to match the folder structure on your web server. I also recommend naming the documents you create after the web pages they'll correspond to. But first, let's review how web pages are named on an Office Live–generated web site and where they reside on the web server.

Office Live's Naming and Storage Conventions

Your web site resides in its own folder on the web server's disk. This folder is called the *root folder*, or simply the *root*. It contains all web pages on your site, including the most important one—the home page.

The home page is often the first page people visit on a web site. To make their life easier, web servers don't require users to type the name of the home page. Whenever users type www.somedomain.com in their browser, the web server automatically sends down the home page of that site. Therefore, a web server has to know which of the several pages on the site is the home page.

Web servers identify the home page by its name. On all sites built with Office Live, the home page must be named default.aspx. It resides in the root folder and its complete web address is http://www.yourdomain.com/default.aspx.

FAQ

What's .aspx? Don't All Web Pages Have to End in .htm or .html?

In the Web's early days, web pages were simply files on a web server. The files contained HTML markup. Just as Word documents have the extension of .doc, HTML files have the extensions .htm or .html. For a few years, a majority of pages on the Web were static HTML pages. Therefore, they ended in .htm or .html.

As the Web got more sophisticated, several technologies sprouted up for generating web pages on the fly. Naturally, each web server had to process a visitor's request depending on the technology it used to serve web pages. Each technology mandated its own naming convention. Microsoft's Active Server Pages (ASP) technology uses the extension .asp, while Sun's JavaServer Pages (JSP) technology uses .jsp. You may have seen other extensions such as .php and .cfm as well.

Office Live uses a technology called ASP.NET, which requires the extension .aspx. Hence, all pages created in Office Live end in .aspx.

You only have to worry about the *default* in default.aspx. Office Live automatically appends the .aspx extension. So I'll refer to web pages as default and products instead of default.aspx and products.aspx.

Web sites usually have subfolders within the root to store special items such as images. Separating images from web pages makes a web site easier to manage. The root of every site built with Office has two subfolders: images and documents. True to their names, they hold images and downloadable documents, respectively.

The roots of typical web sites also contain subfolders that represent the site's major sections. Each subfolder contains pages that appear in the corresponding section. For example, the root may contain a subfolder called products, which may contain pages called widget1.aspx and widget2.aspx. The web address of widget2.aspx would then be www.yourdomain.com/products/widget2.aspx.

■**Note** As you can see, there's nothing magical about web addresses. A web address—also known as a URL—is just the directory path where you can find a given web page on the web server.

Unfortunately, Office Live doesn't let you create any folders or subfolders in the root. All your web pages, images, and documents must reside in the three folders that Office Live creates for you, as summarized in Table 7-1.

Table 7-1. *How Your Web Site Is Organized*

Folder	Folder Contents
root	All web pages you design using Office Live's Site Designer
documents	Files or documents you want visitors to download
images	All images used on your web site

▪**Note** Nothing prevents you from saving an image in the documents folder. However, that's somewhat like labeling a jar in your pantry *Sugar* and storing salt in it.

Naming Web Pages, Images, and Downloadable Files

Web pages, images, and downloadable files is a really long phrase. To make it easier for me to write and easier for you to read, I'll refer to all those files as *resources*. As is the case with your children, you're free to name your resources whatever you please, but if you follow a naming convention, they (resources, not children) are easier to find and manage. I recommend the following conventions for naming resources:

- **Use only letters and numbers in your page names**: Office Live doesn't allow spaces or other special characters in page names. However, you may use hyphens and underscores in the names of images and downloadable files.

- **Name the main pages of sections according to the corresponding sections that you came up with in Figure 7-3**: For example, call the page that appears upon clicking the About link the about page.

- **Name the second-level pages according to the page names that you came up with in Figure 7-3**: Prefix the page names according to the name of the section they appear in. For example, call the Description page in the About section aboutdescription and the Clients page aboutclients. The section-name prefix helps you distinguish pages of the same name in two different sections.

▪**Tip** If you find names such as aboutdescription and aboutclients difficult to read, you can capitalize the first letter of each word so that they read AboutDescription and AboutClients, respectively. But be sure to do so with *all* your pages.

- **Name images by objects they contain, then prefix the image names by the page they appear on**: Separate the page name and the image name with a hyphen. For example, call the image of widget1 `productswidget1-widget1.jpg` if `widget1.jpg` is the name of the image and `productswidget1` is the name of the page it appears on. These names may seem long, but they'll keep images on the same page together in the Image Gallery.

- **Name files in the `documents` folder by the contents of the document**: For example, if the document is a PDF brochure of `widget1`, call it something like `widget1-brochure.pdf`. This nomenclature will keep documents downloadable from the same page together in the Document Gallery.

Creating a Folder Structure

Let's follow these guidelines and create a folder structure on your computer to mimic the folder structure on your web server. Follow these steps:

1. Create a folder named `yourdomain` (substitute the name of your domain here) on your computer in a convenient location, such as the desktop or My Documents. This folder corresponds to the root folder on your web server. All Word documents you'll start creating shortly will go here.

2. Create a subfolder under `yourdomain` and call it `images`. It corresponds to the `images` folder on your web server.

3. Create another subfolder under `yourdomain` and call it `documents`. It corresponds to the `documents` folder on your web server.

I created a staging area for my web site `www.officeliveguide.com` on my desktop in a folder named `officeliveguide.com`. Then I created the `images` and `documents` subfolders in it. Figure 7-4 shows how these folders appear in Windows Explorer.

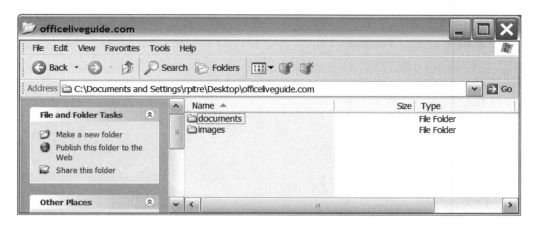

Figure 7-4. *Your staging area should look like this in Windows Explorer.*

Creating Word Documents

After creating the folders, the next step is to create a Word document for every page you'll have on your web site. *Your version* of Figure 7-3 will list all the pages that'll be on your web site. Create a Word document for each. Be sure to follow the naming conventions just discussed.

For example, if I were to create documents based on Figure 7-3, here's what I'd have to do:

1. Create a document named `contact.doc` that corresponds to the top-level page *Contact*.

2. Create documents named `contactaddress.doc` and `contactemail.doc` that correspond to the `Address` and `E-mail` pages, respectively.

3. Create a document named `about.doc` that corresponds to the top-level page `About`.

4. Create documents named `aboutdescription.doc` and `aboutclients.doc` that correspond to the `Description` and `Clients` pages, respectively.

5. Create a document named `products.doc` that corresponds to the top-level page `Products`.

6. Create a document for each product. For example, if I were selling two products, thingamajig and whatchamacallit, I'd create documents named `productsthingamajig.doc` and `productswhatchamacallit.doc`.

7. Create a document named `service.doc` that corresponds to the top-level page `Service`.

8. Create a document for each service. For example, if I had three service plans—silver, gold, and platinum—I'd create documents named `servicesilver.doc`, `servicegold.doc`, and `serviceplatinum.doc`.

Figure 7-5 shows how my staging area would look in Windows Explorer. After you've created a document for every page on your site, your staging area should look similar to mine.

In Figure 7-5, the documents for pages that belong to the same section of the web site are bunched together neatly under the main page of the section. You can thank the naming conventions for it.

You'll use each of these documents to write notes about the content that'll go on the corresponding page. For example, some of the notes in my `aboutclients.doc` could look like the document in Figure 7-6.

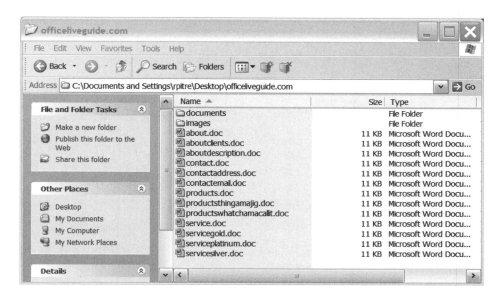

Figure 7-5. *Your staging area should look something like this in Windows Explorer after you create all your documents.*

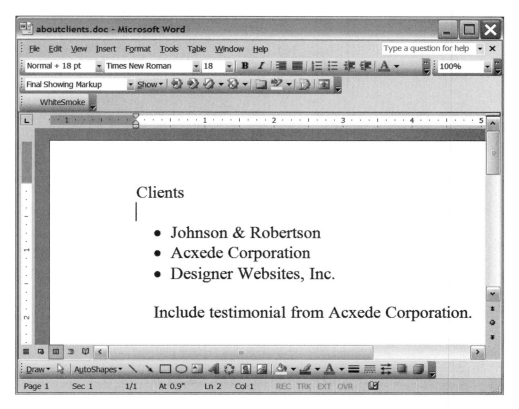

Figure 7-6. *Write notes about the content that will go on a page in the corresponding document in the staging area.*

You'll write the final copy for the page from these notes. If you've already jotted down notes about your pages on random scraps of paper, this is a good time to transfer them to the appropriate documents.

FAQ

Why Bother with a Staging Area?

You may be tempted to skip this step and start creating pages directly on the web site. After all, you may argue, isn't Office Live designed for instant gratification?

Don't do it!

There are two reasons for organizing your resources in folders and subfolders in Windows Explorer:

- **Office Live doesn't have a preview mode**: Creating these documents on your computer gives you chance to validate your design and fix flaws before you go live.

- **Office Live's backup leaves a lot to be desired**: You'll learn more about this in Chapter 14. Having the content of each of your pages in a Word document will enable you to re-create a page from scratch if, god forbid, the need arises.

Summary

Although this is quite a short chapter, it is perhaps the most important one. Planning takes time. When tools like Office Live provide instant gratification by generating web pages with just a few clicks, the temptation to skip the planning stage is overpowering. Don't succumb to it.

In this chapter, you learned

- How to make a blueprint of your web site

- How Office Live organizes your web site on the web server

- The conventions for naming your files, images, and web pages

- How to create a staging area for the web pages, images, and files that make up your web site

In the next chapter, I'll show you how to use the staging area you just created to organize your copy, images, and downloadable files. Once you've organized all your resources, you'll be ready to create web pages.

CHAPTER 8

■■■

Organizing Resources

A web page consists of several elements—HTML markup, images, linked documents, audiovisual content, and even executable scripts. But only the HTML markup on a web page physically resides on it. Other resources, such as images and downloadable files, are stored separately on the web server. Web pages merely contain references and links to these resources.

■Note Advanced web pages may contain a few other goodies such as CSS and JavaScript, along with HTML markup. However, you can safely ignore these items for this discussion.

When you request a web page from a web server, your browser downloads the page and scans it for references and links. Then it requests those resources from the web server as separate files. It assembles and formats all the files into a displayable page according to the instructions in the page's HTML markup. Then it shows you the formatted page.

Because these resources are stored separately from web pages, you must upload them to your web server separately from the pages they appear on. As you learned in Chapter 7, Office Live has special folders on the web server for storing images and downloadable documents. It also has built-in tools to manage and upload these resources to those special folders.

In this chapter, I'll show you how to use these tools. You'll learn how to

- Prepare and upload images to your web server

- Prepare and upload downloadable files to your web server

Preparing Images

Before you can display images on your web pages, you must

- Procure them

- Edit them, if necessary

- Optimize them, if necessary

- Upload them to your web site's Image Gallery

Procuring Images

Many people believe that the Web is one big repository of images and you can copy images from it freely.

Not so!

The first thing you should know about images is that you *cannot* right-click on any image that you fancy on the Web and save it for your own use. Like all creative work, images are copyrighted. Whoever creates the image automatically holds copyrights to it. Even if you don't see a copyright symbol next to an image, you are *not* free to copy it and use it on your web site. Unless you have permission from the copyright holder to use it, copying an image from the Web amounts to stealing.

If you rule out stealing, whether for the sake of morality or out of fear of going to jail, you have four avenues for obtaining images for your web site:

- Find free images or clip art

- Snap pictures with a digital camera yourself

- Scan in pictures or drawings you've drawn

- Buy pictures

Finding Free Images

Although images are copyrighted, the copyright owner may permit you to use them for a fee, and occasionally even free of charge. Several repositories on the Web permit you to use their pictures on your web site.

TIPS FROM THE TRENCHES

Get Free Images, Courtesy of Microsoft

A great place to look for free graphics is the clip-art repository of Microsoft Office at `http://office.microsoft.com/en-us/clipart/default.aspx`.

Although it's called a clip-art repository, it contains thousands of photographs as well. You can search for pictures by keywords. Best of all, you don't have to read a 20-page document written in legalese to figure out whether you may use the images on your web site. In two words, *you may*.

Like Office Live Basics, it's a free service. You'll also find links to several vendors on the site who sell pictures for as little as a dollar.

Get Free Images from Product Manufacturers

If you're looking for images of products that you sell, you may be able to obtain them easily from their respective manufacturers.

Taking Pictures Yourself

You can snap pictures yourself with a digital camera and transfer them easily to your computer. However, keep in mind that most pictures you click will be too massive to use on web pages. You may need to crop and resize them before you can use them on your web site.

Scanning Pictures or Drawings

If you've got hand-drawn or printed drawings, you can scan them. However, remember that you can't scan pictures from printed publications. They're copyrighted just like images on the Web.

Line drawings, freehand drawings, and copies of pictures you clicked with a conventional camera are good candidates for scanning, but you'll probably have to crop and resize them before you can use them on your web site.

Buying Images

If all else fails, you can buy the images you need. Many companies sell disks full of images. These disks cost hundreds of dollars and are basically meant for professional graphic artists.

If you just need a few pictures, your best bet is to buy royalty-free images à la carte from one of the online repositories. Microsoft Office's clip-art gallery, which I mentioned earlier, has links to several repositories. You can buy images from them for as little as a dollar. Here are a few more sites on the Web where you can buy images:

- **Getty Images**: `http://creative.gettyimages.com/source/frontdoor/DefaultRfLanding.aspx`

- **Jupiterimages**: `www.jupiterimages.com`

- **Corbis**: `www.corbis.com`

FAQ

What Are Royalty-Free Images?

Royalty-free doesn't have a universally accepted definition, but, in a nutshell, it means that you pay for an image once and can use it multiple times without having to pay additional fees for subsequent uses. Royalty-free images are *not* free.

Sellers of royalty-free images don't give up the copyright to the image. You can't sell the image or transfer the rights to it to someone else. In that sense, you merely acquire the right to use the image when you "buy" it. Besides, the use of the image is still governed by an end user license agreement (EULA). The conditions in the EULA vary. Therefore, you must fully understand the limitations on the use of an image before you buy it.

In short, you pay for a royalty-free image only once, and you can use it many times as long as you abide by the conditions in the EULA.

No matter how you obtain your images, store them in the `images` folder you created in Chapter 7 in your web site's staging area. Remember to follow the naming conventions I recommended.

Editing Images

Most images you buy or download require little editing. The pictures you click yourself, however, may require some sort of editing for a couple of reasons:

- They may have blemishes, such as shadows or red eyes.

- Their dimensions may be too big or too small for them to fit in their designated spots on your web pages.

FAQ

How Do I Edit Images?

With graphics manipulation software. The best-known graphics application is *Adobe Photoshop*. It's also one of the most expensive. Buying Photoshop just because you have a few images to resize is like buying a horse just because you have a horseshoe.

Office Live has a decent built-in image-editing tool that I'll go over shortly. It can't compete with the likes of Photoshop, but it should suffice for the kind of editing that a small web site requires. If it just won't pass muster, you may want to look into free or low-cost alternatives before splurging on Adobe Photoshop. Here are three free alternatives:

- **Adobe Photoshop Album Starter Edition**: This is a greatly scaled-down version of Photoshop for "fixing" pictures you shoot with your camera. Don't go by the Photoshop in its name. It has very little in common with its big brother. But hey, it's free. You can download it at `www.adobe.com/products/photoshopalbum/starter.html`.

- **Windows Photo Gallery**: Microsoft had its own image-editing products that it recently discontinued. Windows Photo Gallery, which is a part of Windows Vista, uses the technology from Microsoft's erstwhile imaging products. You can open Windows Photo Gallery by clicking on the `Start` button on the Windows taskbar and navigating to `All Programs` ➤ `Windows Photo Gallery`.

- **Paint**: Don't dismiss the Paint applet in Windows. It can come in handy for quickly cropping or resizing an image or for saving it to a different graphics format. You can open Paint by clicking on the `Start` button on the Windows taskbar and navigating to `All Programs` ➤ `Accessories` ➤ `Paint`.

If you're bent on spending money, Corel's *Paint Shop Pro* is a good low-cost alternative.

Optimizing Images

A picture may be worth a proverbial thousand words, but on a web server's disk, it takes up the storage space of more like a hundred thousand words.

Larger images take longer to download. The reason is obvious: the web server has to send more bytes down the wire when you download a bigger image. With the proliferation of broadband, however, the average surfer has a much bigger bandwidth than he ever had before. As a result, he can download larger images relatively quickly.

However, that doesn't mean you shouldn't worry about large images. Look at the image sizes on a typical page from Amazon.com in Figure 8-1. Most product images are in the 2K–3K range. Most standard images, such as the shopping cart and even the logo, are amazingly small. No wonder Amazon.com's pages load quickly despite rich graphical content.

If you want your web site to be fast-loading like Amazon.com, you must optimize your images.

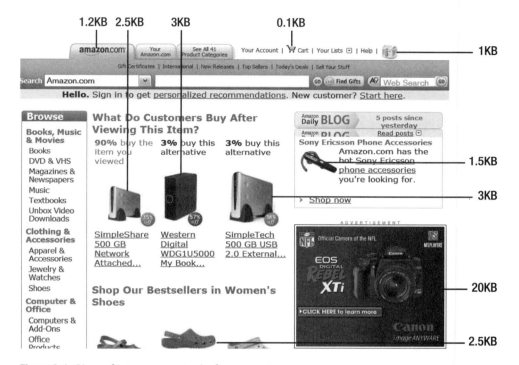

Figure 8-1. *Sizes of images on a typical page on Amazon.com*

Optimizing an image for the Web is a delicate balance between its quality and its size. Higher-quality images are larger. The challenge, then, is to squeeze an image of the best possible quality into a file of least possible size—it's all about compromise.

Images you buy, or download from a free repository on the Web, are usually optimized for use on web pages; you won't have to tinker with them any further. But you almost always have to optimize pictures you click or scan yourself.

Cropping Images

If you click a picture of your son with a digital camera, the picture may contain objects or people besides your son. You can remove everything except your son from the picture by selecting only the part of the picture that your son occupies and saving the selection as another picture. This process is called cropping. Cropping not only removes undesirable or unimportant parts of an image, but it also dramatically reduces the file size.

Figure 8-2. *Cropping reduces the image size.*

In Figure 8-2, the image on the left is a picture that I took with my digital camera of my son swimming with a dolphin. I could post it as it is on my site, but cropping it, as the image on the right shows, reduces not only the picture's dimensions but also its size—without sacrificing any details. And when you visit my site, your browser has to download 40% fewer bytes of information.

Choosing the Right Image Format

Just as you can record the same movie in PAL, NTSC, SECAM, and a few other formats, you can save can save the same image in a wide variety of formats. BMP, GIF, JPEG, PNG, and TIFF are formats you commonly encounter. GIF and JPEG are the most popular ones for web pages, although PNG is gaining in popularity.

Each format uses a different scheme to store images. As a result, each has its strengths and weaknesses. None of them is superior to the others across the board. Besides, you don't have to have all the images on your web site in a single format. You can choose a format that is appropriate for each particular image. Table 8-1 compares the two most popular formats, GIF and JPEG.

Table 8-1. *GIF and JPEG Formats—Feature Summary*

Feature	GIF	JPEG
Pronunciation	Jiff or giff (sounds like *give*)	Jay Peg
Number of colors	256	A few million
File size	Small	Usually larger than GIF
Suitable for	Graphics, clip art, animation, transparent images	Photographs
Not suitable for	Photographs	Pictures with large backgrounds of a single color

When you crop or resize images, you can save them in the appropriate format. Sometimes the best way to choose the right format for an image is to save it in multiple formats. You can inspect each file for quality and size and choose one that you find acceptable on both counts.

Uploading Images to the Image Gallery

Once you collect your images in the images folder in the staging area on your computer, you can upload them to your web site from the Image Gallery section of your Office Live account.

Click on the Image Gallery link in the left navigation pane of Page Manager. You should see the Image Gallery page, as shown in Figure 8-3. Image Gallery has a built-in tool called Image Uploader for uploading images to and deleting images from your web site.

■**Note** Image Uploader works only with Microsoft Internet Explorer, which is why you can't use any other browser to manage your web site.

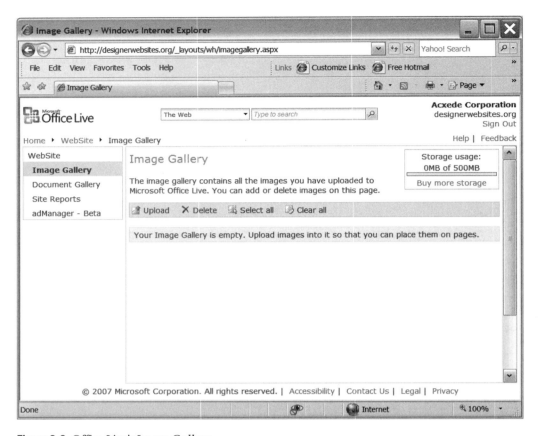

Figure 8-3. *Office Live's Image Gallery*

Image Uploader doesn't reside on the Web. You need to download it from Office Live's web site and install it on your computer.

Installing Image Uploader

To install Image Uploader, follow these steps:

1. Click the Upload link in the blue toolbar on the Image Gallery page. If you haven't already installed the Image Uploader, Office Live will advise you to install it by means of the dialog shown in Figure 8-4.

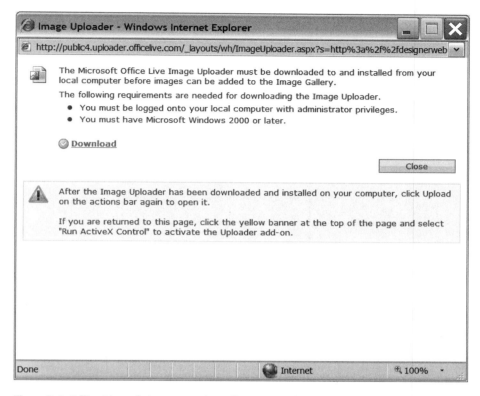

Figure 8-4. *Office Live advises you to install Image Uploader.*

2. Click the red Download link on the dialog. Internet Explorer asks you whether you want to save the installation file or run it, as shown in Figure 8-5.

Figure 8-5. *Internet Explorer asks you whether you want to run the installation program or save it to your computer.*

3. Click Run. Internet Explorer attempts to scare you by displaying the security warning shown in Figure 8-6.

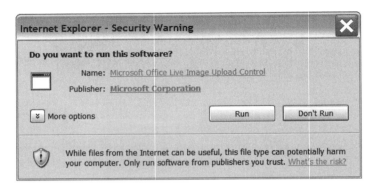

Figure 8-6. *Internet Explorer warns you during the installation. You can ignore the warning.*

4. Ignore the warning and click Run. The Setup Wizard begins with the dialog shown in Figure 8-7.

Figure 8-7. *The Image Uploader Setup Wizard*

5. Click Next. The installation is quite short and painless. Within a minute or so, you should see the Installation Complete message shown in Figure 8-8.

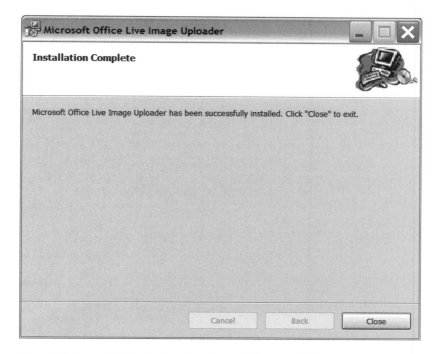

Figure 8-8. *Image Uploader has been installed succesfully.*

6. Click Close to banish the prompt.

Uploading Images

Once you install Image Uploader, you can start uploading images. To do so, follow these steps:

1. Click on the Image Gallery link in the left navigation pane of Page Manager. You should see the Image Gallery page shown in Figure 8-9. The gallery is empty because you haven't uploaded any images yet.

Figure 8-9. *Initial view of the Image Gallery. It's empty because you haven't uploaded any images yet.*

2. Click the Upload link on the blue toolbar. Image Uploader pops up, as shown in Figure 8-10. It has two panes. The pane on the left-hand side shows the folders on your computer. In this pane, you can navigate through your computer's file system just as you do in Windows Explorer. Once you select a folder in the left pane, images in it appear in the right pane. Figure 8-10 shows images in the My Pictures folder on my computer.

At the bottom of the Image Uploader window is the Storage Meter. It shows how much space is available on the web server to upload your images and how much of it you've already used.

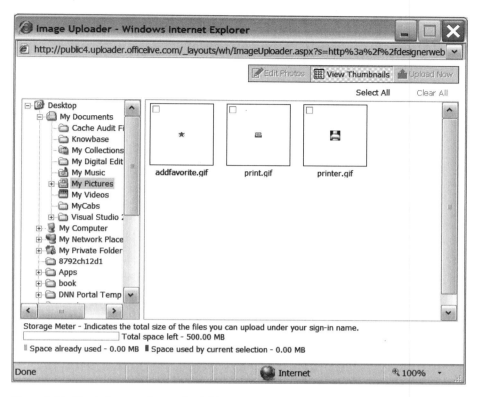

Figure 8-10. *The left pane shows the folders on your computer, and the right pane shows images that you selected in the left pane.*

Note The window in which Image Uploader pops up isn't modal, which means it doesn't always stay on top. If you click anywhere outside it, Image Uploader may get hidden behind other open windows. If it disappears, click on the Upload link on the blue toolbar again to bring it back on top.

3. Navigate to the images folder in the staging area on your computer (the one you created in Chapter 7 to store your images) in the left pane. You should see thumbnails of all the images in it in Image Uploader's right pane. Each thumbnail has a little check box in its top left-hand corner. Check the check boxes on the images you want to upload. You can select all images in the folder by clicking on the Select All link under the button bar in the top right-hand corner of Image Uploader. Right next to it is the Clear All link, which clears all selections in the right pane.

When you select an image for uploading, a bold, blue square appears around it with options to edit or rename it, as shown in Figure 8-11. The tool tip shows the name and the size of the image. The storage meter at the bottom shows the size of all your selections.

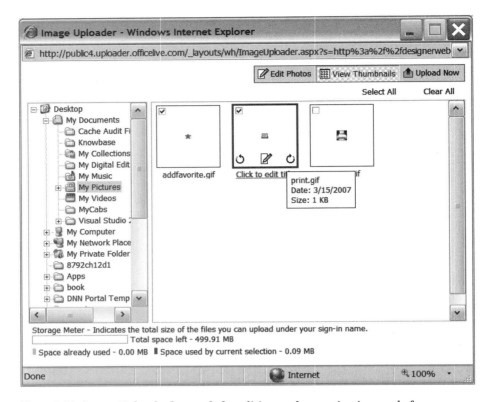

Figure 8-11. *Image Uploader has tools for editing and renaming images before you upload them.*

4. After you select the images you want to upload, the Upload Now button in the button bar becomes enabled. Click on it to upload the selected images—an Upload Progress dialog pops up, as shown in Figure 8-12.

5. When the upload concludes, the dialog goes away, and you go back to the Image Gallery, as shown in Figure 8-13. You can now see thumbnails of all the images you uploaded in the Image Gallery.

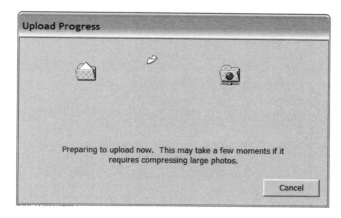

Figure 8-12. *The* Upload Progress *dialog pops up and stays around while the upload is in progress.*

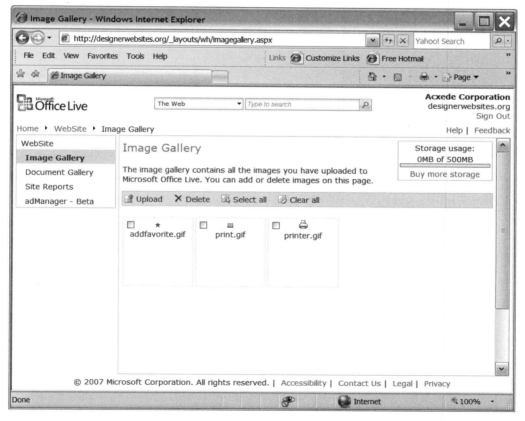

Figure 8-13. *The Image Gallery now displays all the images you've uploaded to your web server.*

Editing and Renaming Images with Image Uploader

Image Uploader allows you to edit images before uploading them. Move your mouse pointer over an image in Image Uploader's right pane. Image Uploader replaces the image's name with a link titled `Click to edit title` and displays three little icons at the bottom of the image, as you can see on the checked image in Figure 8-14.

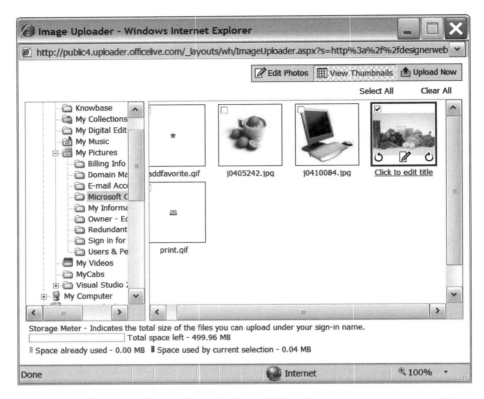

Figure 8-14. *When you select an image in Image Uploader or move your mouse pointer over it, the image becomes editable.*

You can edit or rename the image by clicking the link or icons. Figure 8-15 shows what you can do with an image once you select it for editing.

Now here's the really cool part: when you rename or edit an image in Image Uploader, the original image stays intact. Image Uploader caches all your changes and uploads the altered images to the web server.

■**Caution** When you edit an image with Image Uploader's tools and upload it to the Image Gallery, you aren't left with a copy of the edited image in the `images` folder in your staging area. That's not a good state of affairs. Don't forget to download the edited image and save it in your staging area.

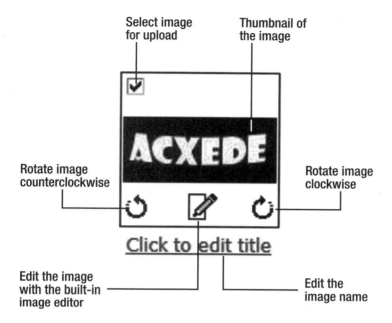

Figure 8-15. *Once you select an image, you can quickly rename or rotate it by clicking on the appropriate links or open it for editing in Image Uploader's editor.*

Renaming an Image

Renaming an image in Image Uploader is very similar to renaming one in Windows Explorer. Select an image in Image Uploader and click on the Click to edit title link under it. A little rectangular box appears in its place, as shown in Figure 8-16.

Figure 8-16. *Renaming images in Image Uploader is very similar to renaming files in Windows Explorer.*

Enter a new name in the box, and click anywhere outside it or press Enter. The new name will appear in place of the old one.

Rotating an Image

Recall that three icons appear at the bottom of an image when you select it. The two icons to the left and right with circular arrows on them are for rotating the image by 90 degrees. I rotated the selected image in Figure 8-14 clockwise by 90 degrees by clicking the button on the right-hand side. You can see the result in Figure 8-17.

Figure 8-17. *The original image is shown on the left, and the image on the right has been rotated by 90 degrees in the clockwise direction.*

When you upload the image, Image Uploader uploads the rotated image but leaves the image on your computer unchanged.

Editing an Image

If you click the icon depicting a paper and a pencil on an editable image, Image Uploader will display an image editor. The editor has two panes. The left pane shows the thumbnail of the original image, and the right pane has a canvas for editing the image.

At the top of the right pane is a toolbar with buttons for editing the image. You can use these buttons to perform the following actions:

- Zoom the image in or out.

- Rotate the image clockwise or counterclockwise 90 degrees at a time.

- Increase or decrease the contrast of the image.

- Increase or decrease the brightness of the image.

- Crop the image.

Figure 8-18 shows the image in the left panel being cropped.

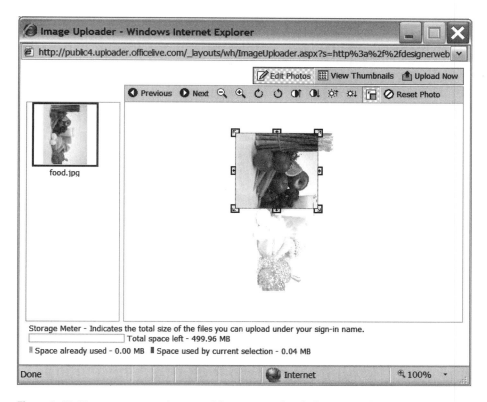

Figure 8-18. *You can crop an image with Image Uploader's image editor.*

If you're not happy with your handiwork at any time, you can click the Reset Photo button in the button bar to restore the image back to its original state. Figure 8-19 shows what each of the buttons on the editor's toolbar is for.

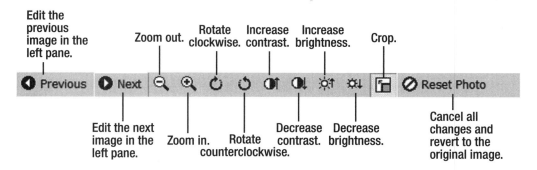

Figure 8-19. *The image editor's toolbar*

Selecting Multiple Images for Editing

Instead of editing one image at a time, you can select several of them at the same time in Image Uploader by checking the check boxes on them and then clicking on the Edit Photos button at the top. Image Uploader opens its image editor, as shown in Figure 8-20.

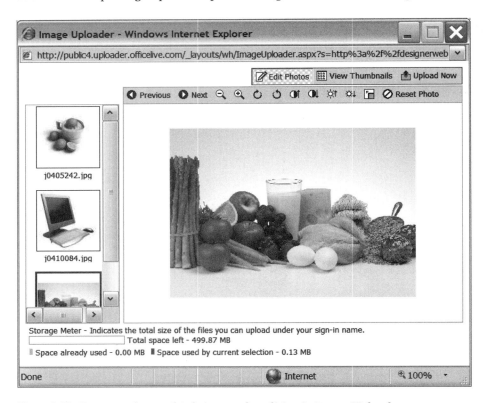

Figure 8-20. *You can select multiple images for editing in Image Uploader.*

The left pane shows all the images you select. The one with a dark blue square around it appears on the canvas in the right pane. You can cycle through the images by clicking the Next and Previous buttons on the button bar.

From the image editor, you can return to Image Uploader by clicking the View Thumbnails button at the top. After you finish working with the selected images, click the Upload Now button at the top to upload them.

Deleting Images from the Image Gallery

To delete images from Image Gallery, follow these steps:

1. In the Image Gallery, check the check boxes of the images you want to delete.

2. Click the Delete link in the blue toolbar. Office Live asks for confirmation, as shown in Figure 8-21.

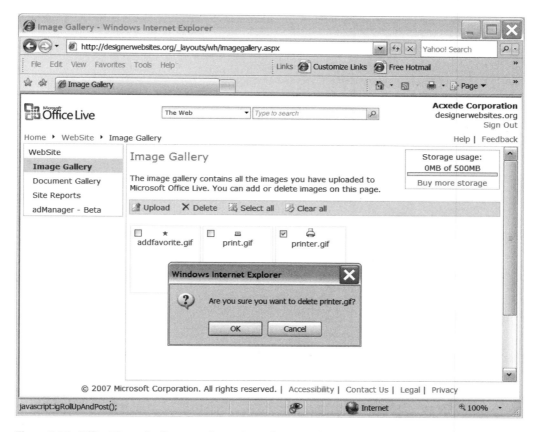

Figure 8-21. *Office Live asks for a confirmation when you delete images from Image Gallery.*

> **3.** Click OK to proceed with deleting the images (or Cancel to back out).

Replacing Images in the Image Gallery

You can't replace images in your Image Gallery simply by uploading them again from Image Uploader. You must delete the images from Image Gallery and then upload them again. If you try to upload images that are already present in the Image Gallery, Office Live will show you the warning in Figure 8-22.

Figure 8-22. *You can't replace images in Image Gallery; you must delete them and upload them again.*

When Image Uploader Misbehaves

Sometimes Image Uploader may fail to perform as advertised. It may not upload images correctly, it may just sit there and do nothing, or it may not come up at all. The best way to fix the problem is to uninstall and reinstall it. Here's how to do it:

1. Go to Control Panel from the Start button on your computer's taskbar and then click on Add or Remove Programs. The Add or Remove Programs applet starts, as shown in Figure 8-23.

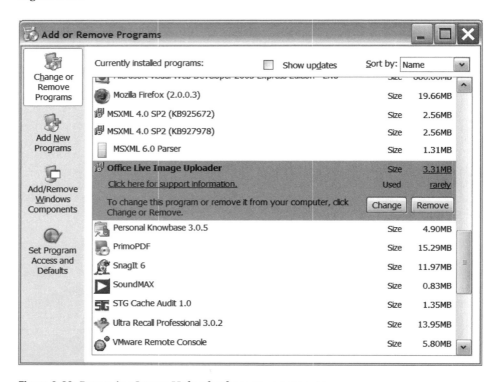

Figure 8-23. *Removing Image Uploader from your computer*

2. Scroll down the list to Office Live Image Uploader and click on it. The entry expands and reveals two buttons: Change and Remove.

3. Click the Remove button. After a few seconds, the Office Live Image Uploader entry disappears from the list. Close the Add or Remove Program and Control Panel windows.

4. Go back to Image Gallery and click the Upload button in the blue toolbar. Office Live prompts you to download and install Image Uploader again.

Preparing Downloadable Files

Downloadable files are files that a visitor to a web site can transfer from the site's web server to his computer typically by clicking on a link on a web page. Before you can place links to your files on your web pages, you must

- Save them in an appropriate format

- Upload them to your web site's Document Gallery

You should consider providing downloadable files from your web site in three situations:

- **When you want to deliver a document you already have in print, while maintaining its original visual formatting**: For example, you might have a product brochure or the sample chapter of a book that you want to publish. The most common way of doing so is to deliver it as a PDF file.

- **When you want to deliver several files in a single download**: For example, you might have many images of the same product. The most common way of delivering them in a single download is to deliver them as a ZIP file.

- **When you want to deliver non-HTML files**: For example, you might want to post links to word-processor documents, spreadsheets, presentations, executable programs, or plain-text files. If you don't want to deliver them as PDF or ZIP files, you can deliver them in their original format.

Choosing the Appropriate Document Format

Let's look at the most common file formats that you could use for your downloadable files—PDF, ZIP, and Microsoft Office document formats—in more detail.

PDF Files

Portable Document Format (PDF) is the ideal format for posting downloadable documents on your web site. Here's why:

- **PDF documents are platform-independent**: It doesn't matter whether you have a Windows PC, an Apple Macintosh, or a Unix- or Linux-based computer. As long as you have a PDF reader on your computer, you can read any PDF document. Adobe makes Adobe Reader, a free PDF reader, for most operating systems.

- **A person opening a PDF document doesn't have to know how the document was created, nor does he need the application used to create it**: Let's say you create a brochure with WordPerfect and post it on your web site. Anyone who downloads it would require WordPerfect on his machine to open and read your brochure. However, if you convert your document to PDF, anyone who downloads it couldn't care less how you prepared the brochure. He can simply open and read it with a PDF reader.

- **A person reading your document doesn't need to have the fonts you use in your brochure installed on his computer**: All fonts used in a PDF document are embedded in it. Even if you use an esoteric font, anyone reading your brochure will see it exactly as you saw it when you prepared it.

- **PDF documents can't contain macro viruses**: Therefore, unlike Microsoft Word documents or Microsoft Excel spreadsheets, PDF documents are safe to download.

Creating PDF Files

You need a PDF generator to create PDF files from documents. PDF is *not* a proprietary specification. Although Adobe invented it, PDF is available publicly. Therefore, anyone can make software to create PDF files, not just Adobe.

FAQ

Doesn't Everyone Have Adobe Acrobat on His Computer?

You're probably thinking of Adobe Reader. Adobe Acrobat and Adobe Reader are two different products. Adobe Reader, which is installed on most computers, *cannot* create PDF files. Its name says it all—it only reads PDF files that have been created using applications that can create PDF files.

While Adobe Reader is free (which is why you'll find it on most computers), Adobe Acrobat will set you back about $300.

There are several PDF generators on the market. Naturally, Adobe makes a product that is capable of creating PDF files. It's called Adobe Acrobat. But it does much more than just creating PDF files. For example, you can create printable forms with it and sign your documents digitally.

To create downloadable documents for your web site, you don't need Acrobat's advanced features. Any application capable of generating a file in PDF format will do just fine. There are several such applications on the market, and quite a few of them are absolutely free—no advertisements, no strings attached.

TIPS FROM THE TRENCHES

Get PrimoPDF—It's Free

A PDF converter I like and use extensively is PrimoPDF (www.primopdf.com).

You can download the installer from the site and run the EXE file. The installer installs a printer driver. From then on, PrimoPDF appears as a printer on your computer. Now you can convert any document to PDF. Say you want to convert a Microsoft Word document to PDF. To do so, follow these steps:

1. Open the document with Microsoft Word.

2. Navigate to File ➤ Print.

3. In the Print dialog, click on the Printer Name drop-down.

4. Choose PrimoPDF as the printer (remember, the PrimoPDF installer installed it).

5. Click OK. A PrimoPDF dialog appears.

6. Enter a name for your PDF document, and click OK.

That's it. Your PDF document is created. Now you can post it to your web site, e-mail it, or simply look at it and admire your handiwork. If you have trouble along the way, refer to an online manual at `www.primopdf.com/free-pdf-userguide.asp`.

Because PrimoPDF emulates a printer, you can convert absolutely any printable document to PDF. In general, I don't like free applications. Office Live Basics is an exception, and so is PrimoPDF.

Use Google Docs & Spreadsheets—It's Free, Too

If you don't want the hassle of downloading and installing PrimoPDF, you can create an account with Google Docs & Spreadsheets (`http://docs.google.com`). It converts any stored document to PDF with a single click.

It's hard not to be impressed by PDF's capabilities. But before you go out and convert every document in sight to PDF, there's one thing you ought to be aware of: PDF files can get *very* large, very quickly, especially if they contain lots of images. To get the file down to a reasonable size, you may have to get rid of a few images. You could also break the document up into several smaller documents.

ZIP Files

A ZIP file is really an archive that contains one or more files. The files in the archive are compressed to minimize their size. Like smaller images, smaller files are desirable on the Web because you can download them faster. After downloading the archive, you can "extract" the files in it—a process that restores the files to their original form.

Creating ZIP files

Windows has built-in support for creating ZIP files—a process called *zipping*—and for extracting files from a ZIP archive, which is called *unzipping*.

To create a ZIP file from one or more files, follow these steps:

1. Select the files you want to zip in Windows Explorer.

2. Right-click on one of the selected files and move your mouse over the Send To menu option. A secondary menu appears, as shown in Figure 8-24.

3. Click Compressed (zipped) Folder in the secondary menu. The menus go away, and the ZIP archive you just created appears in the folder, as shown in Figure 8-25.

4. The zipped folder usually has the name of the file you right-clicked on. In Figure 8-25, I right-clicked on presentation.ppt; so my zipped folder is called presentation.zip. Rename it to something suitable.

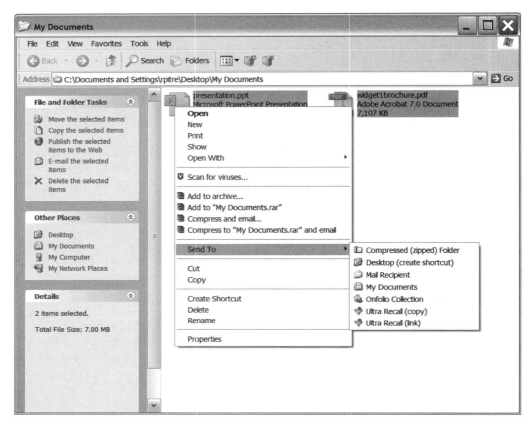

Figure 8-24. *You can create ZIP archives in Windows without any additional software.*

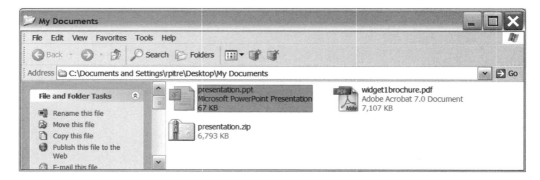

Figure 8-25. *ZIP archives usually appear in the same folder as the files in them.*

Microsoft Office Document Formats

While PDF and ZIP files are the most common downloadable files, there are times when making other types of files available for download makes sense. If you speak at conferences, for example, you might want to make the PowerPoint presentation for a talk available on your web site. Or there might be times when you want your clients to use a specific Microsoft Word template while giving you job specifications. You might then want to make the template available for download on your web site. You can certainly zip these documents, but sometimes it's just easier to make them available in their native formats.

You can make most Microsoft Office documents like Word documents, Excel spreadsheets, and PowerPoint presentations available for download. Your visitors will be able to open them right in their browsers.

Uploading Files to the Document Gallery

All Office Live web sites have a special repository for downloadable files: the documents folder, which you read about in Chapter 7. You can manage the contents of this folder from your web site's Document Gallery.

■**Caution** You *must* check the documents you upload for viruses. Most antivirus programs give you an option to right-click on a folder in Windows Explorer and scan it for viruses. You should make it a habit to check the documents folder in your staging area for viruses before you upload documents to Documents Gallery.

Uploading Files

To upload documents from your computer to Document Gallery, follow these steps:

1. Click on the Document Gallery link in the left navigation panel of Page Manager. You'll see the page shown in Figure 8-26. You can upload new files to your server or delete existing ones from this page.

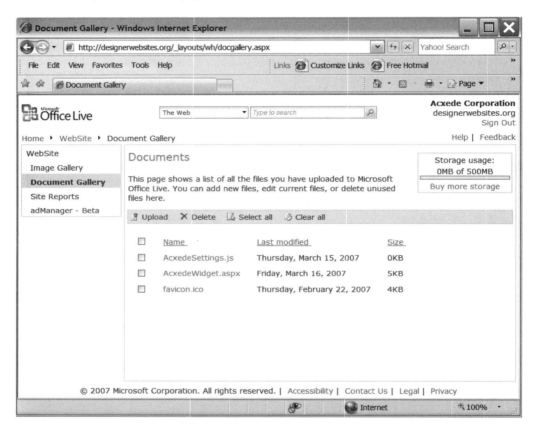

Figure 8-26. *You manage the downloadable documents on your web site from the Document Gallery.*

2. On the blue toolbar across the center of the page, click Upload. You'll see the Document Uploader dialog shown in Figure 8-27.

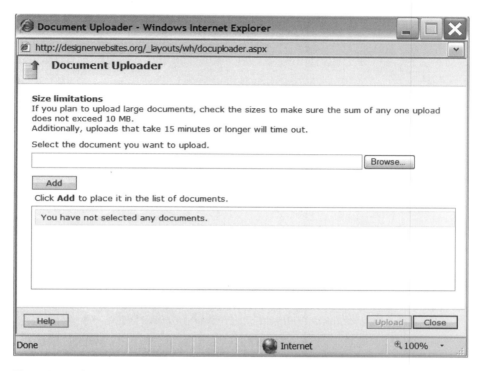

Figure 8-27. *The* Document Uploader *dialog*

3. Uploading documents is much like attaching documents to e-mail messages. Click the Browse... button to see the Choose file dialog shown in Figure 8-28.

4. Navigate to the documents folder on your computer where you've stored all your downloadable files. Choose a file and click the Open button. The Choose file dialog closes, and the name of the file you select appears in Document Uploader, as shown in Figure 8-29.

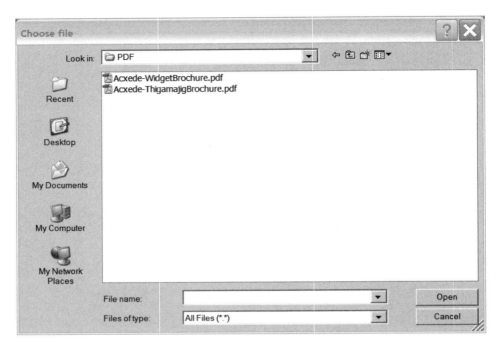

Figure 8-28. *The* Choose file *dialog of Document Uploader is just like the* Choose file *dialog you see in standard Windows applications such as Word.*

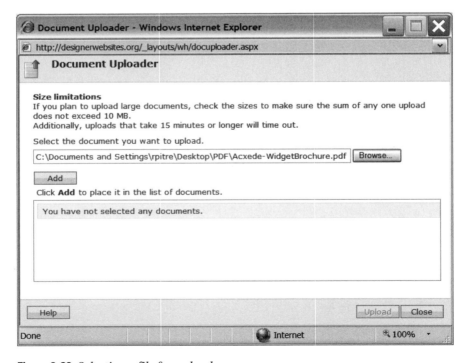

Figure 8-29. *Selecting a file for upload*

5. Click the Add button under the file name. The entry moves down to the box below, as shown in Figure 8-30.

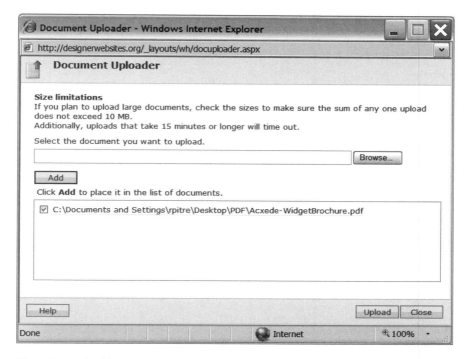

Figure 8-30. *The files you select appear in the list of documents to be uploaded.*

6. You can add more files by clicking the Browse... button again and repeating the process. All the files you select appear in the Document Uploader, as shown in Figure 8-31.

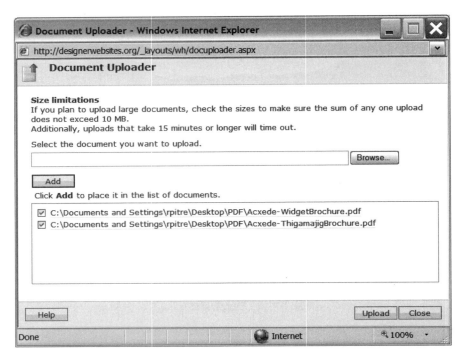

Figure 8-31. *You can select several files at a time and upload them in a single batch.*

Although you can upload multiple files at a time, keep in mind that the total size of all files you upload as a batch can't exceed 10MB. This 10MB limit isn't really rigid, but the larger the size of the files, the longer it takes to upload them. If an upload exceeds 15 minutes, Office Live aborts it.

■**Note** Usually it's a good idea not to test the limits of uploads. Depending on the speed of your Internet connection, large uploads may exceed a time limit of 15 minutes, which Office Live imposes. Besides, if an upload fails, for whatever reason, you'll have to go through the motions all over again. I prefer uploading in batches of 5MB or less.

---

7. After you select all the files, click the `Upload` button at the bottom. After a brief delay, or a long one if your Internet connection is slow, Document Uploader informs you that it uploaded the files successfully, as Figure 8-32 shows.

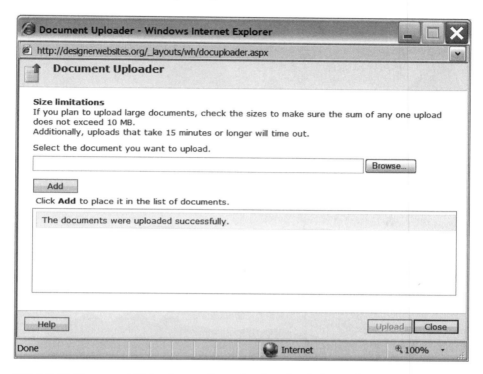

Figure 8-32. *Document Uploader confirms that it uploaded your documents successfully.*

8. Click the Close button to close Document Uploader and return to Document Gallery. You should see the documents you just uploaded listed in Document Gallery, as shown in Figure 8-33.

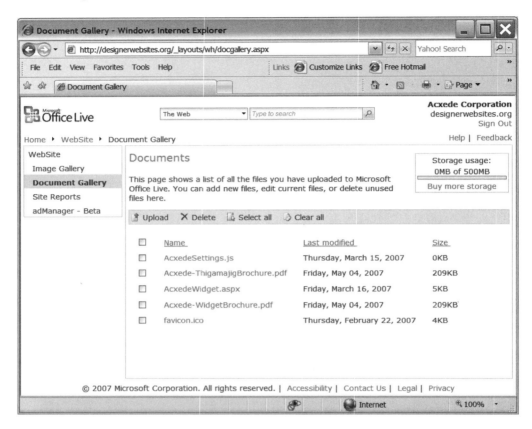

Figure 8-33. *The uploaded documents appear in Document Gallery.*

Deleting Documents

From time to time, you'll want to delete documents from the Document Gallery. To do so, follow these steps:

1. Navigate to Document Gallery and check the check boxes next to the documents you want to delete.

2. Click the Delete button on the blue toolbar. Document Gallery asks for confirmation, as shown in Figure 8-34.

Figure 8-34. *Document Gallery asks you to confirm the deletion of the selected documents.*

3. Click Cancel to back out or OK to go ahead and delete the documents. Either way, you get back to Document Gallery.

Replacing Documents in Document Gallery

You can't replace documents in Document Gallery simply by uploading them again from Document Uploader. You must delete the documents from Document Gallery and then upload them again. If you try to upload documents that are already present in Document Gallery, Office Live will show you the warning in Figure 8-35.

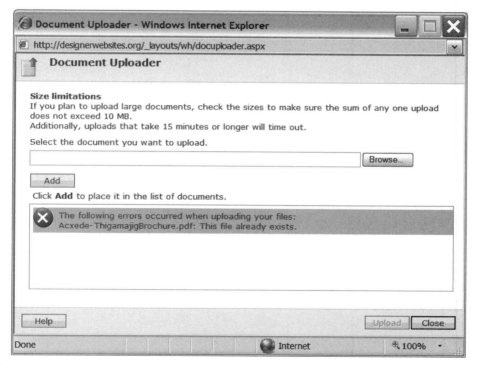

Figure 8-35. *You can't replace documents in Document Gallery simply by uploading them again; you must delete them from Document Gallery first.*

Summary

I covered a lot of ground in this chapter. I showed you how to obtain and upload images to your web server, and I introduced you to a couple of tools for converting downloadable documents to suitable formats before uploading them to your web server. Here are the important points to note from this chapter:

- Web pages contain references to images and downloadable documents, which are stored separately on the web server.

- You can look for free images. You can also take the pictures yourself, scan them, or buy them.

- Images that you snap yourself or scan might need further editing and optimization.

- Images on your web site are stored in the `images` folder under your web site's root directory. Use the Image Gallery to upload images to the `images` folder.

- Image Gallery requires you to install a tool called Image Uploader to edit and upload images. When you attempt to upload an image for the first time, Office Live asks you to install Image Uploader.

- Image Uploader isn't the greatest image editor, but it should serve the needs of most small web sites.

- If you need more advanced image-editing features, you should look into other free or low-cost image editors before going all the way and buying Adobe Photoshop.

- Downloadable documents on your web site are stored in the `documents` folder under your web site's root directory. Use the Document Gallery to upload documents to the `documents` folder.

- You can let visitors download pretty much any kind of file, but the common types of files people expect to download are PDF, ZIP, and Microsoft Office documents.

- You can create ZIP files from Windows Explorer without additional tools. To create PDF files, you require a PDF generator.

Okay, you've now done all the preparatory work. If you've been (impatiently) asking the question, "When are we going to start designing the #!$*^@% web pages, for heaven's sake?" the answer, at last, is "Right now!" That's what I'll show you how to do in the next chapter.

■ ■ ■

CHAPTER 9

Choosing Site-Wide Settings

When you design a web site, you have to make several design decisions. Some of them affect the web site as a whole, while others affect individual web pages. How your site's header will look, for example, is a decision that affects all pages on your site. Who receives e-mails that visitors send from the Contact Us page, on the other hand, is a decision relevant only to the Contact Us page.

Office Live has a separate tool for incorporating each of the two kinds of decisions into your web site's design: *Site Designer* is the tool for choosing site-wide settings, and *Page Editor* is the tool for designing individual web pages. Together, the two tools constitute *Web Designer*, Office Live's integrated site design environment.

In this chapter, I'll tackle Site Designer and show you how to choose site-wide design settings for your web site. I'll give you a tour of Page Editor and explain how to design individual web pages in the next chapter.

Introducing Web Designer

To launch Web Designer, Office Live's integrated site design environment, follow these steps:

1. Bring up Page Manager in your browser. A blue toolbar stretches across the page, as shown in Figure 9-1. Site Designer and Page Editor are the first two icons on it. Clicking either of them launches Web Designer.

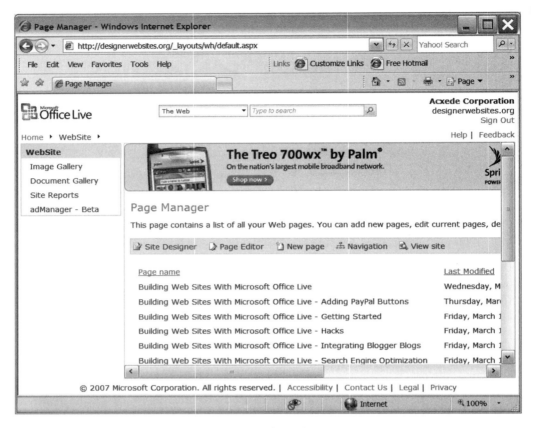

Figure 9-1. *You invoke Office Live's Web Designer from the Page Manager.*

2. Click the Site Designer icon. The Web Designer page, shown in Figure 9-2, loads. It has two tabs: Page Editor and Site Designer. The Site Designer tab is the active tab, because you clicked on the Site Designer icon in Page Manager. Had you clicked the Page Editor icon, the Page Editor tab would have been the active tab.

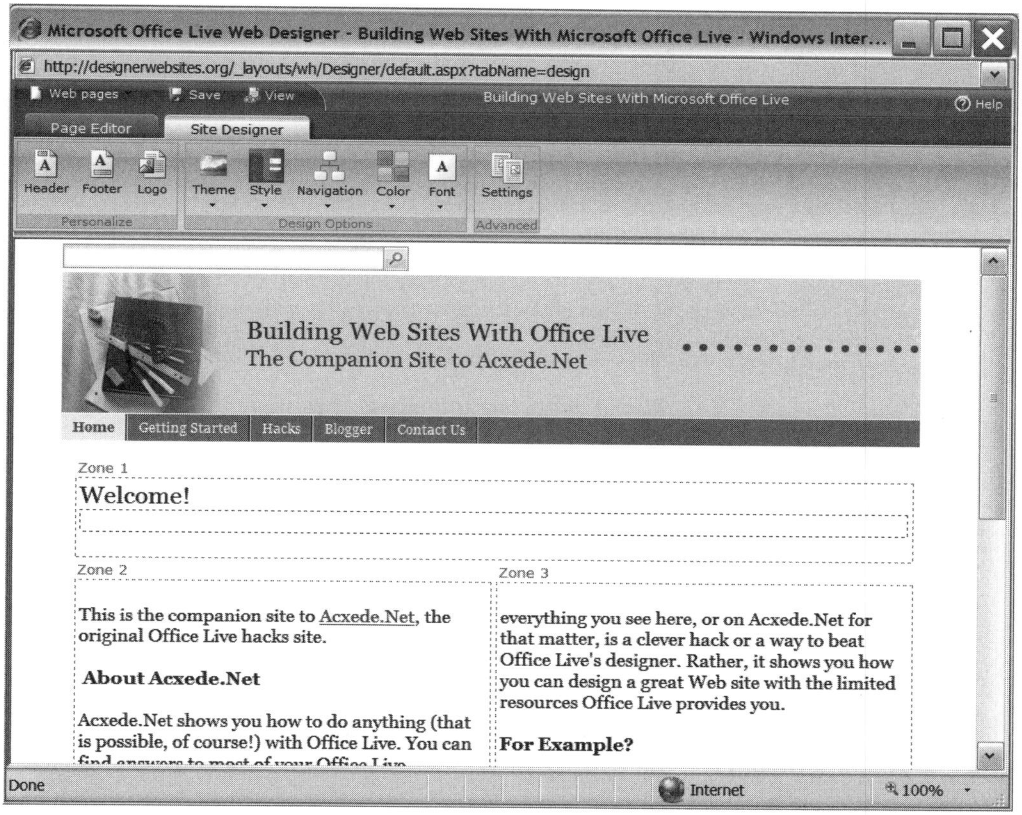

Figure 9-2. *Office Live's Web Designer*

Web Designer's Ribbon

The first thing you'll notice about Web Designer is that it doesn't have navigation links like the other web pages on Office Live's site. Instead, it boasts a Microsoft Office 2007–style Ribbon. The Ribbon is the oversized, taller-than-normal menu bar with tabs on it, as shown in Figure 9-3.

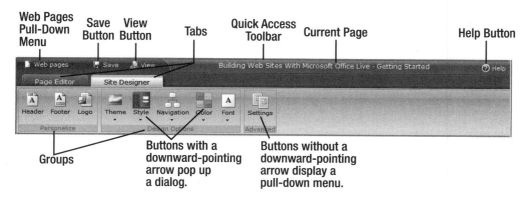

Figure 9-3. *Anatomy of Web Designer's Office 2007–style Ribbon*

At the top of Web Designer's Ribbon is the `Quick Access Toolbar`. It contains five items:

- **`Web pages` pull-down menu**: You can select which web page on your site you want to work with by pulling down this menu.

- **Save button**: You can save all unsaved changes in Web Designer by clicking this button.

- **`View` button**: You can preview the web page currently displayed in Web Designer in a new browser window by clicking this button.

- **Name of the current page**: You can quickly see which page you're editing by looking at the name of the current page. This is an informational entry only.

- **`Help` button**: You can summon Office Live's help pages by clicking this button.

Below the `Quick Access Toolbar` are *tabs* that group related commands. Web Designer's Ribbon has two tabs:

- **`Page Editor` tab**: You can manipulate individual web pages using the buttons and links on this tab.

- **`Site Designer` tab**: You can set site-wide design option with the buttons and links on this tab.

Each tab on the Ribbon houses containers called *groups*. A group's name appears in a thin gray area at the bottom of the group. Each group contains a set of related *buttons* or other selectable options. Some buttons have a little downward-pointing arrow. When you click one of these buttons, a pull-down menu with selectable options comes up. Others don't have the downward-pointing arrow. When you click one of these buttons, a web dialog pops up, where you can set several properties at a time.

The Current Page

The body of the page you're presently working on appears below the Ribbon (see Figure 9-2). If you don't select a page to work on, the home page of your web site, `default.aspx`, automatically becomes the current page and appears below the Ribbon.

Click on the `Page Editor` tab. The Ribbon changes to show groups and buttons that are relevant for editing an individual page. Notice that the web page displayed under the Ribbon stays put even if you toggle between the tabs.

Previewing and Saving Changes

Whenever you make changes to the current page in the Page Editor or change a site-wide setting in Site Designer, the current page in Web Designer immediately reflects the changes. A little asterisk appears in the title bar of the `Web Designer` page to indicate that Web Designer has pending changes. An asterisk also appears immediately to the right of the page name in Web Designer's `Quick Access Toolbar`, as shown in Figure 9-4.

Asterisks indicate that some changes on the page haven't been saved, even though you can see them in Web Designer. You will lose them unless you save them by clicking the Save button.

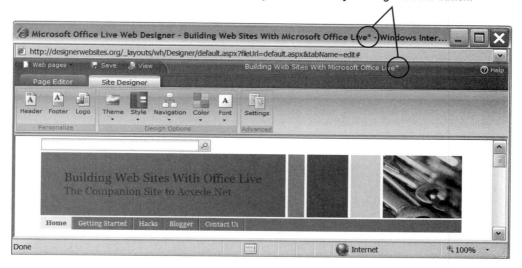

Figure 9-4. *Asterisks in the page title and the browser's title bar indicate that changes to settings or pages are pending.*

Think of the current page as the preview mode for changes you make in Web Designer. But as long as you see the asterisks, the changes aren't saved, even though you can see them on the current page.

To save the changes, you must click the Save button on the Quick Access Toolbar. When you do so, the asterisks disappear to indicate that all changes have been saved. If you attempt to close the Web Designer page without saving pending changes, Office Live will pop up the message shown in Figure 9-5, asking you whether you really want to abandon them.

Figure 9-5. *If you don't save the changes you made in Web Designer, Office Live will give you another chance to save them.*

Over the course of the remainder of this chapter and the two chapters that follow, you'll make several changes in Web Designer. Instead of mentioning the asterisks and the confirmation dialog in Figure 9-5 every time, I'll save a few trees by simply asking you to save your changes.

Working with Site Designer

Click on the Site Designer tab to return to Site Designer. Its Ribbon has three groups of buttons: Personalize, Design Options, and Advanced. Let's explore each of them further.

TIPS FROM THE TRENCHES

Make a Note of Your Settings

In the course of this chapter, you'll be setting site-wide design options for your web site. It's a good idea to make a note of the settings. This will come in handy if you make a mistake in the future and save the wrong settings. To do so, follow these steps:

1. Create a new folder in the staging area on your computer and name it documentation.

2. Create a new Word document in the newly created documentation folder, and name it SiteSettings.doc. If you're the lazy type, I've even prepared a document for you to use.[1]

3. As you move from setting to setting, jot down your selections in this document.

This may feel like a chore to you now, but believe me, you'll thank yourself (and me) for it one day.

Personalization Options

You can customize your web site's header and footer, as well as the logo you wish to display on your web pages, by manipulating the Personalize options.

Setting Your Site's Header

Click the first menu item, Header, on the Ribbon. The Customize Header -- Webpage Dialog, shown in Figure 9-6, pops up.

You can customize three header settings in this dialog: Site Title, Site Slogan, and Web search.

---

1. You can download it from this book's companion sites, which are mentioned in the Introduction.

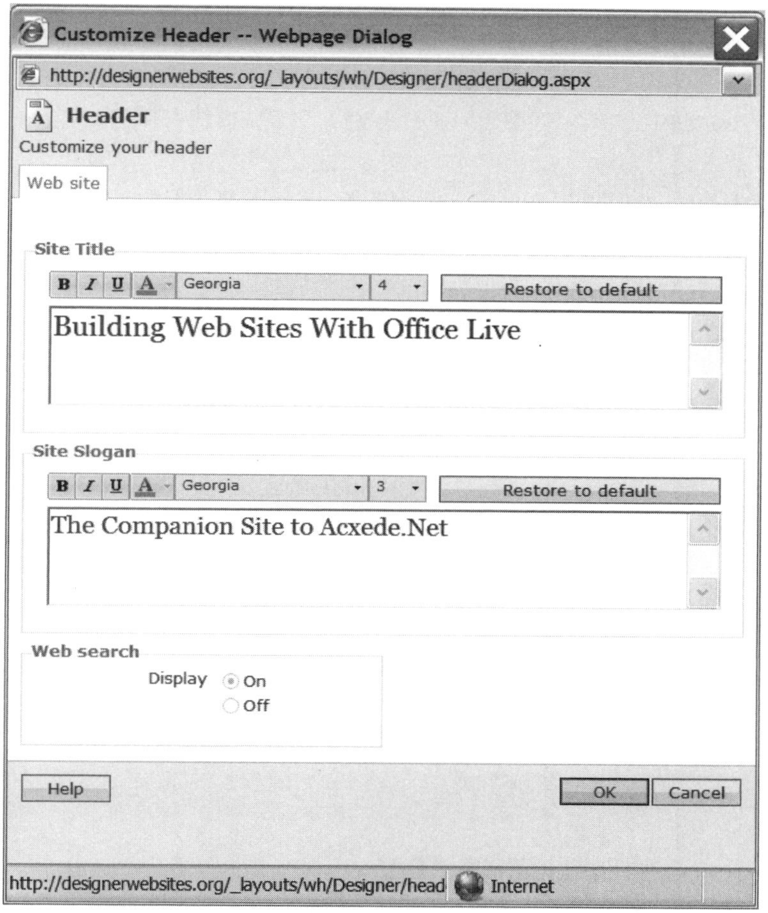

Figure 9-6. *Setting your web site's headers*

Site Title

Site Title is, well, the title of your site. Enter it in the miniature editor and format it using the options on the editor's menu bar. The number of formatting options isn't exactly overwhelming, but you have all the basic options you need: bold, italics, underline, font color, font face, and font size. You'll see this editor on several dialogs that Site Designer pops up.

Site Slogan

Site Slogan is sometimes called a *tag line*. It's a great way of telling your visitors what your site is all about. Catchy tag lines often help identify a brand, as the following tag lines illustrate:

- **Subway**: Eat fresh.
- **De Beers**: A diamond is forever.
- **Avis**: We try harder.

- **American Express**: Don't leave home without it.

- **Nike**: Just do it.

- **MasterCard**: There are some things money can't buy. For everything else there's MasterCard.

Enter your slogan here, if you have one, and format it using the little editor, as you did with `Site Title`.

Web Search

The `Web search` option on the `Customize Header -- Webpage dialog` is a setting that lets you choose whether you want to show or hide the `Web search` box in the top left-hand corner of all web pages on your web site. If you subscribe to Office Live Essentials or Office Live Premium, I recommend hiding the search box. Do so by selecting the `Off` radio button.

If you're an Office Live Basics subscriber, you'll find the `On` radio button selected and both radio buttons grayed out. In effect, you can't select the `Off` option. The `Web search` box will always show up at the top of all your pages.

■Note In Chapter 11, I'll show you how to hide the `Web search` box in Office Live Basics. However, this only works to an extent, because the search box flickers before disappearing.

FAQ

Why Hide the Search Box?

A facility to search the content of your site is generally considered a great asset. However, the search box that Office Live puts on your web pages isn't for searching the content of your site. It's for searching the *entire Web*.

You often see such boxes on amateur web sites. That shouldn't lead you to believe that they're a good feature. Search engines, such as Google and Windows Live, want you to put these boxes on your pages because *they* stand to gain potential advertising revenue from searches initiated from your pages.

Browse through any corporate web site, including Microsoft's own, and you'll be hard-pressed to find a Web search box on any of them. The reason is obvious: unless you want to build a search engine, these boxes make little sense on your site.

During Office Live's beta days, you could hide the Web search box. Microsoft decided to change its stance when it released the final version. The problem is that many people don't want to have a search box on all their pages for the reasons I just mentioned. Naturally, they weren't too thrilled about the change. Many have voiced their displeasure on Office Live's forums. Hopefully, Microsoft will listen.

Click `OK` to save the settings.

Figure 9-7 shows these elements in the header of my web site. At the top of the header is the Web search box that Office Live has forced upon me. Below it, in big bold letters, is the site title Building Web Sites With Office Live. The site slogan, The Companion Site to Acxede.Net, is the final element of the header.

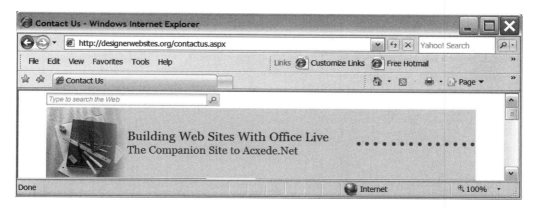

Figure 9-7. *How headers appear to your visitors*

Setting Your Site's Footer

Click the second menu item, Footer, on Site Designer's Ribbon. The Customize your footer -- Webpage Dialog, as shown in Figure 9-8, pops up.

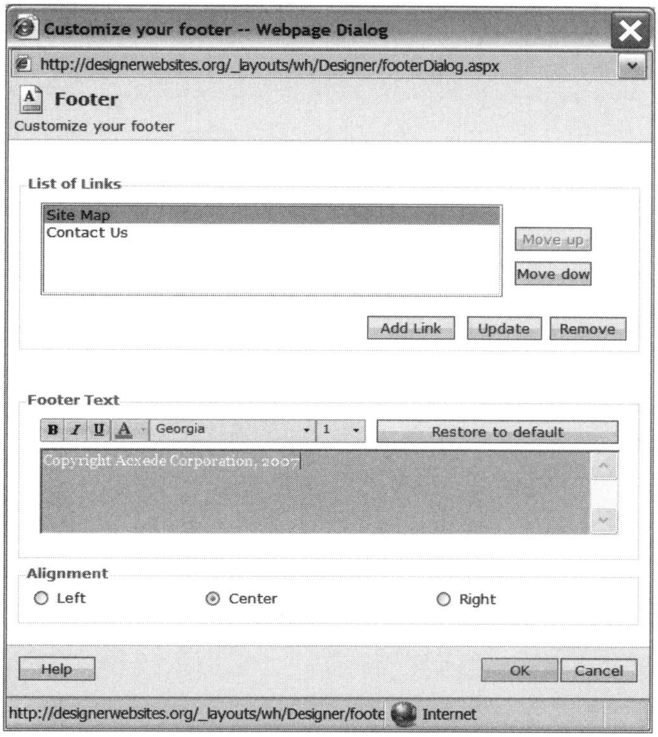

Figure 9-8. *Setting your web site's footer*

You can customize three footer settings in this dialog: List of Links, Footer Text, and Alignment.

List of Links

You'll usually find links to pages that display site policies, terms, conditions, and other legal mumbo jumbo in a web site's footer. Figure 9-9 shows the footers on Microsoft's web site www.microsoft.com. You can add such links to your web site too.

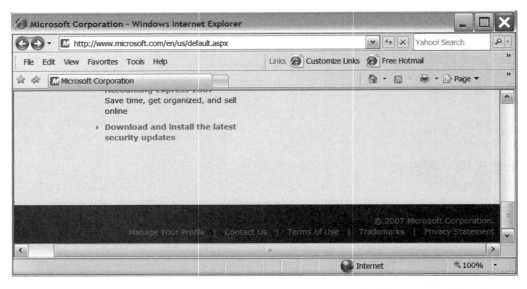

Figure 9-9. *The footer of Microsoft's web site shows links to pages related to terms and conditions.*

"What links?" you might ask. This is a good question, because you haven't built these web pages yet. However, pretend for a moment that you have. I'll show you how to add links to the footer while we're still talking about the footer. You don't have to add them right away. You can come back and add them after you build the pages. But if you know which links you want to show in your site's footer, you can create them right away. They just won't lead anywhere until you create the web pages they point to.

To add a link to the footer, follow these steps:

1. Click on the Add Link button on the Customize your footer -- Webpage Dialog. The Link Properties -- Webpage Dialog pops up, as shown in Figure 9-10.

Figure 9-10. *Adding a link to your web site's footer*

2. Enter a name for the link in the `Link Name` box. This name will appear as the text of the link in the footer.

3. If the link points to a web page on your site, enter a forward slash(`/`), and then enter the address of the web page this link points to in the `Link Address` box. The forward slash indicates that the page resides in the home directory of your web site. By using this shortcut, you can avoid entering long addresses such as `http://www.yourdomain.com/home.aspx`. However, if the link points to a page that's not on your web site, you must enter its complete web address, long or not.

4. Click `OK` to save the link and banish the dialog.

Repeat these steps for every link you wish to add to the footer.

Footer Text

The footer text appears at the very bottom of your web pages. This is a good location for your copyright message. Enter it in the miniature editor, and format it using the options on the editor's menu bar.

FAQ

How Do I Type the Copyright Symbol?

You always find the copyright symbol in site footers, and yet, there's no key on the keyboard to type it. Here are two ways to placate your lawyers:

1. Cut and paste the copyright symbol from Microsoft Word.

2. Turn on Num Lock, hold down the Alt key, and type 0169 on the numeric keypad. This trick won't work if you type the digits using the number keys above the letters on your keyboard.

Alignment

You can align your web site's footer elements to the left edge, the center, or the right edge of your web pages. Select the appropriate radio button in the Customize your footer -- Webpage Dialog to choose the setting for your site. Click the OK button to close the dialog.

Figure 9-11 shows these elements in the footer of my web site. At the top of the footer bar are three links—Home, Site Map, and Contact Us—which I set using the first option in the Customize your footer -- Webpage dialog.

Figure 9-11. *How footers appear on your web pages*

Below these links is the footer text claiming the copyright for the web site, which I set using the second option in the dialog.

The links and the text in Figure 9-11 are centered because I chose the Center alignment option. Had I chosen the Left or Right options, the entire footer text would have appeared at the left or the right edge, respectively, of the footer bar.

Inserting Your Logo

Click the third item, Logo, on Site Designer's Ribbon. The Change your Logo -- Webpage dialog, as shown in Figure 9-12, pops up.

Follow these steps to insert your logo:

1. If you've already uploaded your logo, it will appear in the images pane when the dialog opens. If you haven't uploaded your logo yet, click the Upload pictures button. Image Uploader pops up. Select your logo from your computer's hard drive and upload it. It appears in the images pane of the Change your Logo -- Webpage Dialog.

2. Click on your logo in the images pane. As you can see in Figure 9-12, a dark square appears around it to indicate your selection.

3. Choose a Location for the logo. Your options are Top and Next to title. If you choose Top, the logo will appear above the header, as shown in Figure 9-13. This option makes sense if you have a wide logo that will span the entire width of the header.

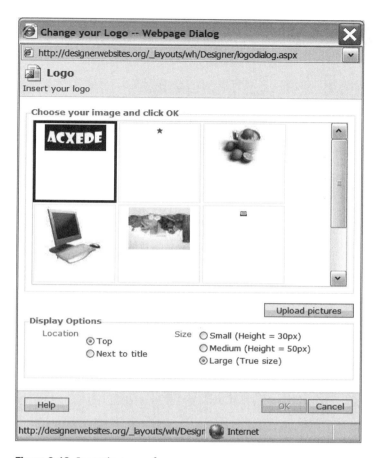

Figure 9-12. *Inserting your logo*

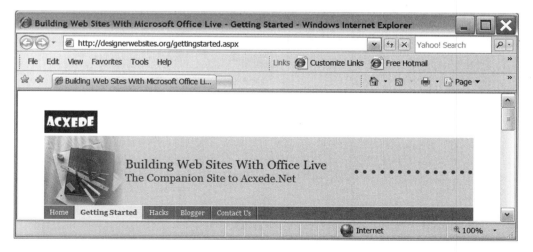

Figure 9-13. *Logo positioned above the header*

4. If you have a small logo, you may want to display it within the header bar. To do so, choose Next to title. The logo appears within the header bar, as shown in Figure 9-14.

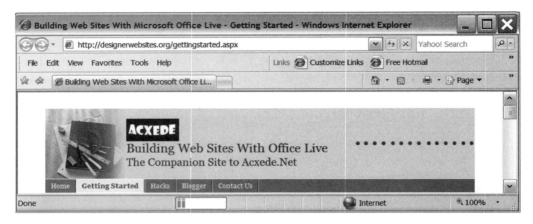

Figure 9-14. *A logo positioned* Next to title *sometimes appears above it.*

You might be tempted to ask why this option isn't called Above the title, because that's where the logo appears in Figure 9-14. You would normally expect the Next to title option to display your logo as in Figure 9-15.

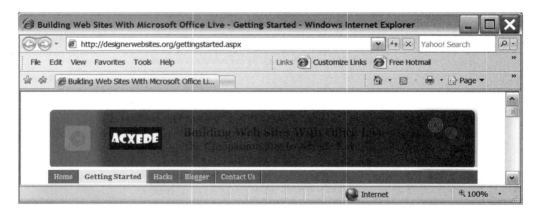

Figure 9-15. *You would expect a* Next to title *display to look like this.*

Notice that the header bar in Figure 9-15 is different from the one in Figure 9-14. The header bar changed because I selected a different *theme*. How your site's title, slogan, and logo are displayed depends on a combination of

- Your site's width

- The font size you choose for the title and slogan

- The theme you choose

- The style you choose

- The width and height of your logo

I haven't walked you through all these settings yet; I'll introduce them in the next section. At this point, keep in mind that the final appearance of your site's header elements depends on several settings in the Site Designer. You'll have to tweak these settings to achieve the precise effect you desire.

You can alter the size of your logo by selecting the Size option on the Change your Logo -- Webpage Dialog. You can have Office Live automatically resize your logo's height to either 30 or 50 pixels, or you can leave it at its original size.

■Note It's a good idea to generate your logo with precise dimensions. If you ask Office Live to resize it, the logo may become fuzzy. Besides, browsers have to do extra work to resize the image, which delays the loading of a page in a visitor's browser.

Design Options

One of the most difficult challenges in web design is to come up with visually appealing styles and themes. For all the individual elements of a web site to blend into a consistent design, you must choose colors, fonts, and images that complement each other. With so many choices in each category, this can be an overwhelming task. Thankfully, Office Live comes loaded with design options preconfigured by Office Live's graphic artists. You can use these options to design a professional-looking web site in just a few mouse clicks.

Site Designer has five design options to choose from:

- Theme

- Style

- Navigation

- Color

- Font

Let's see how each affects your site's design. To focus on these elements, I've removed the site title and the site slogan from some of the figures that follow.

Choosing a Theme

The theme is basically the picture that goes in the site's header. In Figure 9-16, a picture of wrenches appears on the extreme right of the header area, because I chose an Automotive theme.

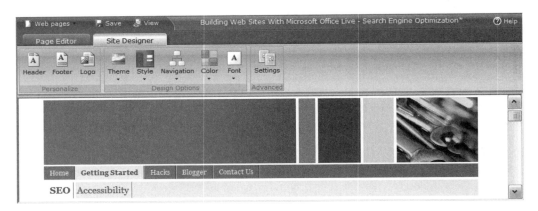

Figure 9-16. *A theme determines which picture appears in the header.*

Office Live's graphic designers have come up with many images appropriate for various kinds of businesses. Click on the Theme button on the Ribbon. A pull-down menu appears, as shown in Figure 9-17. You can choose the line of business you're in by clicking on an option on the left side of the pull-down menu. A selection of images appropriate for your choice appears on the right side of the pull-down menu. You can choose one of them as the picture for your web site's header.

FAQ

I Don't Like Any of These Pictures—Can I Upload My Own?

No. You must choose one of the pictures from the theme menu. Office Live automatically adds a few folders to your web sites for storing themes and other design elements. You don't have access to those folders.

If you're an experienced Web designer, this limitation can be quite frustrating. However, what may be a limitation to some can actually simplify life considerably for anyone with little or no design experience.

If one of the several pictures available just won't do for you, I'll show you how to get around this limitation and customize your web site's headers in Chapter 11.

Follow these steps to select a theme for your site:

1. Click the Theme button on the Ribbon. The Themes menu opens.

2. Click on a line of business on the left side of the Themes menu. A selection of pictures appears to the right.

3. Click on one you like. A rectangle appears around it.

4. Click on the little *x* in the top right-hand corner of the Themes menu to close it.

You'll see the result of your selection right away on the current page in the Site Designer.

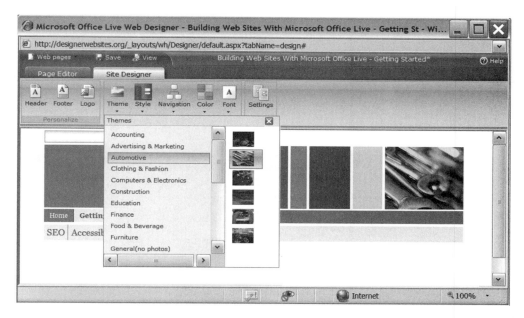

Figure 9-17. *You can choose themes and the pictures associated with them from the* Themes *menu. Office Live provides several pictures for every type of business it has themes for.*

Choosing a Style

A style determines the layout of your site's header. You can display the theme you choose in several different styles. Figure 9-18 shows the theme in Figure 9-16 with a different style.

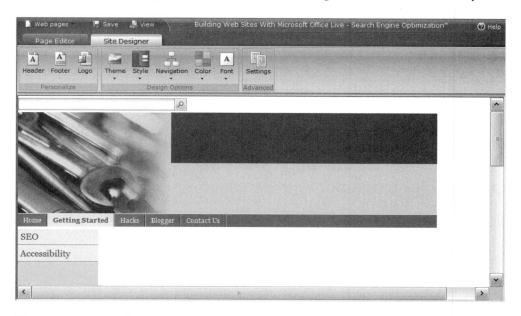

Figure 9-18. *You can change the layout of the header by selecting a different theme.*

Notice that although the picture of wrenches is basically the same, it's a larger version of a cropped section of the image shown in Figure 9-16.

As with themes, Office Live has several style choices. Click on the Style button on the Ribbon. You can choose a style you like from the pull-down menu that appears, as shown in Figure 9-19.

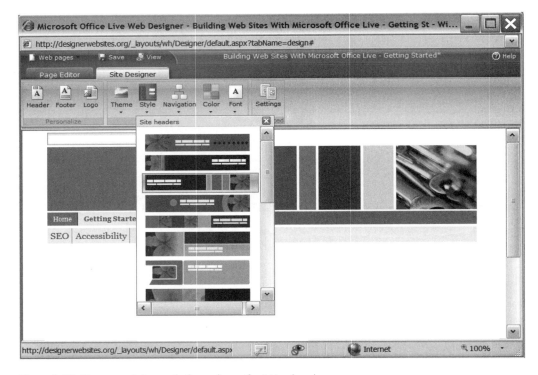

Figure 9-19. *You can pick a style from from the* Site headers *menu.*

Follow these steps to select a style for your web site:

1. Click the Style button on the Ribbon. The Site headers menu opens.

2. Click on a style you like. A rectangle appears around it.

3. Click on the little *x* in the top right-hand corner of the Site headers menu to close it.

You'll see the result of your selection right away on the current page in the Site Designer.

Choosing a Navigation Layout

The navigation layout determines where your site's navigation links appear. Office Live supports two levels of navigation. The levels don't have formal names, so I'll simply call them *first-level* navigation links and *second-level* navigation links. Navigation levels enable you to divide pages on your web site into logical sections.

Each first-level link leads to a web page that you can logically think of as the main page of a section. Links to all pages in that section appear as second-level links on the main page. Figure 9-20 shows an example of the two levels of navigation. Home, Getting Started, Hacks, Blogger, and Contact Us are first-level links, which lead to the main pages of sections called Home, Getting Started, Hacks, Blogger, and Contact Us, respectively. When you click on, say, the Getting Started link, the Getting Started page comes up in the browser. It displays links to pages called SEO, Accessibility, Credibility, and Color Schemes. These links are only visible while you're in the Getting Started section. Therefore, they're second-level links under Getting Started.

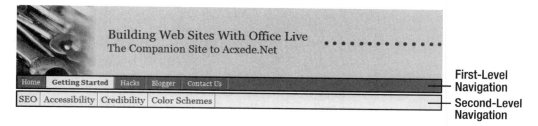

Figure 9-20. *Office Live supports two levels of navigation.*

Office Live offers a choice of three navigation layouts. To see them, click on the Navigation button on the Ribbon. You should see a pull-down menu, as shown in Figure 9-21.

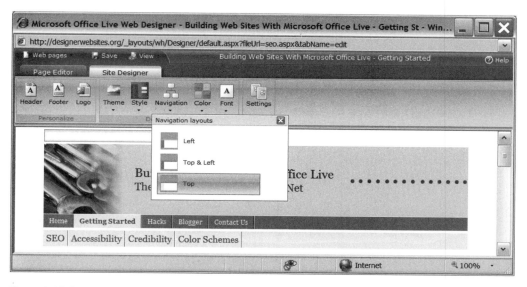

Figure 9-21. *You can access navigation layouts from the* Navigation *menu.*

The presently selected layout in Figure 9-21 is Top, so both levels of navigation appear at the top. Figure 9-22 shows the site with the Top & Left navigation layout in which the first-level navigation links are at the top and the second-level navigation links are on the left.

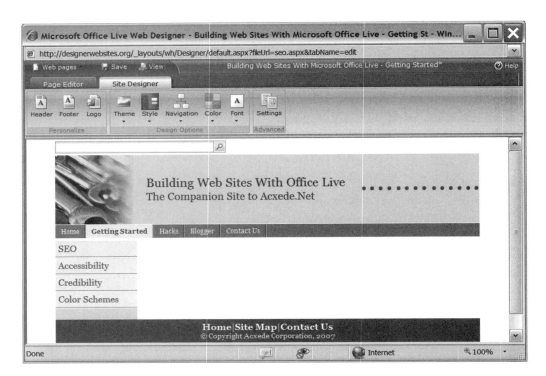

Figure 9-22. *In the* Top & Left *navigation layout, the first-level navigation links are at the top, and the second-level navigation links are to the left.*

Figure 9-23 shows the site with the Left layout in which both levels of links appear on the left. The Getting Started section is expanded, and the second-level links below it appear in the expanded area.

Follow these steps to select a navigation layout for your site:

1. Click the Navigation button on the Ribbon. The Navigation layouts menu opens.

2. Click on a layout you like. A rectangle appears around it.

3. Click on the little *x* in the top right-hand corner of the Navigation layouts menu to close it.

You'll see the result of your selection right away on the current page in the Site Designer.

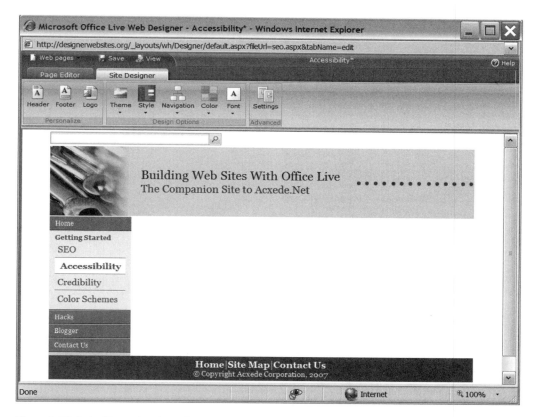

Figure 9-23. *In* Left *navigation, the navigation links at both levels are on the left.*

Choosing a Color Theme

Choosing complementary colors for the various elements of your site can be far from easy. Fortunately, Office Live's graphics designers have made it really easy for you. You don't have to choose colors for individual elements. Instead, you simply choose a color theme, and Office Live automatically applies the appropriate color to each element.

Click on the Color button on the Ribbon. You should see the pull-down menu shown in Figure 9-24.

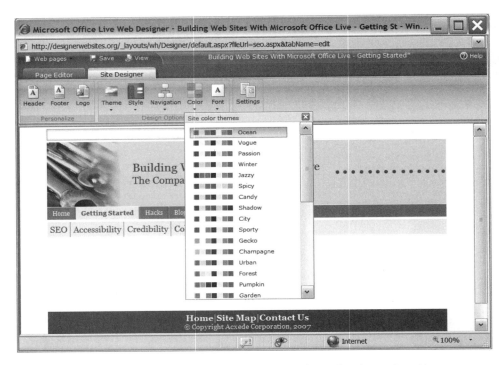

Figure 9-24. *You can access preconfigured color themes from the* Site color themes *menu.*

The color theme depicted in Figure 9-24 is Ocean. I changed it to Jazzy. You can see the result of the change in Figure 9-25.

■**Note** Although this book is printed in black and white, you'll be able to see different shades of gray in Figure 9-24 and Figure 9-25. Or you can simply take my word for it! But a better way to see color themes in action is to actually try them out on your site.

FAQ

I Don't Like the Color Themes—Can I Make My Own?

No. You must choose one of the color themes in Site Designer.

I think most people are better off using one of the available options. Coming up with harmonious color themes is more difficult than it first appears to be. Just look at the atrocious color combinations all over the Web if you don't believe me.

Site Designer doesn't have hundreds of choices, but each color theme has colors that complement each other. The end result is a visually pleasing web page.

Yes, if you're a professional web designer, the available choices will hamper you. But keep in mind that Office Live isn't meant for professional web designers.

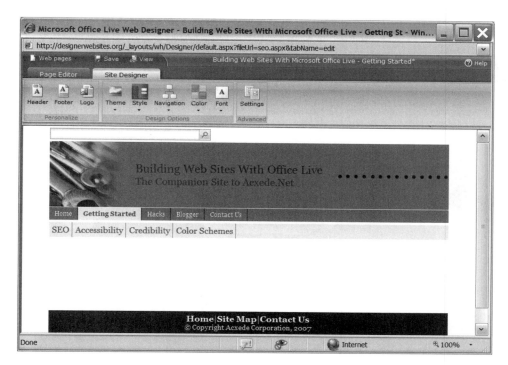

Figure 9-25. *The same web page looks dramatically different with a different color theme.*

Let's choose a color theme for your site. Follow these steps:

1. Click the Color button on the Ribbon. The Site color themes menu opens.

2. Click on a color theme you like. A rectangle appears around it.

3. Click on the little *x* in the top right-hand corner of the Site color themes menu to close it.

You'll see the new color theme immediately on the current page in the Site Designer.

Choosing a Default Font

As with colors, choosing the right combination of font face and font size isn't easy. Again, Office Live's graphic designers come to your rescue. You simply choose a font, and Office Live applies it in appropriate sizes to various elements on your site.

To choose a font, click on the Font button on the Ribbon. You should see a pull-down menu, as shown in Figure 9-26.

The font shown in Figures 9-25 and 9-26 is Georgia. If I change it to Verdana, the font on all navigation links as well as the links in the footer will instantly change to Verdana, as you can see in Figure 9-27.

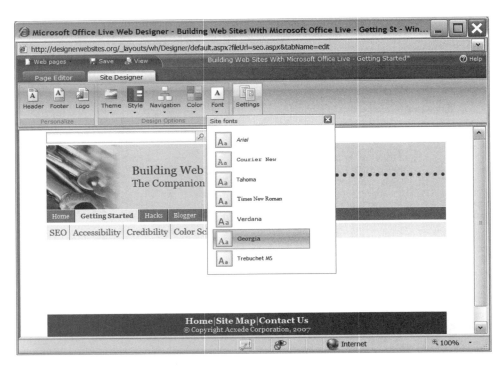

Figure 9-26. *You can pick a font from the* Site fonts *menu.*

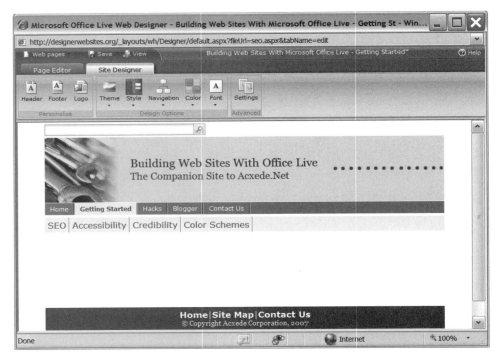

Figure 9-27. *If you change the site font, the font will change across the entire web site.*

The page in Figure 9-27 doesn't have any text on it. Had text been present, its font would have changed to Verdana as well. As a rule, changing the font setting in Site Designer has the effect of changing the font of all the text on the site. However, there are a couple of exceptions:

- **Any fonts you set in Site Designer specifically aren't affected**: The font setting of the site title, site slogan, and the copyright message didn't change in Figure 9-27. That's because you set those fonts explicitly using the little editors in the Customize Header dialog.

- **Any fonts you specify using HTML markup in the body of your page won't be affected**: You haven't written any HTML markup yet. But when you do (in Chapters 10 and 11), remember that site-wide font settings won't affect fonts you specify explicitly in your markup.

FAQ

Why Doesn't Office Live Provide a Wider Choice of Fonts?

If you want a visitor to your web site to see your web pages in the same font as you specified, that font must be installed on the visitor's computer.

Many of the fonts installed on a typical computer don't come with the operating system. They're installed by software packages such as Microsoft Office. However, you can't expect everyone to have Microsoft Office and the fonts that come with it. If the font you choose for your web pages isn't available on a visitor's computer, the browser will usually default it to Times New Roman on PCs and Times on the Mac. This may throw the formatting of your pages off.

The seven fonts available in Site Designer are *web-safe* fonts—that is, they're installed on almost all computers. You can't go wrong by choosing any of them, although I recommend using Verdana or Georgia for the reasons I mentioned in Chapter 6.

Let's choose a font for your site. To do so, follow these steps:

1. Click the Font button on the Ribbon. The Site fonts menu opens.

2. Click on a font you like. A rectangle appears around it.

3. Click on the little *x* in the top right-hand corner of the Site fonts menu to close it.

You'll see all text on the current page in the Site Designer change to the font you just selected.

Advanced Settings

Click on the Settings button in the Advanced group on the Ribbon. The Advanced site options -- Webpage dialog, as seen in Figure 9-28, pops up. It has three settings: Page width, Page alignment, and Display background color.

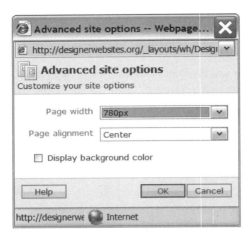

Figure 9-28. *Office Live's* Advanced site options, *which happen to be quite elementary.*

Page Width and Page Alignment

You can choose a page width of either 780 pixels or 100%. If you choose 780 pixels, the next setting, Page alignment, will become relevant. You can choose to align the page to the center, left, or right of a browser window. For a width setting of 100%, the alignment is irrelevant, because the page takes up all of the browser window's area.

In Figure 9-27, and in almost every figure you've seen in this chapter so far for that matter, the width is set to 780 pixels. That's why you see white space to the left and right of the page content.

When you set the page width to 100%, the content of the page spans across the entire width of the browser window. The browser automatically adjusts the page content to fit the dimensions of the browser's window. Figure 9-29 shows how the page would look at 100% width.

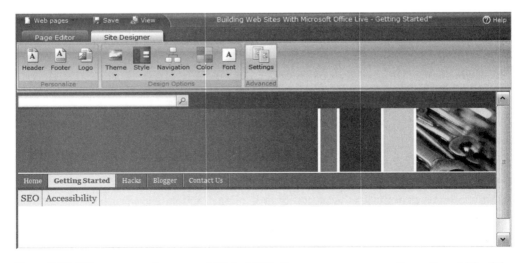

Figure 9-29. *When you set the page width to 100%, the page spans across the entire width of the browser window.*

FAQ

Which Width Setting Is Better—780 pixels or 100%?

As bigger monitors get cheaper, the trend these days is to set the width to 100% because the site automatically adjusts to the width of the monitor. Personally, I like to set the width depending upon how much content goes on your pages.

If pages are light on content, a setting of 100% tends to produce pages with a couple of lines of text at the top and a vast empty area underneath. Then people attempt to fill it with irrelevant images, advertisements, animations, and other equally useless eye candy. Personal or small-business sites typically have less content, so for these, I prefer to set the width at 780 pixels.

If, on the other hand, you're designing a portal site, you need every square inch of space you can get. For such sites, 100% width is generally a given.

Most web sites designed with Office Live will fall under the first category. Therefore, a width setting of 780 pixels will usually be appropriate. However, if your site has a good bit of content, by all means set the width to 100%.

Display Background Color

Every color theme you choose in Site Designer has a background color associated with it. You can display it or hide it by checking the Display background color checkbox under Advanced Settings. I've opted to display the background color in Figures 9-29 and 9-30, which is why you see a colored background around the Web search box (it is 100% width elsewhere on the page) in Figure 9-29 and around the entire page content in Figure 9-30.

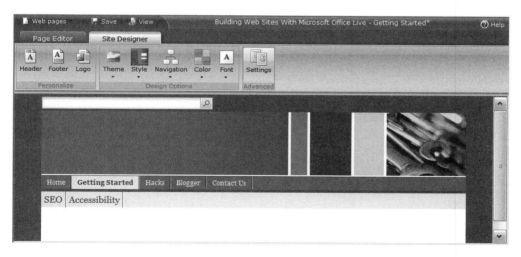

Figure 9-30. *Background color, if enabled, fills in the white space around the page content.*

Choose the Page width and Page alignment settings you'd like to have on your site. Check the Display background color if you want Office Live to display background color on your web pages; otherwise, clear it. Then click OK to close the Advanced site options -- Webpage dialog.

Don't forget to click the Save button on the Quick Access Toolbar to save your changes.

Summary

In this chapter, I showed you how to choose and set site-wide design options for your web site. You should now know how to perform the following tasks:

- Set your web site's headers and footers.

- Select and set your web site's theme and style.

- Choose a color theme and a default font.

- Set the location of navigation menu items.

- Set width and background options.

- Document all your choices.

The basic framework of your site is now in place. In the next chapter, you'll (finally!) start designing and editing individual web pages for your site.

■ ■ ■

CHAPTER 10

Building Web Pages

We've covered a lot of ground in Chapters 6 through 9. By now you know what constitutes a good web site, how to plan your site, how to collect resources that go on your web pages, and how to build a skeleton of your site by setting site-wide options in Site Designer. The only thing left to do is add web pages to your site.

In this chapter, I'll show you how to use the other half of Web Designer, the Page Editor. Specifically, you'll learn how to

- Edit page content using Page Editor's tools

- Place links to your web pages in your site's navigation hierarchy

- Set the properties of a page

- Add metatags to your pages so that search engines can find them readily

- Add textual, graphical, and tabular content to your web pages with Page Editor's tools

- Add new pages to your web site

- Delete pages from your web site

Page Editor is a feature-rich tool. It's going to take you a while to explore everything it has to offer. While it might be tempting to start designing your site's web pages right away, a slightly more patient approach is prudent. First, I'll walk you through Page Editor's features. I suggest trying them out with test pages before building your pages.

Exploring Page Editor

To start exploring Page Editor's features, sign in to your Office Live account and bring up Page Manager. You've no doubt seen this page several times by now. However, this time you'll look at all that it has to offer instead of simply clicking a link on it and trotting off somewhere else.

TIPS FROM THE TRENCHES

Use Pages from the Starter Site to Familiarize Yourself with Page Editor

The pages you see listed in Figure 10-1 are from the starter site that Office Live generates for you after you sign up. Most of you will end up deleting these pages and creating your own. However, don't delete them right away, because they make terrific guinea pigs for trying out Page Editor's features.

I suggest you work through this chapter and learn how to use Page Editor by manipulating these pages fearlessly. Once you're familiar with Page Editor, delete these pages and start building the *real* ones.

Let's concentrate on the section of Page Manager shown in Figure 10-1.

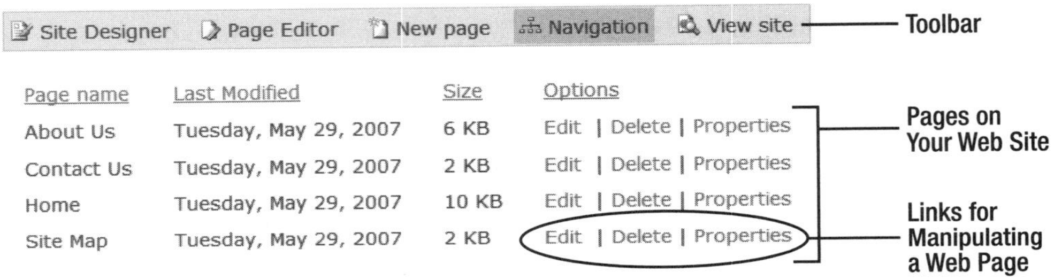

Figure 10-1. *Page Manager lists all the pages on your web site.*

At the top is the familiar toolbar. Below it is the list of pages on your web site. Each entry in the list of pages contains the name of the page, the day it was last modified, its size, and a set of three links to manipulate the page.

FAQ

What If I've Already Deleted the Pages That Office Live Created for Me?

Don't worry if you've already deleted or altered some of the pages from the starter site. Office Live doesn't allow you to delete your home page, so no matter what you did, you'll always see the home page in Page Manager. That's the page I use to demonstrate most of Page Editor's features. However, demonstrating some features requires additional pages, so if you only have the home page on your site, you can either skip ahead to the "Creating a New Page" section and follow the directions to create additional pages, or you can simply look at the figures that accompany this discussion.

By the way, the default title of the home page is Home. If you change it to something else, the new title will appear under the Page name column in Figure 10-1.

Properties of a Page

Click the Properties link next to the Home page in Page Manager. The Choose page properties
-- Webpage Dialog, shown in Figure 10-2, opens.

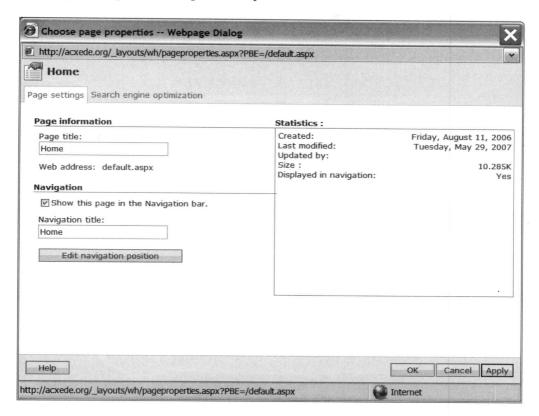

Figure 10-2. *Properties of a page in the* Choose page properties -- Webpage Dialog

This dialog features two tabs:

- Page settings
- Search engine optimization

Let's explore the contents of each in detail.

Page Settings

The Page settings tab is the active tab in Figure 10-2. It has three sections:

- Page information
- Navigation
- Statistics

I'll go through each setting and show you how you can change it.

Page Information

In the `Page information` section, you can set a page's *page title* and check its *web address*. The *page title* is the text that appears in the browser's title bar when you bring up a web page in a browser.

■Note Office Live sometimes refers to the page title as `Page name`. See the header of the first column in Figure 10-1 for an example of such a reference.

The last part of the URL in the browser's address bar is called the page's *web address*. It's really the name of the file in which the web page's HTML markup is stored on the web server. You can specify the web address for a new web page when you create it, but you can't edit it after you create the page.

Office Live uses the terms title, name, and header ambiguously and often interchangeably. Figure 10-3 identifies the page title and the web address on a web page, along with two additional elements—the navigation title and the page header—which I'll get to shortly.

Page Title

Web Address

Navigation Title

Page Header

Figure 10-3. *In Office Live terms, you can see the page title, the web address, the navigation title, and the page header on this page.*

TIPS FROM THE TRENCHES

Choose Page Titles with Care

The title of a page is one of its most important attributes. Search engines use page titles in deciding how to index pages. Thinking of page titles that shed light on the page's content can take you a long way in optimizing your pages for search engines.

Take the home page's title, for example. It's simply Home. There are a few million pages on the Web called Home. To distinguish your page, you must give it a more relevant title.

However, that's easier said than done. A good way to come up with titles for your pages is to look at what other great web sites do. Let's see a few examples from some prominent web sites:

- Amazon.com: Online Shopping for Electronics, Apparel, Computers, Books, DVDs & more

- eBay - New & used electronics, cars, apparel, collectibles, sporting goods & more at low prices

- Google

- Microsoft Corporation

- Walmart.com - Always Low Prices!

- Business Financial News, Business News Online & Personal Finance News at WSJ.com - WSJ.com

- Ford Motor Company Home Page

You can see that corporate web sites simply have their name in the title, while e-commerce sites tend to have their name and a brief explanation of what they do.

Personally, I prefer the way e-commerce sites name their pages with a corporate name and a brief business description. But no matter what you do, call your home page something other than Home.

Editing Page Information Settings

The only Page information setting you can edit is the Page title. Follow these steps to edit it:

1. Click on the Properties link next to the home page in Page Manager. The Choose page properties -- Webpage Dialog, shown in Figure 10-2, pops up.

2. The present title of the page is displayed in the Page title box. Change it to something that reflects your web site's purpose. For this illustration, I'll name mine Office Live Guide - Microsoft Office Live Tips, Tricks, and Hacks.

3. Click OK. The dialog closes, and Page Manager reloads in your browser. Note the name of the page in Page Manager. It changes to the new title—in my case, Office Live Guide - Microsoft Office Live Tips, Tricks, and Hacks.

4. Click the View site button on Page Manager's blue button bar. A new browser window displaying your home page opens. The title bar of the window displays the new title as well.

Navigation

The Navigation section houses controls that determine how the page appears in your web site's navigation system (see Figure 10-2). The first control is the Show this page in the Navigation bar check box. If this box is checked, the page will appear on the navigation bar. If it's unchecked, the page won't appear on the navigation bar.

The second control is a text box for the page's *navigation title*, which is the text of its link on the navigation bar. The navigation title is relevant only if the box above it is checked. In Figure 10-2, the box is checked and the navigation title is Home. Therefore, the link to the page, or its navigation title, reads Home, as you can see in Figure 10-3.

The third control is the Edit navigation position button. Clicking it opens up a dialog that lets you move the page around on the navigation bar, as you'll see in just a bit.

Editing Navigation Settings

Follow these steps to edit the navigation settings:

1. Click on the Properties link next to the home page in Page Manager. The Choose page properties -- Webpage Dialog, shown in Figure 10-2, pops up.

2. Uncheck the Show this page in the Navigation bar check box.

3. Click OK. The dialog closes, and Page Manager reloads in your browser.

4. Click the View site button on Page Manager's blue button bar. A new browser window displaying your home page opens, as shown in Figure 10-4. Note that the link for the home page, which you saw in Figure 10-3, disappears.

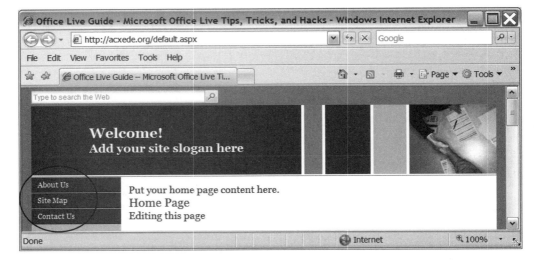

Figure 10-4. *A link to your home page doesn't show up in the navigation bar, because you decided not to show it.*

Follow these steps to enable the link again:

1. Click on the Properties link next to the home page in Page Manager to open the Choose page properties -- Webpage Dialog again.

2. Check the Show this page in the Navigation bar check box.

3. Change the navigation title to Home Page.

4. Click OK. The dialog closes, and Page Manager reloads in your browser.

5. Click the View site button on Page Manager's blue button bar. A new browser window displaying your home page opens, as shown in Figure 10-5. Note that the page's title in the browser's title bar changes to reflect the change you made earlier in the "Editing Page Information Settings" section. Also, the link for the home page reappears on the navigation bar, but it now reads Home Page.

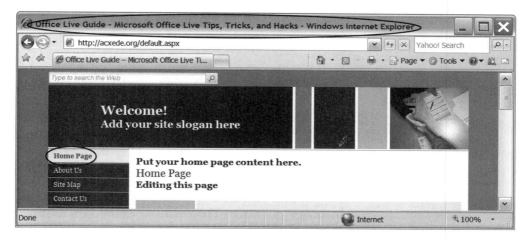

Figure 10-5. *The link to the home page reappears in the navigation bar, and the page's title changes in the browser's title bar.*

Changing Navigation Position

Click the Edit navigation position button. The Navigation -- Webpage Dialog, shown in Figure 10-6, appears.

Follow these steps to change the home page's position in the navigation bar:

1. Click on Home Page in the Select the page you want to move box on the left side of the dialog. Office Live highlights the entry in this box as well as the entry in the Page order box to its right.

2. Click the Move dow button. *The Dow* falls by 100 points and wipes out a few hundred million dollars from the stock market. Just kidding. The text on the button should have read Move down; the developer of the dialog made the button too narrow. Anyway, the page moves down one notch in the page order box, as shown in Figure 10-7. Notice that the Move up button is now enabled, if you want to move the page back up one notch.

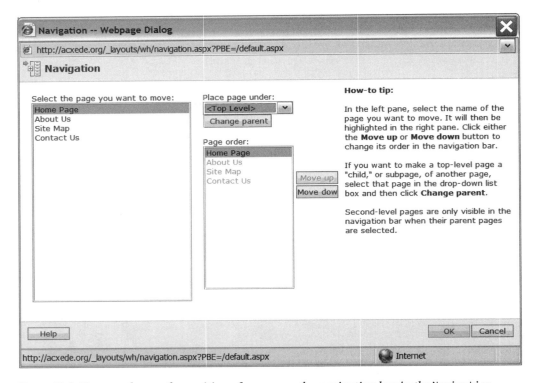

Figure 10-6. *You can change the position of a page on the navigation bar in the* Navigation -- Webpage Dialog.

Figure 10-7. *The page moves down one notch in the* Page order *box on the right.*

3. Click OK. You'll return to the Choose page properties -- Webpage Dialog. Click OK again to return to Page Manager.

4. Click View site. You'll see your home page in a browser window, as shown in Figure 10-8. Note that Home Page is now the second link on the navigation bar.

Figure 10-8. Home Page *is now the second link on the navigation bar.*

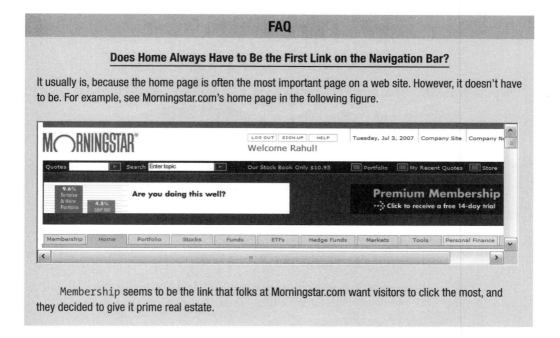

Changing Navigation Level

As you might recall from Chapter 9, your site has two navigation levels. You can move a web page from one level to the other by following these steps:

1. Click on the Properties link next to the home page in Page Manager to open the Choose page properties -- Webpage Dialog again.

2. Click the Edit navigation position button. The Navigation -- Webpage Dialog reappears. Home Page is selected in both boxes on the page (see Figure 10-7).

3. Let's move the home page to the second level and make the About Us page its parent. To do so, click the arrow on the Place page under selection box. All first-level pages appear in the drop-down. Select About Us.

4. Click the Change parent button below the selection box. The Navigation Webpage Dialog now looks like Figure 10-9.

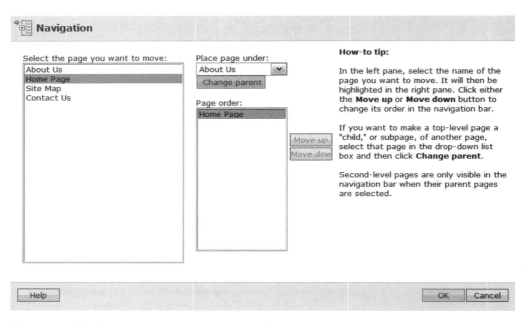

Figure 10-9. *The* About Us *page is now* Home Page's *parent.*

5. Click OK. Return to the Choose page properties -- Webpage Dialog, and click OK again to return to Page Manager.

6. Click View site. You'll see your home page in a browser window, as shown in Figure 10-10. Note that Home Page is now the second link on the navigation bar.

You don't want to leave the home page at the second level. Follow these steps to move it back to the first level and make it the first link on the navigation bar:

1. Click on the Properties link next to the home page in Page Manager to open the Choose page properties -- Webpage Dialog again.

2. Click the Edit navigation position button. The Navigation -- Webpage Dialog reappears. Home Page is selected in both boxes on the page (see Figure 10-11). Note that Home Page is indented below the About Us page to indicate that it is now at the second level of navigation and that the About Us page is its parent.

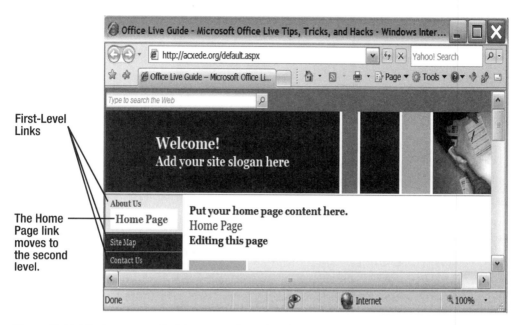

First-Level Links

The Home Page link moves to the second level.

Figure 10-10. *The* Home Page *link is now indented under the* About Us *link, because you made the* About Us *page the* Home Page*'s parent.*

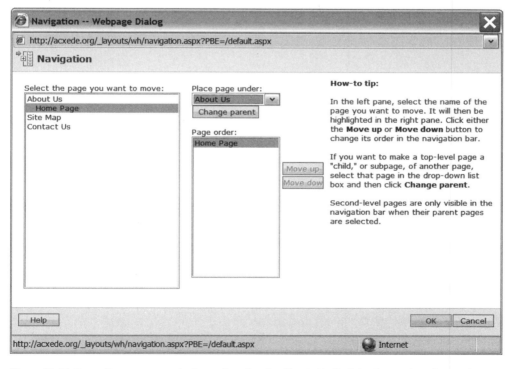

Figure 10-11. Home Page *appears indented under the* About Us *link in the* Navigation Webpage -- Dialog *as well.*

3. Let's move the home page back to the second level. Click the arrow on the Place page under selection box. All first-level pages appear in the drop-down. Select <Top Level>.

4. Click the Change parent button below the selection box.

5. Click the Move up button until Home Page moves to the top of the Page order box.

6. Click OK. You return to the Choose page properties -- Webpage Dialog. Click OK again to return to Page Manager.

7. Click View site. You'll see your home page in a browser window as it was in Figure 10-5 before you changed its navigation position.

Statistics

The Statistics section displays, at a glance, when the page was created, when it was updated last and by whom, what its size is, and whether it's visible in the navigation bar. When you change a page's properties or its contents, Office Live updates these statistics.

Viewing Updated Page Statistics

To see how your changes so far have affected the home page's statistics, follow these steps:

1. Click on the Properties link next to the home page in Page Manager to open the Choose page properties -- Webpage Dialog again.

2. The Statistics section in the dialog looks like Figure 10-12. Compare it with the statistics section in Figure 10-2. You'll notice that Office Live has updated the Last modified date.

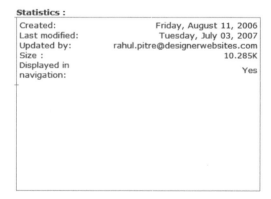

Figure 10-12. *The statistics of a page change when you update it's the page's properties or its content.*

3. Your Windows Live ID appears next to the Updated by entry. The Created date doesn't change, but the Last modified date changes to reflect the date when you made the changes.

Search Engine Optimization Settings

Figure 10-13 shows the `Search engine optimization` tab of the `Choose page properties --
Webpage Dialog`. It features two settings:

- `Keyword metatags`

- `Description metatag`

I'll describe each setting and show you how to edit it.

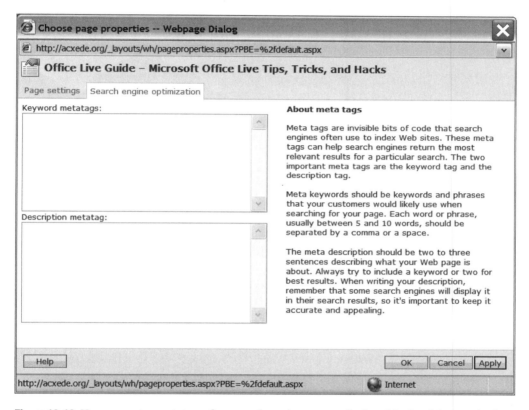

Figure 10-13. *You can enter metatags that search engines use to find and index this page in the
two text boxes on the* `Search engine optimization` *tab.*

Keyword Metatags

Keyword metatags are words that capture the essence of the content of the web page they
appear on. For example, the keyword metatags for a web page about a book might include the
book's title, author, publisher, and subject as keywords.

There is considerable debate about the value of keyword metatags. The consensus is that
many modern search engines ignore them and that they're not as important as some people would
like to believe. Still, it doesn't hurt to include them on your pages, for whatever they're worth.

Enter up to ten words that describe the content of the page, separated by commas, in the
`Keyword metatags` box.

Description Metatag

Page authors can describe what's on a web page in the `Description metatag` box. Many search engines display the contents of this metatag in search results. Take Amazon.com, for example. Figure 10-14 shows the metatags on Amazon.com's pages.

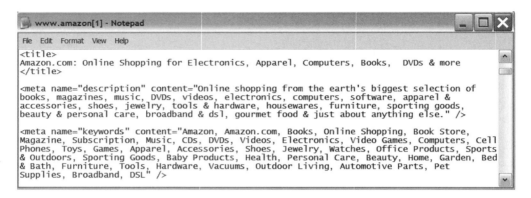

Figure 10-14. *Amazon.com's metatags*

The description metatag reads:

Online shopping from the earth's biggest selection of books, magazines, music, DVDs, videos, electronics, computers, software, apparel & accessories, shoes, jewelry, tools & hardware, housewares, furniture, sporting goods, beauty & personal care, broadband & dsl, gourmet food & just about anything else.

Now look at what the search results look like when I search for *amazon* in Google (see Figure 10-15).

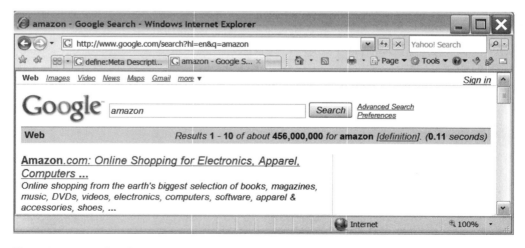

Figure 10-15. *Results of searching for* amazon *in Google*

The text in the description metatag appears in the search results right below the link. Therefore, you must put some thought into the text of the description metatag.

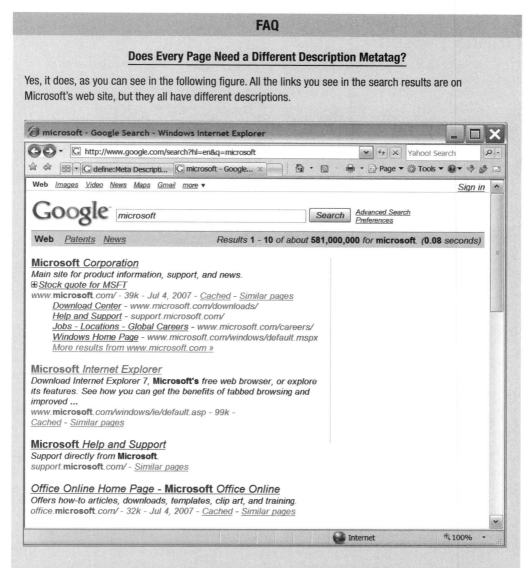

FAQ

Does Every Page Need a Different Description Metatag?

Yes, it does, as you can see in the following figure. All the links you see in the search results are on Microsoft's web site, but they all have different descriptions.

You can learn from the description metatags on pages on prominent web sites that are like yours. To see the metatags on any web page, bring up the page in Internet Explorer. Pull down the Page menu and click on View Source (or View ➤ Source, depending on the version of Internet Explorer you're using). The HTML markup of the page displays in a Notepad window. Then scroll down until you find the word *meta*.

Good descriptions go a long way toward optimizing your site for search engines. Don't type in something just for the sake of adding some text.

Try to come up with description text that is catchy, readable, and precise. It's a good idea to include a keyword or two as well. Enter the description in the `Description metatag` box.

Click `OK` to save your entries and close the `Choose page properties -- Webpage Dialog`.

Editing a Page

Click the `Edit` link next to the home page in Page Manager. The `Web Designer` page shown in Figure 10-16 pops up.

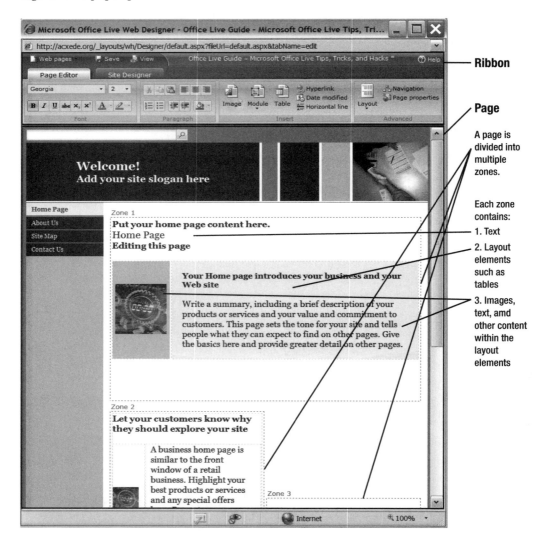

Figure 10-16. *A page is divided into multiple zones. Each zone contains text, images, and possibly other types of content.*

At the top of the page is the Ribbon. It's the same Ribbon you worked with while you learned how to use the Site Designer in Chapter 9, except that this time the Page Editor tab is the active tab.

Below the Ribbon, in edit mode, is the body of the web page you're editing. I'll call this page the *editable page*. Presently, that page happens to be the home page. The editable page displays the site-wide design elements, such as the header and the navigation bar. You can't edit them in Page Editor, but you can do so by switching to the Site Designer tab at any time. As its name suggests, Page Editor is strictly for editing page content.

Page Editor's Ribbon

Figure 10-17 shows Page Editor's Ribbon. I discussed the anatomy of the Ribbon in great detail in Chapter 9 (for a quick recap, see Figure 9-3).

Figure 10-17. *Page Editor's Ribbon has four groups:* Font, Paragraph, Insert, *and* Advanced.

The Ribbon has four groups of buttons: Font, Paragraph, Insert, and Advanced. I'll explore each of them in more detail, but I won't cover them in order. I'll start with the Advanced options, go back to the Font and Paragraph options, and finally address the Insert options.

Advanced Options

Figure 10-18 shows Page Editor's Advanced options, which include three buttons: Layout, Navigation, and Page properties.

Figure 10-18. *The* Advanced *options in Page Editor*

Layout Options

You've seen buttons like the Layout button before in Site Designer. They have a down arrow that opens a pull-down menu with selectable options. The Layout button is no exception. Click it to pull down the menu shown in Figure 10-19.

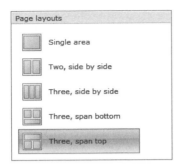

Figure 10-19. *The* Page layouts *options in Page Editor*

The menu shows five layout options. Every web page you design with Office Live's Web Designer must have one of these layouts.

A layout is simply a frame of reference to format and organize content on a page. It gives you a visual clue for placing the content. The best way to understand layouts is to visualize how artists draw a face. They first draw an oval to represent the face and then draw vertical and horizontal lines across it as guides for drawing the eyes, the nose, and the mouth. The initial picture looks something like the sketch on the left in Figure 10-20. Then using the lines as guides, they draw the features. The lines don't belong in the final picture; they just create a frame of reference to ensure that the eyes are at the same level, that the nose is roughly at the center relative to the eyes, and that the final sketch looks like the sketch in the middle and not like the sketch on the right.

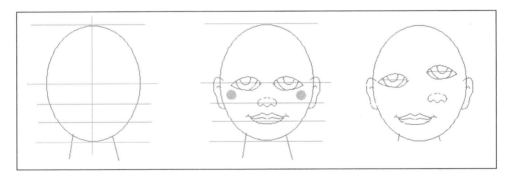

Figure 10-20. *Without the reference lines in the sketch on the left, the final sketch is likely to look like the sketch on the right instead of the sketch in the middle.*

Every web page you create in Web Designer must have a layout associated with it. You can pick any of the layouts shown in Figure 10-19.

Depending on the layout you choose, Office Live places a number of *zones* on your editable page. If you choose the Single area layout, the page will have only one zone. If you pick the Two, side by side layout instead, you'll get two zones side by side, and so on.

The home page of the starter site that you've been using so far has the three, span top layout. That means the page has three zones; one zone spans the width of the page at the top, and the other two zones appear side by side below the first. If you change its layout to Single area, the page will transform to the layout shown in Figure 10-21.

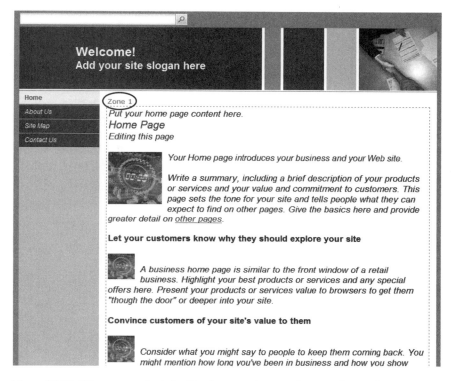

Figure 10-21. *When you select the* Single area *layout, the page has only one zone.*

To experiment with the layouts, choose a different layout from the menu in Figure 10-19. The editable page will change right away to reflect the new layout.

All the content on a web page goes into a zone. You can't arbitrarily place content below the Contact Us link in the left navigation bar, for example. It must reside inside a zone.

Adding text to zones is easy. Click inside a zone and type text as you would in a word processor. You can adorn the text with effects such as different fonts, colors, backgrounds, and emphasis, as you'll see in just a bit.

Navigation Options

To the right of the Layout button on the Ribbon is the Navigation button. Click it. The Navigation -- Webpage Dialog, which you saw earlier in Figure 10-6, pops up. In effect, clicking this button is equivalent to bringing up the Navigation -- Webpage Dialog from the Choose page properties -- Webpage Dialog, as you saw earlier on.

In fact, there is yet another way of arriving at the Navigation -- Webpage Dialog. The blue toolbar that spans across Page Manager has a Navigation button, as shown in Figure 10-22. Clicking it also pops up the Navigation -- Webpage Dialog.

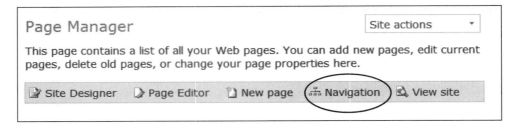

Figure 10-22. *Yet another way of manipulating the navigation hierarchy of your web site*

Once you open the dialog, you can manipulate the navigation hierarchy of not only the editable page but also of any page on your site, just like you did earlier in this chapter.

Page Properties

Below the Navigation button on the Ribbon is the Page properties button. Click it. The Choose page properties -- Webpage Dialog, which you saw earlier in see Figure 10-2, pops up. Like the Navigation button above it, this button also provides an alternate way to alter page properties while you edit a page.

Font Options

Figure 10-23 shows Page Editor's Font options. You've probably seen these options in your word processor, spreadsheet, graphics program, and pretty much anywhere you type text.

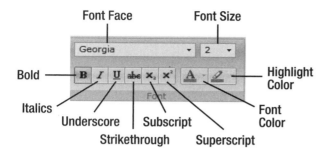

Figure 10-23. Font *options in Page Editor*

Font Face

The font-face drop-down box lets you set the font of the text you select. Figure 10-24 shows your font choices. Notice that these are the same six fonts you saw in Site Designer in Chapter 9.[1]

Figure 10-24. *Fonts available in Page Editor*

To apply a font to the text on your page, select the text and then select the font face in the drop-down box. The font of the selected text will change right away on the editable page.

Font Size

The font-size drop-down box lets you set the font size of the text you select. Figure 10-25 shows your font size choices.

The font sizes range from 1 to 7, because they are expressed using HTML conventions. The more common *point* sizes you're used to seeing in word processors are shown in parentheses.

To apply a font size to the text on your page, select the text and then select the font size in the drop-down box. The size of the selected text will change immediately on the editable page.

---

1. Refer to the "Choosing a Default Font" section in Chapter 9, where I discussed why these are the only available options and why Verdana and Georgia are the preferred options.

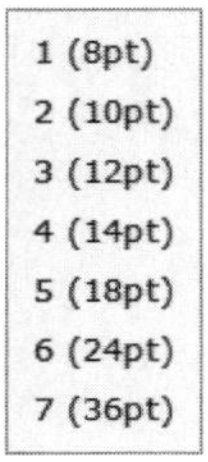

```
1 (8pt)
2 (10pt)
3 (12pt)
4 (14pt)
5 (18pt)
6 (24pt)
7 (36pt)
```

Figure 10-25. *Font sizes available in Page Editor*

Font Color

All the text you type in Page Editor is black by default. Page Editor gives you a choice of 115 colors, so you can emphasize some text by changing its color.

To set the color of some of the text on your page, select the text and then click the font-color button on the Ribbon. The color selector, shown in Figure 10-26, pops up.

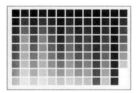

Figure 10-26. *Font colors available in Page Editor*

Click on the color that you want to emphasize the selected text with. The color of the selected text on the editable page will change immediately.

Highlight Color

To highlight some of the text on your page, select the text and then click the highlight-color button on the Ribbon. The color selector that you saw in Figure 10-26 pops up again. Click on the color you want to highlight the selected text with. The selected text is immediately highlighted on the editable page.

More Font Options

In addition to the font options you just saw, you can add the following effects to the text on your pages by selecting the text and clicking the appropriate button in the Font group of the Ribbon:

- Bold
- Italic
- Underline
- Strikethrough
- Subscript
- Superscript

Paragraph Options

The Paragraph options in Page Editor, shown in Figure 10-27, help you format paragraphs of text on your web pages.

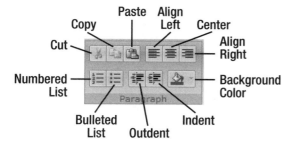

Figure 10-27. *Paragraph formatting options in Page Editor*

The Paragraph group has the following buttons, which work like the standard editing options in a word processor:

- **Cut**: Cuts the selected text and places it on the clipboard
- **Copy**: Copies the selected text to the clipboard
- **Paste**: Inserts the text on the clipboard at the cursor location
- **Align left**: Aligns the paragraph to the left margin of its container
- **Center**: Centers the paragraph with respect to its container
- **Align right**: Aligns the paragraph to the right margin of its container
- **Background color**: Allows you to change the background color of the selected text
- **Indent**: Indents the paragraph
- **Outdent**: Outdents the paragraph
- **Bulleted list**: Converts the selected text to a bulleted list
- **Numbered list**: Converts the selected text to a numbered list

Insert Options

Along with text, web pages display other goodies, such as images and hyperlinks, as well. Page Editor's Insert options offer you a way to manipulate these elements on your web pages.

Working with Images

You can only add images from the images folder on your web site to your web pages.

Adding Images   To add an image to a web page, follow these steps:

1. Open it in edit mode in Page Editor. Figure 10-28 shows the home page in edit mode.

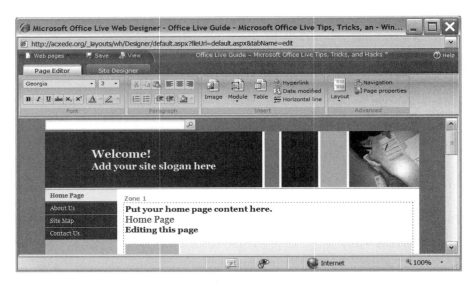

Figure 10-28. *Page Editor's edit mode*

2. Let's say you want to place an image right next to the page header. Place the cursor right after the phrase Home Page and click the Image button on the Ribbon. The Pick an image -- Webpage Dialog, shown in Figure 10-29, opens. It displays all the images in your Image Gallery.

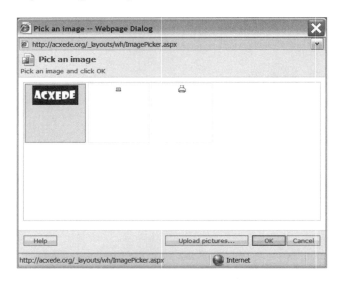

Figure 10-29. *You'll see this dialog wherever you can add images in Page Editor.*

3. Select the image you want to display on your web page and click OK. The image appears at the cursor's location, as shown in Figure 10-30.

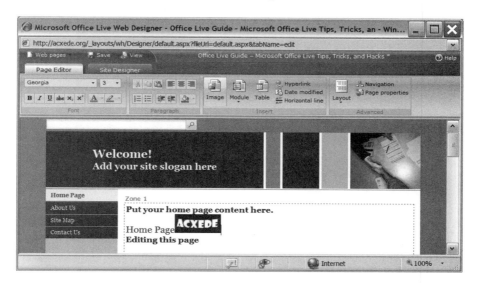

Figure 10-30. *The inserted image appears at the cursor location.*

4. Click on the image. Little squares, called *drag handles*, appear at its edges, indicating that you've selected it. You can now drag the image around on the web page and even resize it if you want to. Remember, however, that if you resize images this way, they'll get distorted.

5. Right-click on the image. The pop-up menu shown in Figure 10-31 appears. It lists ways of manipulating the image.

Figure 10-31. *Context-sensitive pop-up menu for images*

6. Click Float left. The image gets aligned to the left margin of the zone with respect to the text after it, as shown in Figure 10-32.

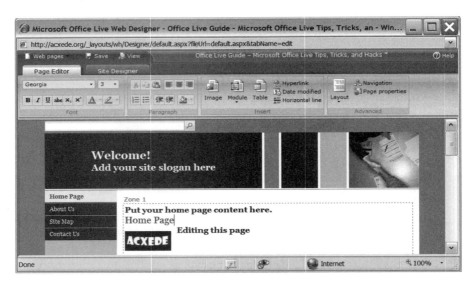

Figure 10-32. *Floating the image to the left*

7. Right-click on the image again to bring up the pop-up menu. This time, click Float right. The image aligns with the right margin of the zone, as shown in Figure 10-33.

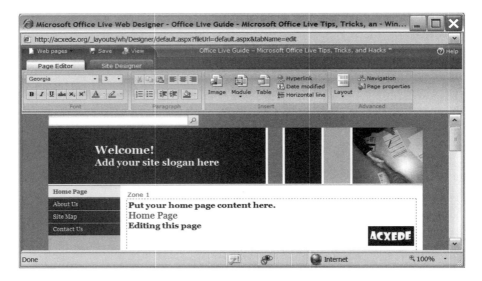

Figure 10-33. *Floating the image to the right*

8. When you float an image right or left, the text in the zone wraps around it. If you don't want the text to wrap, click No text wrapping on the pop-up menu. The image will return to its original position.

Deleting Images   You might have noticed the `Delete` option on the image's pop-up menu. You can click on it to delete the image, or you can simply select the image by clicking on it and hit the Del key on your keyboard.

Working with Hyperlinks

Adding hyperlinks to your web pages is as easy as adding images. Let's say you want to turn the text `Editing this page` into a hyperlink. To do so, follow these steps:

1. Select the text and click on the `Hyperlink` button on Page Editor's Ribbon. The `Insert link -- Webpage Dialog`, as shown in Figure 10-34, pops up.

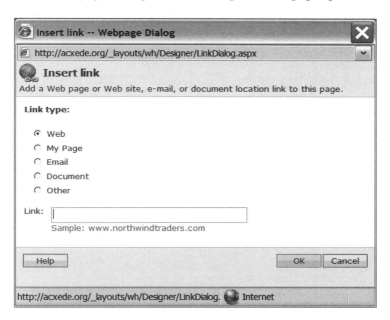

Figure 10-34. *The* `Insert link -- Webpage Dialog` *gives you several ways of adding hyperlinks to your pages.*

2. Click the radio button next to the type of link you want to add. The hyperlink you propose to add can be one of the following five types:

   a. `Web`: This link points to any arbitrary web address. You must enter a `Web` link as a web address without the `http://`, as in `www.somedomain.com`.

   b. `My Page`: This link points to a web page on your web site. You must enter it as a forward slash (/) followed by the page name, as in `/directions.aspx`. The forward slash tells Office Live that the link points to a page on your site.

   c. `Email`: This link points to an e-mail address. You must enter it as a complete e-mail address, as in `you@yourdomain.com`.

d. Document: This link points to a document in the documents folder of your web site. You must enter it as a forward slash (/) followed by the word documents, followed by another forward slash, followed by the name of the document, as in /documents/ directions.aspx. The /documents/ part tells Office Live that the link points to a document in the documents folder of your site.

An easier way to add the link is to click the Select document... button, which appears below the Link textbox when you choose Document under Link type. The File Chooser -- Webpage Dialog, shown in Figure 10-35, pops up, displaying all the documents in your Document Gallery.

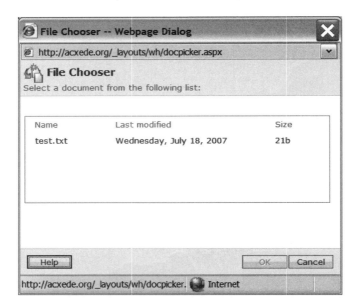

Figure 10-35. *You see Page Editor's* File Chooser *dialog wherever you can choose a file in Page Editor.*

Click on the document you want this link to point to. It gets highlighted. Then click OK. You'll return to the Insert link -- Webpage Dialog, shown in Figure 10-36. Notice that the name of the document you selected appears in the Link textbox.

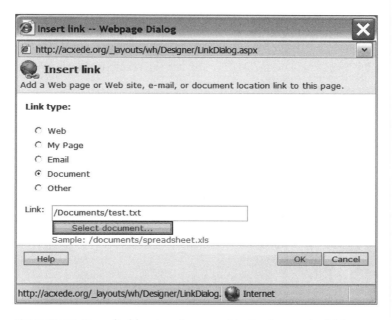

Figure 10-36. *Hyperlinking to a document in the* documents *folder*

   e. Other: This link points to any arbitrary web address not covered by the first four types of links. You'll typically use it to point your link at a secured site, as in https://www.somesecureddomain.com, or an FTP site, as in ftp://someftpdomain.com.

3. Click OK. The dialog closes, and you return to the home page, which displays your link, as shown in Figure 10-37.

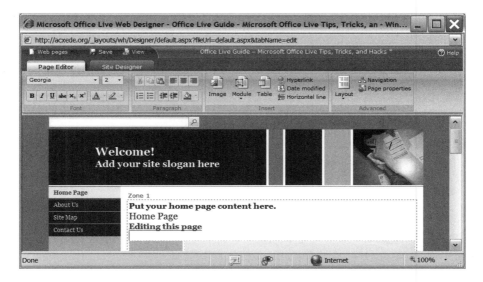

Figure 10-37. *Hyperlink on a page*

If you don't select some text before clicking the `Hyperlink` button, the link's address will appear at the cursor location. For example, I just placed the cursor after the text `Home Page` and then clicked the `Hyperlink` button. In the `Insert link -- Webpage Dialog`, I chose to add a `Web` link pointing to `www.acxede.net`. You can see the result in Figure 10-38.

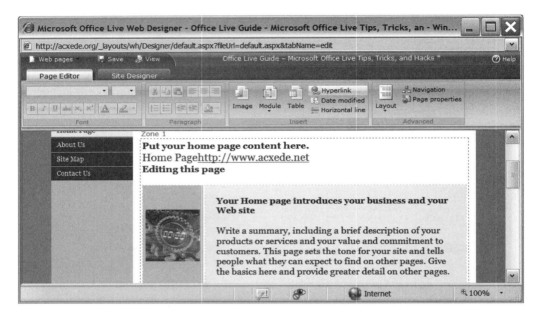

Figure 10-38. *The URL you enter appears in the link if you don't select text on your page before adding a hyperlink.*

Editing Hyperlinks   To edit the hyperlink, follow these steps:

1. Right-click on it in Page Editor. A pop-up menu appears, as shown in Figure 10-39.

Figure 10-39. *The context-sensitive pop-up menu for hyperlinks*

2. Choose the `Create/edit hyperlink` option. The `Insert link -- Webpage Dialog` appears.

3. Edit the link in the `Link` text box and click `Apply`.

Deleting Hyperlinks   The `Delete` option in the hyperlink's pop-up menu in Figure 10-39 might lead you to believe that clicking on it will remove the hyperlink. Actually, it does much more; it deletes the text as well. If you want to leave the text as it is but remove only the hyperlink, you must edit the hyperlink, clear the Link textbox, and click the Apply button.

Working with Timestamps

At times, you might want to inform a visitor to your site about when a specific page, or the entire site for that matter, was updated. Page Editor has a built-in tool for adding timestamps.

Typical examples of pages where a timestamp is appropriate are Terms of Use, Privacy Policy, Disclaimer, and other pages that carry legalese. By adding a timestamp to these pages, you can lead your lawyers to believe that you value their counsel.

Some people like to put a timestamp at the bottom of their site's home page as well. Since you have the starter site's Home page handy, let's add a timestamp to it.

Adding a Timestamp   Figure 10-40 shows the Home page on my starter site.

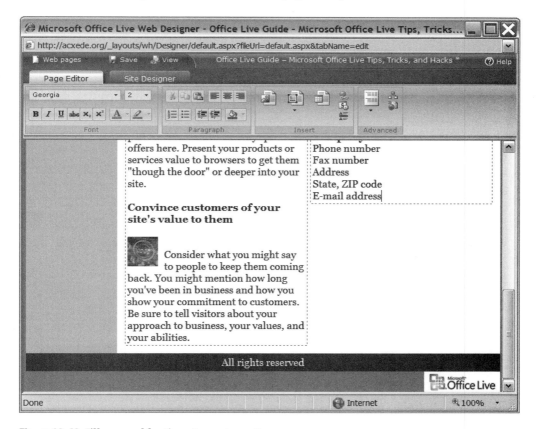

Figure 10-40. *I'll soon add a timestamp to my* Home *page.*

The bottom of the page is a good place for the timestamp. Let's add it to the bottom of the right-hand column below E-mail address. To do add it, follow these steps:

1. Position the cursor below E-mail address. Press the Enter key on your keyboard a couple of times to leave some whitespace between the E-mail address and the timestamp.

2. Click the Date modified button in the Insert group of the Ribbon. The Page last modified -- Webpage Dialog, as shown in Figure 10-41, pops up.

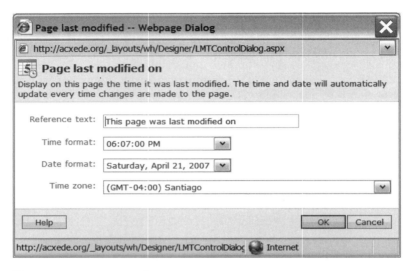

Figure 10-41. *Properties of a timestamp*

3. Select formats for date and time in the dialog. Select the time zone you're in and enter reference text, which is the legend in your timestamp.

   Note that you aren't selecting an actual date and time; you're only choosing the *format* in which the date and time should appear. So the date Saturday, April 21, 2007, which you see in the dialog, shouldn't be a cause of concern. Office Live will automatically add the correct date and time every time you edit the page.

4. Click OK to close the dialog.

You return to Page Editor, and the timestamp you just added appears where the cursor was. Figure 10-42 shows the home page with the timestamp.

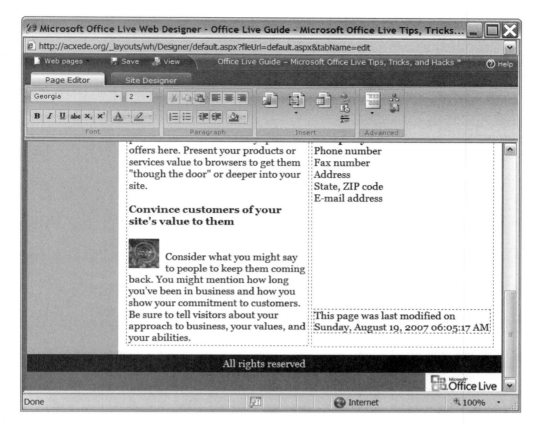

Figure 10-42. *A timestamp appears at the bottom of my* Home *page.*

Deleting a Timestamp   Deleting a timestamp is easy. Just click on it in Page Editor. Drag handles appear at its edges, indicating that you've selected it. Press the Del key on your keyboard to say good-bye to the timestamp.

Working with Horizontal Lines

Horizontal rule is the HTML term for a straight line that spans your web page. Calling a humble line a *horizontal rule* makes it sound really important and allows web designers to charge you a small fortune for drawing one. But since Office Live bypasses web designers and deals directly with you, it refers to a horizontal rule as a *horizontal line*.

Horizontal lines typically separate blocks of content on a page. For example, I might want to separate the timestamp I just added in Figure 10-42 from the contact information above it. A horizontal line fits the bill perfectly.

Adding a Horizontal Line   To add a horizontal line, place the cursor where you want it to appear on your page, and click the Horizontal line button in the Insert group on the Ribbon. A line appears instantly, as shown in Figure 10-43.

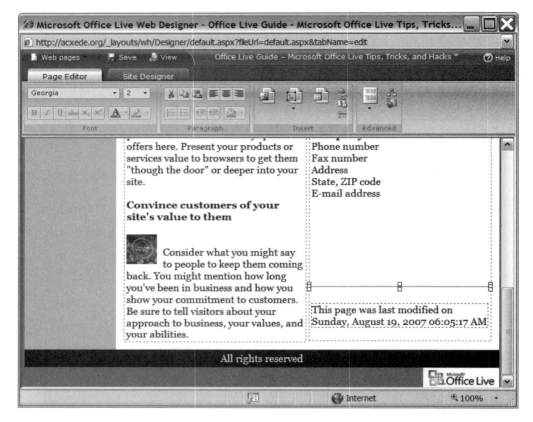

Figure 10-43. *Adding a horizontal line*

Deleting a Horizontal Line   Double-click on the horizontal line to select it, then press the Del key on your keyboard. The horizontal line goes away.

Working with Tables

Web pages often display tabular data. HTML supports a construct called *table* (duh!) to satisfy this requirement. Tables come in handy even in the absence of tabular data. You can use them to arrange text, images, and other content. The home page of your starter site, for example, uses tables to arrange the placeholder images and text.

Constructing tables the HTML way is rather painful, so Office Live lets you create and edit tables just as you would in a word processor.

Adding a Table   Let's add a table to the Home page. To do so, follow these steps:

1. Place the cursor at the location where you want to add the table.

2. Click the Table button in the Insert group on Page Editor's Ribbon. The Create Table -- Webpage Dialog, as shown in Figure 10-44, pops up.

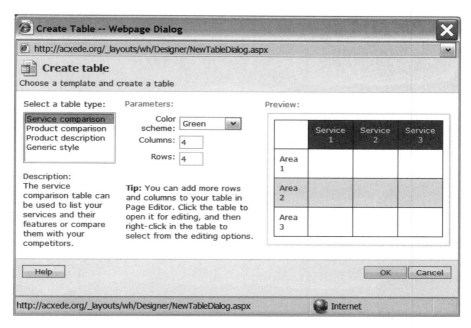

Figure 10-44. *You can specify the attributes of your table in the* Create Table -- Webpage Dialog.

■Note Changing the number of rows or columns in the Create Table -- Webpage Dialog has no effect on the preview.

---

3. You can make your table look the way you want it to by tweaking the options in this dialog. A preview pane on the right shows the effect of your selection on the look and feel of the table. Let's see what each option does:

   a. Select a table type: Office Live's designers have created a few table templates for you to use. Although the templates have names like Service comparison and Product description, you don't necessarily have to use them only for displaying tabular data about products and services. And you may not want to use the boilerplate format of these templates at all. Just think of them as templates you can use for any purpose.

   b. Color scheme: Once you pick a table type, you can apply one of several color schemes to it. The color schemes add background colors to the table's header and alternate rows. As you change color schemes, the preview changes as well.

   c. Columns and Rows: You can use these options to specify how many rows and columns your table should have.

4. Select the options you want and click OK.

A table appears at the location of the cursor, as shown in Figure 10-45.

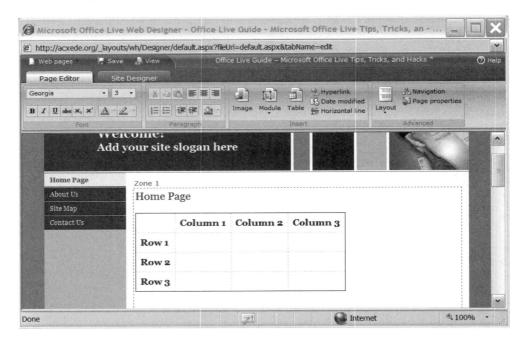

Figure 10-45. *How a table appears in Page Editor*

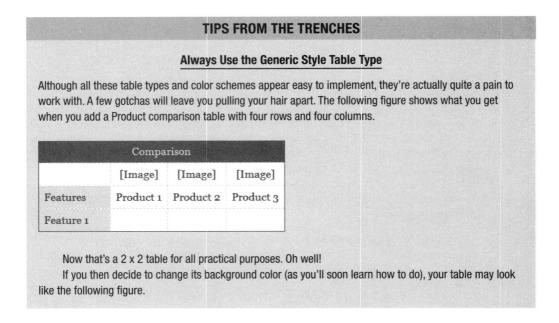

"That looks weird," you might say. "How about changing the color of the cells individually?" Sorry, no can do.

All right. Forget about this table type. Choose the `Service comparison` table instead. The following figure shows a 4 x 4 (or rather, a 3 x 3) version of it.

	Service 1	Service 2	Service 3
Area 1			
Area 2			
Area 3			

So far, so good. Now if you add another row to this table (which I'll show you how to do in a moment as well) at the bottom, you'd expect the bottom row to have a colored background, because you'd expect alternate rows to have a colored background. The following figure shows what you get instead.

	Service 1	Service 2	Service 3
Area 1			
Area 2			
Area 3			

Your best bet, therefore, is to opt for the `Generic style` table type, which doesn't have any of these idiosyncrasies simply because it's free of all formatting.

Formatting a Table   You can customize the look and feel of a table in many ways. Right-click one of the cells in the table. The context menu shown in Figure 10-46 pops up.

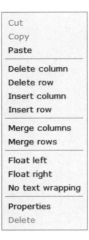

Figure 10-46. *The context-sensitive pop-up menu for table cells*

Notice that some of the options are grayed out. The reason is that they apply to the table as a whole and not to the rows and columns that constitute it. Since you clicked inside a cell before bringing up the menu, Page Editor assumes that you want to work with table cells and grays out options that don't make sense in this context. Here's a list of the options and what they do:

- Paste: Pastes the contents of your clipboard in the current cell

- Delete column: Deletes the entire column the current cell is in

- Delete row: Deletes the entire row the current cell is in

- Insert column: Inserts a new column to the *left* of the column the current cell is in

- Insert row: Inserts a row *above* the row the current cell is in

- Merge columns: Brings up the Merge Columns -- Webpage Dialog, as shown in Figure 10-47

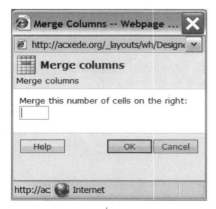

Figure 10-47. *You can merge cells on a column from the* Merge Columns -- Webpage Dialog.

Enter the number of cells to the *right* of the current cell that you want to merge with the current cell and click OK. Page Editor merges those cells.

- Merge rows: Brings up the Merge Columns -- Webpage Dialog, as shown in Figure 10-48

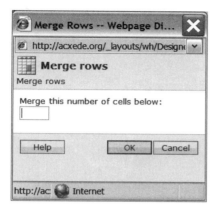

Figure 10-48. *You can merge cells on a row from the* Merge Rows -- Webpage Dialog.

Enter the number of cells *below* the current cell that you want to merge with the current cell and click OK. Page Editor merges those cells.

■**Note** Although the previous two options are called Merge columns and Merge rows, respectively, they don't merge entire columns and rows. They merely merge the cells adjacent to the current cell. If you want to merge a column with the one to its right, you'll have to do this exercise with the cell in every row in the first column.

Manipulating a Table   The properties you choose when you add a table to your page are not set in stone. You can change them whenever you wish. Follow these steps to do so:

1. Move the cursor over one of the edges of the table. The cursor changes to a cross. Click the right mouse button. Drag handles appear on the edges of the table, and the pop-up menu shown in Figure 10-49 pops up.

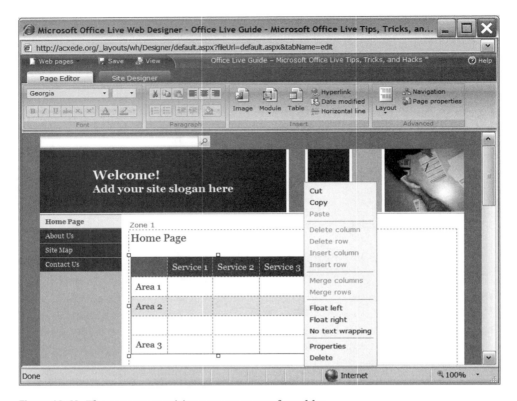

Figure 10-49. *The context-sensitive pop-up menu for tables*

This is the same pop-up menu that you saw in Figure 10-45, but this time, the links that apply to individual cells, rows, and columns are grayed out. Here's what each of the available options can do:

- Cut: Cuts the table from the page and copies it the clipboard.

- Copy: Copies the table to the clipboard. If you cut or copy a table, you can paste it elsewhere on the page or even on another page.

- Float Left: Aligns the table to the left edge of the zone it's in.

- Float Right: Aligns the table to the right edge of the zone it's in.

- No text wrapping: Prevents the text on the page from wrapping around the table.

The last two options on the menu are Properties and Delete, which I'll address in the next two sections.

Changing the Properties of a Table   When you select Properties, the dialog shown in Figure 10-50 opens up.

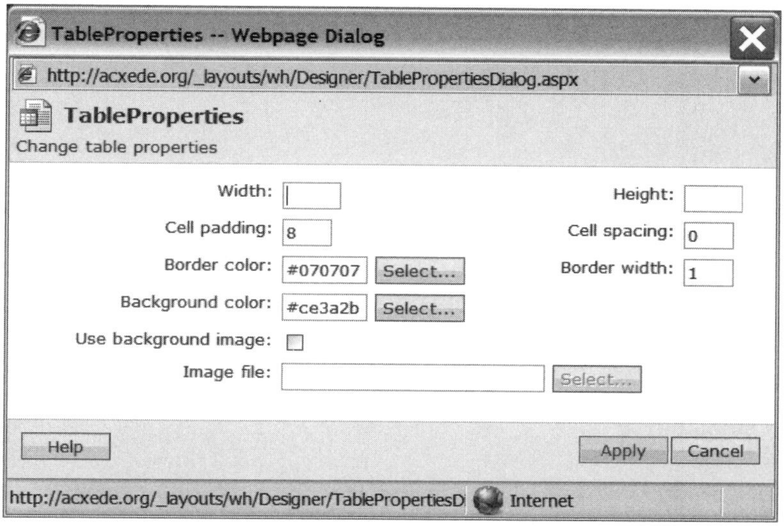

Figure 10-50. *Properties of a table*

You can adjust the dimensions of the table in this dialog and set its visual properties. Here's what each property will do:

- Width: Sets the width of the table. If you change this setting, the width of all the columns will change proportionately.

- Height: Sets the height of the table. If you change this setting, the height of all the rows will change proportionately.

- Cell padding: Sets the padding, or the empty space, between the contents of a cell and its borders. If you enter 0, the contents of table cells will be very close to the grid lines. This will make your table look ugly. Choose a higher value to increase the distance between a cell's content and its borders.

- Cell spacing: Sets the spacing, or the empty space, between the borders of adjacent cells.

- Border color: Sets the color of the grid lines in the table. You must enter an HTML color code to set this property, but don't worry if you don't know what HTML color codes are. Just click on the Select… button next to the Border color box, and a nice little color picker pops up, as shown in Figure 10-51.

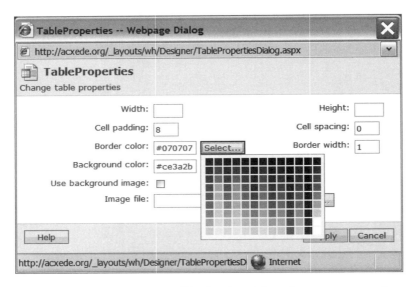

Figure 10-51. *You can see Page Editor's color picker wherever you can choose colors.*

Click on a color you want your table's grid lines to have. The color picker goes away, and the HTML code for the color you selected appears in the Border color box.

- Border width: Sets the width of the gridlines in the table. Usually 1 is a good setting for border width. To make the gridlines bolder, enter a bigger number. Enter 0 if you don't want grid lines.

- Background color: Sets the background color for the entire table. Like the border color, you must set the background color as an HTML color code. The color picker comes to your rescue again. Click the Select… button next to the box, and choose the color you want.

- Use background image: Sets an image as the background of the table. This is useful if you want to add a watermark to your table, for example. To add a background image, check the Use background image check box. The Select… button next to the Image file box becomes enabled. Click it to bring up the familiar Image Uploader. Select an image from the image gallery or upload a new one.

Click Apply when you're done. You return to the page in Page Editor, and your table sports the new look.

Adding Content to Table Cells   Place the cursor in the cell you want to add content to. Now type text or add an image, a hyperlink, a module, or any other type of content to the cell, just as you would add directly to a zone on your page.

Deleting a Table   To delete a table, click on one of its edges until drag handles appear, indicating that you've selected it. Press the Del key on your keyboard to get rid of the table for good.

Working with Modules

Most of what you've added to web pages so far has been static content. Page Editor lets you add dynamic content to your pages using *modules*. Each module is a little bundle of predefined dynamic content.

Normally, you'd need server-side code to add dynamic content to your pages. Modules make it a simple matter of drag-and-drop instead.

The Contact Us Module   Every web site needs a way for visitors to send inquiries, messages, feedback, or complaints. The usual way to do this is through a Contact Us form that the visitors fill out. The contents are then e-mailed to the webmaster.

Sending an e-mail from a web page is not straightforward; you need some sort of server-side code. The Contact Us module encapsulates that code. All you have to do is drop the module on a page, and Office Live takes care of the rest.

To add and set up a Contact Us module on your web page, follow these steps:

1. Place the cursor at the location where you want to add the module.

2. Click the Module button in the Insert group on Page Editor's Ribbon. Select the Contact Us module from the Modules menu that drops down. The Contact Us -- Webpage Dialog, as shown in Figure 10-52, pops up.

Figure 10-52. *Setting the e-mail address in a* Contact Us *module*

3. The dialog asks you to enter a single field: the e-mail address at which you want to receive messages sent from this page. If you want the messages to go to multiple e-mail addresses, enter them separated by commas or semicolons.

4. Click OK. The Contact Us dialog goes away, and an e-mail submission form appears on your web page, as shown in Figure 10-53.

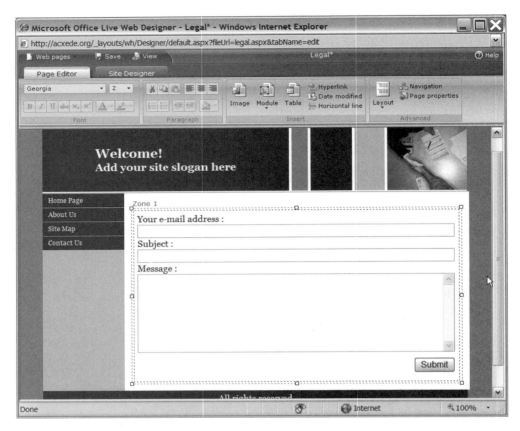

Figure 10-53. *A web page with a* Contact Us *module*

The HTML Module   Although one of Office Live's main objectives is to cater to the web design needs of people who don't know HTML, writing HTML is sometimes the only way to perform some tasks on a web page. Take scripting, for example. If you want to add JavaScript code that interacts with HTML elements on your pages, the only way to add it to your pages is to write custom HTML. The HTML module gives you the ability to do so.

To add and set up an HTML module on your web page, follow these steps:

1. Place the cursor at the location where you want to add the module.

2. Click the Module button in the Insert group on Page Editor's Ribbon. Select the HTML module from the Modules menu that drops down. The HTML -- Webpage Dialog, as shown in Figure 10-54, pops up.

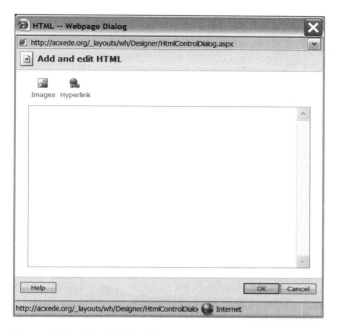

Figure 10-54. *The HTML editor in an* HTML *module*

3. The dialog has a mini editor in which you can type HTML markup. I'll type some simple HTML markup to prove to you that the module really works. Figure 10-55 shows my markup.

Figure 10-55. *Typing HTML in an* HTML *module's editor*

4. If you wish to add a hyperlink or a link to an image, you can do so using the Images and Hyperlinks icons above the editor.

5. Click OK. The HTML -- Webpage Dialog closes, and you return to Page Editor, which renders the HTML you just typed as a browser would. Figure 10-56 shows what the page looks like.

Figure 10-56. *Office Live renders the HTML you add using an* HTML *module.*

Follow these steps to edit your HTML markup:

1. Right-click on the HTML module in Page Editor. The pop-up menu shown in Figure 10-57 appears.

Figure 10-57. *An* HTML *module's context-sensitive pop-up menu*

2. Choose `Properties` on the pop-up menu.

3. The `HTML -- Webpage Dialog`, as shown in Figure 10-58, pops up. Notice that the formatting of the mark is different from what you entered initially. That's a nuisance, but you have to live with it.

Figure 10-58. *The HTML editor forgets the formatting.*

4. Make changes to your markup, and click `OK` to return to Page Editor.

TIPS FROM THE TRENCHES

You can add all kinds of interesting features to your web pages with HTML modules. Here are two examples.

Displaying a Video Clip from YouTube

You can display a video clip from YouTube (www.youtube.com) on a web page on your site. To do so, drag an HTML module to your page and add the following code to it:

```
<object type="application/x-shockwave-flash"
style="width:550px; height:400px;"
data="http://www.youtube.com/v/xxxxxxxx">
<param name="movie" value="http://www.youtube.com/v/xxxxxxxx" />
</object>
```

Change the width and height of the clip, shown in bold, to the dimensions you want the video clip to have. You also have to change the URLs, also shown in bold, that point to the movie clip on YouTube.

Displaying a Flash Movie

You can display a Flash movie on your web pages too. To do so, drag an HTML module and add the following code to it:

```
<object classid="clsid:D27CDB6E-AE6D-11cf-96B8-444553540000" ➡
codebase="http://download.macromedia.com/pub/shockwave/cabs/flash/ ➡
swflash.cab#version=6,0,40,0" width="550" height="400" id="myMovieName">
<param name=movie value="myFlashMovie.swf">
<param name=quality value=high>
<param name=bgcolor value=#ffffff>

<embed src="/Documents/myFlashMovie.swf" quality=high bgcolor="#ffffff"
width="550"  height="400"
name="myMovieName" align="" type="application/x-shockwave-flash"
pluginspage="http://www.macromedia.com/go/getflashplayer">
</embed>

</object>
```

Change the width and height of the clip, shown in bold, to the dimensions you want the video clip to have. You also have to change the name of the flash movie file from `myFlashMovie.swf` to whatever your movie is called.

This code assumes that your Flash movie is in the Document Gallery. Therefore, you must upload the movie file to the Document Gallery.

You'll find more such snippets you can add to your pages at `www.acxede.net`.

The Map & Directions Module   You can add a map of a location, such as your office, and provide driving directions on your web site by using a `Map & directions` module.

Follow these steps to add and set up a `Map & directions` module on your web page:

1. Place the cursor at the location where you want to add the module.

2. Click the `Module` button in the `Insert` group on Page Editor's Ribbon. Select the `Map & directions` module from the `Modules` menu that drops down. The `Map & directions --` `Webpage Dialog`, as shown in Figure 10-59, pops up.

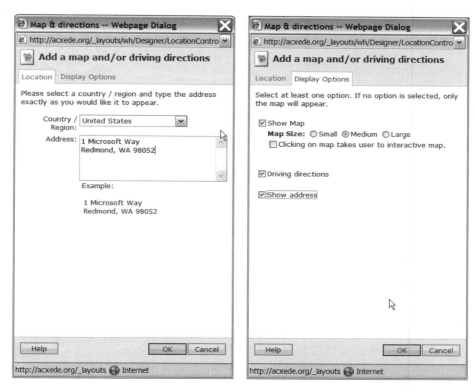

Figure 10-59. *Properties of a* Map & directions *module*

3. The module features two tabs: Location and Display Options. On the Location tab, you enter the address of the location you want to map. If you want to provide a map and directions to your office, for example, you should enter your office address here. The Display Options tab offers options that determine how Office Live renders the map on your web pages.

4. To display a map, check the Show Map check box and choose a display size.

5. If you'd like the map to be clickable, check the Clicking on map takes user to interactive map check box.

6. You can choose to display driving directions as well by checking the Driving directions check box. If you check this, a link to driving directions will appear under the map.

7. If you want the module to display the address you enter, check the Show address check box.

8. Click OK. The Map & directions -- Webpage Dialog closes.

As you can see in Figure 10-59, I selected all the options. Figure 10-60 shows the map Office Live generated for me.

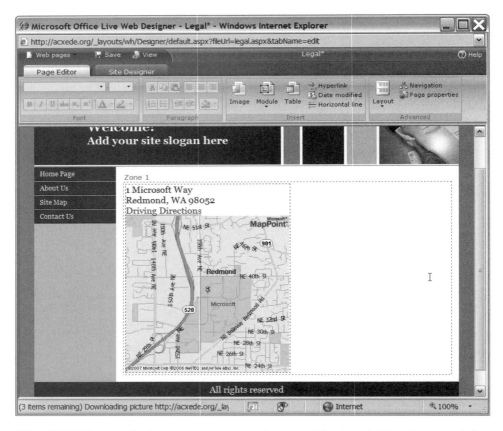

Figure 10-60. *You can display a map on your web pages with a* Map & directions *module.*

Note that the module displays the address I entered as well as the driving directions. If you click on the Driving Directions link, you'll arrive at the Driving directions page on the Microsoft Live Search web site, as shown in Figure 10-61.

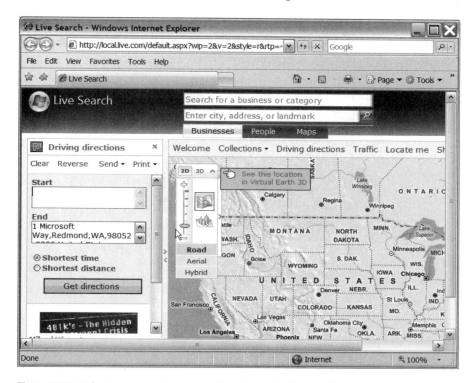

Figure 10-61. *The* Driving directions *link from the* Map & directions *module on your web page takes you to Microsoft Live's* Driving directions *page.*

The Slideshow Module You can use a Slideshow module to create a moving slide show on your web site. Follow these steps to add and set up the slide show on your web page:

1. Place the cursor at the location where you want to add the module.

2. Click the Module button in the Insert group on Page Editor's Ribbon. Select the Slideshow module from the Modules menu that drops down. The Stocks -- Webpage Dialog, as shown in Figure 10-62, pops up.

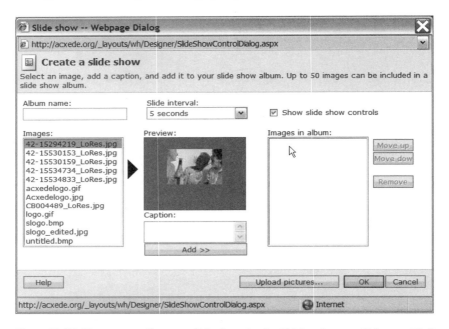

Figure 10-62. *You can configure a slide show in the* Slide show -- Webpage Dialog.

3. Every slide show you create is called an *album*. Enter a name for it in the Album name box. This name will appear in the slide show on your web page.

4. You can see all the images in your Image Gallery in the Images list box below the Album name. If you want to upload more images, click the Upload pictures... button at the bottom. Image Uploader pops up. Upload the necessary images.

5. In the Images list box, click on the name of an image you want to include in your slide show. The Preview pane to its right shows a thumbnail of the image. Add a caption for it in the Caption box below the Preview pane. The caption appears below the image when it comes up in the slide show.

6. Click Add >>. The image appears in the Images in album list box on the right, as shown in Figure 10-63.

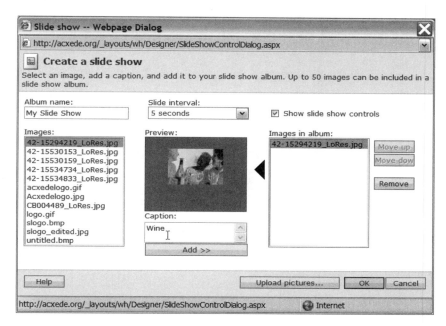

Figure 10-63. *Selecting images for your slide show*

7. Add all the images you want to include in your slide show in the same fashion. The images show up in the slide show in the sequence they appear in the Images in album list box. You can change the sequence by selecting an image and then clicking the Move up or Move dow buttons.

8. Choose how long you want to display each slide in the slide show by selecting an interval in the Slide interval drop-down.

9. Check the Show slide show controls check box if you want to display VCR buttons below your slide show.

10. Click OK. The dialog closes and you return to Page Editor, which displays a placeholder for your slide show, as shown in Figure 10-64.

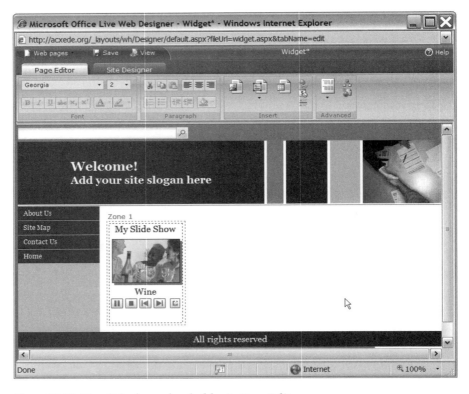

Figure 10-64. *The slide show placeholder in Page Editor*

11. Click Save in the Ribbon's Quick Access Toolbar and then click View. A new browser window opens to display your slide show, as shown in Figure 10-65.

Figure 10-65. *Your slide show in action*

■**Note** A slide show can accommodate a maximum of 50 images.

The Stock list Module   You can use a Stock list module to add stock quotes delayed by 20 minutes to your web pages.

Follow these steps to add and set up a Stock list module on your web page:

1. Place the cursor at the location where you want to add the module.

2. Click the Module button in the Insert group on Page Editor's Ribbon. Select the Stock list module from the Modules menu that drops down. The Stocks -- Webpage Dialog, as shown in Figure 10-66, pops up.

Figure 10-66. *You can select ticker symbols to display stock quotes on your web pages.*

3. To add a symbol, type it in the Add a symbol box and click Add. The symbol appears in the Move or delete a symbol list at the bottom. You can delete a symbol by selecting it and clicking the Delete button, or you can move the symbol up or down in the list by clicking on the Up or Down buttons in the list.

4. If you don't know the ticker symbol for a stock, you can click on the `Find a symbol` link next to the `Add` button. Office Live takes you to the MSN Money site, shown in Figure 10-67, where you can look up the symbol.

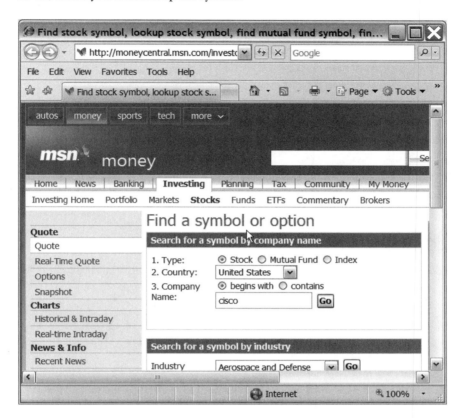

Figure 10-67. *To help you find a ticker symbol, a* `Stock list` *module provides a link to MSN Money.*

■Note The `Find a symbol` link merely takes you to the MSN Money site. You must look up the symbols and enter them manually in the `Stocks -- Webpage Dialog`.

---

5. Enter all the symbols you want, and click OK. The Stocks -- Webpage Dialog closes, and you return to Page Editor, where you can see the quotes for your stocks, as shown in Figure 10-68.

Figure 10-68. *Your own little stock quote page*

The Weather Module You can add a local weather forecast to your web pages with a Weather module.

Follow these steps to add and set up a Weather module on your web page:

1. Place the cursor at the location where you want to add the module.

2. Click the Module button in the Insert group on Page Editor's Ribbon. Select the Weather module from the Modules menu that drops down. The Weather -- Webpage Dialog, as shown in Figure 10-69, pops up.

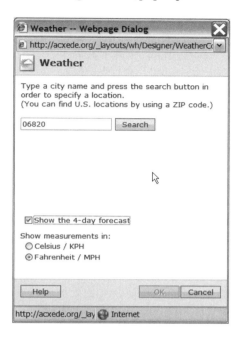

Figure 10-69. *The properties of a* Weather *module*

3. Enter a ZIP code for the place you want to add the forecast for. If you want to show an extended four-day forecast, check the Show the 4-day forecast check box. You can choose to show your forecast in degrees Celsius or degrees Fahrenheit.

4. Click Search. The Weather -- Webpage Dialog refreshes and displays the city that your ZIP code represents, as shown in Figure 10-70.

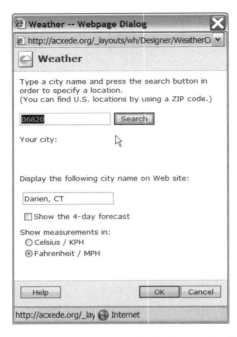

Figure 10-70. *Office Live finds the city for the ZIP code you enter.*

5. Click OK. The Weather -- Webpage Dialog closes, and you return to Page Editor, where you can see the weather forecast for your ZIP code, as shown in Figure 10-71.

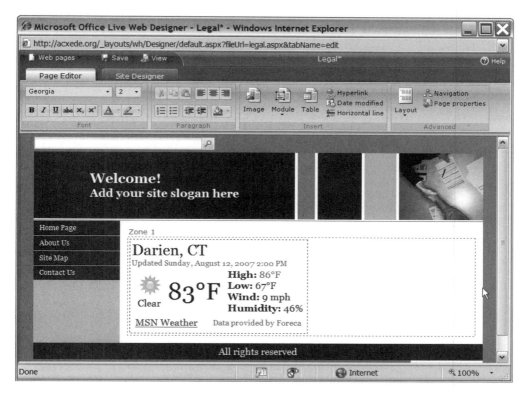

Figure 10-71. *An MSN weather forecast on your web site*

FAQ

Can I Get Rid of the MSN Weather Link that a Weather Module Displays?

The short answer is *no*.

Modules such as a `Weather` module, a `Stock list` module, and a `Map & directions` module display data provided by external data providers. Displaying a link back to the provider's site is usually a requirement for using the service. So you can't suppress such links.

■**Tip** You can edit the properties of any module by right-clicking on it and choosing `Properties` from the context-sensitive menu that pops up.

Creating a New Page

So far, you've been working with the pages in the starter site that Office live created for you. Let me now show you how to create new web pages. Follow these steps to create a new page:

1. Click on the New page icon on Page Manager's blue toolbar. The Create Web page -- Webpage Dialog, as shown in Figure 10-72, pops up.

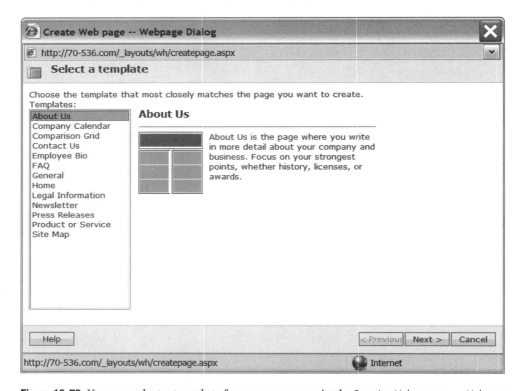

Figure 10-72. *You can select a template for your new page in the* Create Web page -- Webpage Dialog.

The dialog asks you to select a *template*. Templates are prototypes of various types of pages that Office Live's graphic designers have created for you. The Home template is a prototype for the home page, for example, and the Legal Information template is a prototype for any page with legalese, such as Terms of Use, Disclaimers, Copyrights, and Privacy Policy. The idea is to give you a preformatted page that you can get up and running quickly simply by changing the text on it.

2. Select the General template, and click Next. The Create Web page -- Webpage Dialog appears, as shown in Figure 10-73.

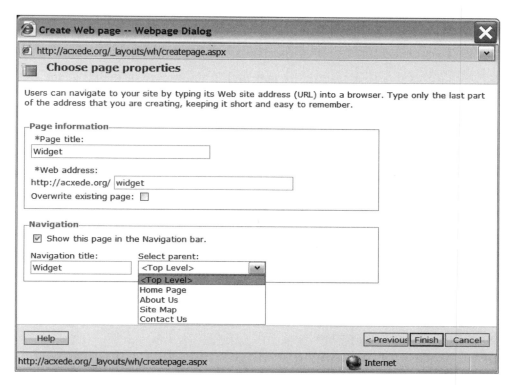

Figure 10-73. *While creating a new page, you must specify essential information such as a title and a web address for the page.*

3. Enter a title for this page. Recall that the title appears in the browser's title bar when someone views the page.

4. Enter a web address for this page. This is the name under which a file with an `.aspx` extension will be stored in your web site's root directory.

5. If you already have a page with the same web address and you wish to replace it with the one you're creating now, check the `Overwrite existing page` check box.

6. The `Show this page in the Navigation bar` check box is selected by default, because you'd normally want a page to appear in your web site's navigation menu. Notice that the title you entered in step 3 automatically appears in the `Navigation title` box. You can change it if you want to. The text in this box appears in the link to this page on the navigation menu.

   Since your site has two levels of menus, you get to select the level at which you want this page to appear. If you select the `<Top Level>` option in the `Select parent` drop-down, the page will appear at the first level. If you select any other option, this page will appear at the second level of navigation below the page you select in this drop-down.

Of course, there are times when you won't want the page to appear in the menu navigation, because it has link to it in the body of another page. In such cases, uncheck the Show this page in the Navigation bar check box.

7. Click Finish. Office Live creates a new page for you and opens it up in Page Editor, as shown in Figure 10-74.

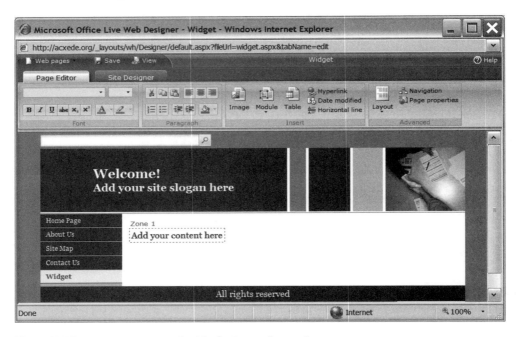

Figure 10-74. *A new page created with the* General *template*

8. Notice that the title bar of the browser shows the title I chose for this page in Figure 10-74: Widget. Also notice the new navigation link, Widget, in the navigation menu.

You can now add content to this page just as you did to the pages on the starter site.

Using Page Templates

The `Create Web page -- Webpage Dialog` lists quite a few templates. Let's see what those are and how to choose the appropriate template while creating a new page.

You can divide these templates into three broad categories:

- The `General` template

- Common templates

- Dynamic templates

■Note These template category names are of my creation. They're not part of standard Office Live vocabulary.

The General Template

Sometimes, you just want to start with a clean slate and lay out your own page. That's what the `General` template is for. It's the prototype of a blank page. When you start with the `General` template, you have the flexibility of adding content in whatever manner and format you wish.

Common Templates

Common templates are prototypes for pages you'll commonly find on web sites. Every site has a home page, for example, and many sites display newsletters, employee biographies, and legal information. Office Live makes your life easier by providing you canned templates for creating these pages quickly. You'll find the following common templates in Office Live's `Create Web page -- Webpage Dialog`:

- `Home`

- `Company Calendar`

- `Comparison Grid`

- `Employee Bio`

- `Legal Information`

- `Newsletter`

- `Product or Service`

You can think of common templates as special cases of the general template. Take a look at the `Company Calendar` template in Figure 10-75, for example.

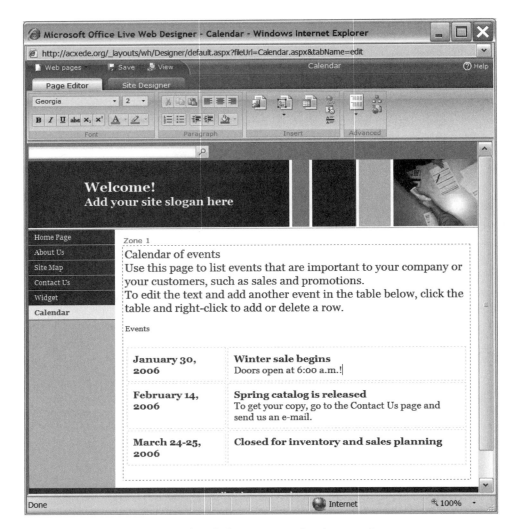

Figure 10-75. *A new page created with the* Company Calendar *template*

This page looks like the page in Figure 10-74, which uses the general template, except this one has some placeholder content that you can type over.

Figure 10-76 shows a page created with the Newsletter template.

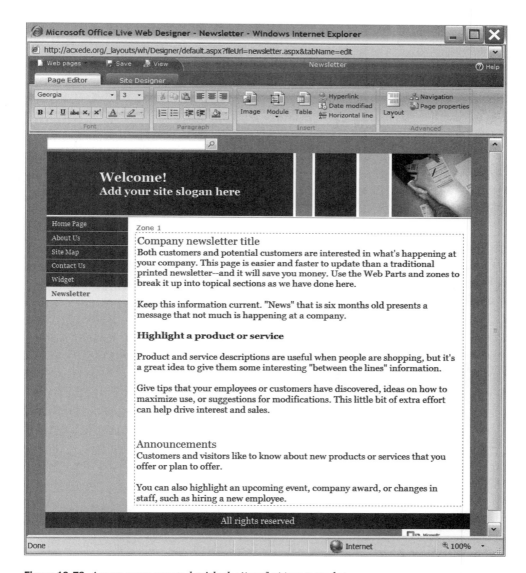

Figure 10-76. *A new page created with the* Newsletter *template*

This page isn't all that different from the other two you've seen, except, again, for the placeholder content.

A screenshot of every template would serve little purpose here. Instead, I encourage you to try out each templates to get an idea of what kind of content should go on each type of page.

Dynamic Templates

Dynamic templates provide a quick way to add dynamic pages to your web site. You can think of these as prototype pages with dynamic modules on them. The Contact Us template, for example, is a page with a Contact Us module plopped onto it. The Contact Us page in your starter site is created using the Contact Us template. Office Live has three dynamic templates:

- Contact Us
- FAQ
- Site Map

The Contact Us Template

Figure 10-77 shows a page created using the Contact Us template.

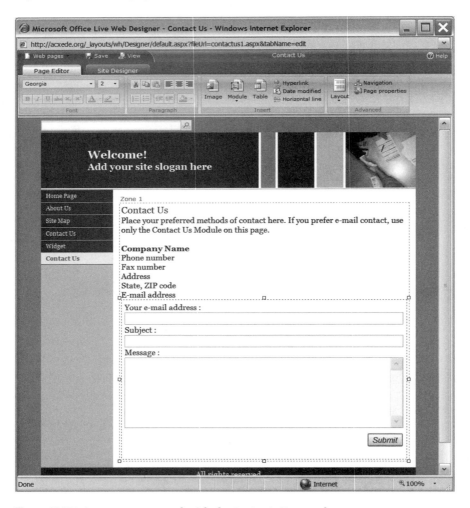

Figure 10-77. *A new page created with the* Contact Us *template*

Other than the General template, this is one of the few templates worth using. (Unfortunately, sites normally need only one Contact Us page.) To create it, follow these steps:

1. Create a new page using the Contact Us template.

2. Replace the placeholder text with your contact information.

3. Right-click on the Contact Us module on the page and select Properties. The Contact Us -- Webpage Dialog, as shown in Figure 10-78, pops up.

Figure 10-78. *Setting an e-mail address for the* Contact Us *page*

4. Enter the e-mail address at which you want to receive mail sent from this page. You can enter more than one e-mail address if you wish. Just separate the addresses with a comma or a semicolon.

5. Click OK to return to Page Editor.

6. Save the page.

Tip You can reuse the Contact Us page on your starter site instead of deleting it and creating it again.

The Site Map Template

A page created using the Site Map template creates a site map for your site automatically. Figure 10-79 shows the site map of the starter site.

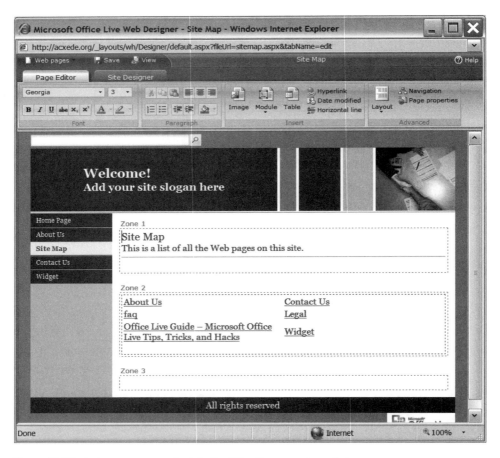

Figure 10-79. *A site map created with the* Site Map *page template*

As you can see, every page on the site, except for the Site Map page itself, is faithfully represented on the site map with a hyperlink. That's great. You didn't have to do any work to generate the site map.

There's a problem with the page, though. You can't control the order in which these pages appear in the site map, nor can you control how the hyperlinks are formatted. The home page of this site is called Office Live Guide – Microsoft Office Live Tips, Tricks, and Hacks. However, in the site map in Figure 10-79 it appears as if Office Live Guide – Microsoft Office and Live Tips, Tricks, and Hacks were two different pages.

Therefore, I recommend not using this module. If your site requires a site map, you'll be better off creating one manually using an HTML module and adding hyperlinks to it.

Selecting an Appropriate Template

Despite the many template options, my favorite template is the General template. I'm not fond of the common templates, because as you saw earlier, they differ only in the placeholder content they display. However, they force a format on you that you may not want to adhere to at a later date. Changing the format of a common template is more work than starting with the General template and customizing the page to your liking. Therefore, I recommend using the General template for creating most of your pages.

Deleting a Web Page

You may want to delete a web page from your site for two reasons:

- If it has outlived its purpose, such as a web page that features a specific promotion or a sale

- If you messed it up thoroughly while building it, and you'd like to start from scratch again

---

■**Caution** Once you delete a web page, there's *no way* to undelete it. The only way to get it back is to create it again from your documentation. Think twice before deleting your pages.

Either way, follow these steps to delete the unwanted page from your site:

1. Go to Page Manager and scroll down until you can see the page you want to delete.

2. Click the Delete link next to the appropriate page. Office Live asks you if you really want to delete the page by showing you the confirmation dialog shown in Figure 10-80.

Figure 10-80. *Page Editor asks you to confirm that you really want to delete a page.*

3. If you've made up your mind to do away with the page, click OK. Office Live deletes the page and returns you to Page Manager. The page you just deleted will no longer appear in the list in Page Manager.

TIPS FROM THE TRENCHES

Deleting Your Web Site's Home Page

As you just saw, deleting web pages from your web site is easy. Except in one case—your site's home page. If you attempt to delete your home page, you'll see the following dialog.

This is *not* a bug. Recall that when you bring up Web Designer, the home page appears in it if you don't specifically select a page to edit, so it makes sense that you can't get rid of it. Besides, you can't really have a web site without any pages in it. Therefore, Office Live prevents you from deleting your home page.

But what if it's beyond repair and you want a new home page? Follow these steps:

1. Click on the New Page icon on Page Manager's blue toolbar. The Create Web page -- Webpage Dialog, shown here, pops up.

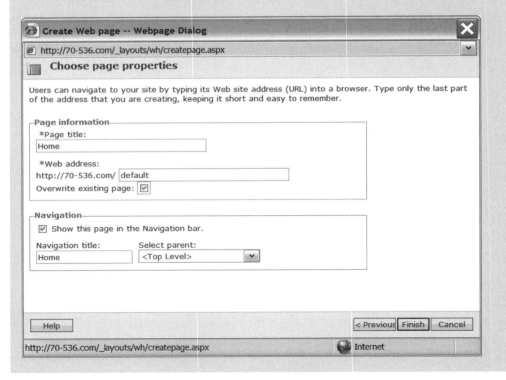

2. Give the page whatever title you want it to have. Then enter `default` as the web address, and check the `Overwrite existing page` check box.

3. Click `Finish`.

   You'll return to Page Manager with a spanking new home page.

Building Pages

Now that you're comfortable with manipulating web pages in Page Editor, it's time to go back to the list of pages you made for your site in Chapter 7 and create every page in the list.
   Follow these steps to get your web site up and running quickly:

1. Go to Page Manager and delete all the pages from the starter site. Remember, you can't delete the home page, so replace it with a new one. Use the `General` template if you want more control of the styling of the home page.

2. Open the folder on your computer that you've used as the staging area.

3. Create a page corresponding to each of the documents in your staging area. Follow the naming conventions discussed in Chapter 7. Remember to enter meaningful titles for your pages and set them up correctly in the menu navigation hierarchy. Use the `General` template whenever you want full control over the content of the page. Use the `Contact Us` template for the `Contact Us` page.

4. You should now have the skeleton of your site. Use your new skills to populate each page with content from the documents in your staging area.

5. Click the `View site` button on Page Manager's blue toolbar. Believe it or not, that's your own web site!

Summary

This chapter explored Office Live's Page Editor, which lets you create your web pages without writing any HTML markup. Remember these important points when creating web pages with Page Editor:

- Each web page must have a unique name. The home page of your web site is always named `default.aspx`.

- Every web page has a title. Search engines use the title extensively, so it pays to put some thought into coming up with meaningful page titles.

- You can code keyword and description metatags on every page. Many experts now believe that search engines don't make use of keyword metatags, but it still doesn't hurt to code keyword metatags, for whatever they may be worth. Many search engines show the description from the description metatag in search results. Therefore, as with the page title, it's a good idea to come up with catchy and relevant descriptions.

- Office Live supports two levels of navigation. You can place a given web page on either of the two levels, and you can easily move the page's position on the navigation menus.

- Each web page that you create in Page Editor is made up of one or more zones. Zones act as containers of content. You can see zones only while you design pages in the Page Editor. They provide a frame of reference for placing content on a web page and formatting it.

- You can add text, images, or any kind of content to zones. You can then format the text and add special effects such as fonts, colors, and emphasis to the text in the zones.

- You can add elements such as images and hyperlinks to your pages simply by clicking a button the Ribbon and setting a few properties. You don't need to code HTML.

- You can easily format the content on your pages with Microsoft Word–style tables.

- Using Office Live's modules, you can inject canned features such as stock quotes into your web pages and even build specialized web pages for tasks such as accepting feedback from visitors via e-mail.

Your site's now ready! In the next chapter, I'll show you a few hacks to take it to the next level.

CHAPTER 11

Hacking Office Live

The word *hacking* often conjures images of illegal, criminal, and antisocial activities. Hackers in the news manage to break into the computers of financial institutions and steal large amounts of money from helpless old ladies. Hackers in movies have tattoos, wear black leather outfits and bleak expressions, and usually hold governments to ransom. They sit in rooms full of electronic gadgetry, stare at green terminals, and type cryptic commands that have the power to blow up national monuments, the president's family, or commercial jets full of screaming women and children.

These images are flawed, for hacking is actually quite an honorable profession and a highly intelligent pursuit. Although people often refer to the bad guys as hackers, the correct term for them is *crackers*. Hackers, in reality, are the *good* guys who beat the crackers at their own game by making a computer do things it wasn't designed to do. Celebrity hackers enjoy a rock-star status among geeks.

In this chapter, I'll show you how to hack Office Live. Don't worry. You won't be doing anything sinister that would blow up Office Live's servers or bring the secret service to your doorstep. You'll just learn how to work around some of the limitations Office Live's Web Designer imposes upon you. Specifically, I'll show you how to

- Use IFRAMEs to show external content on your web pages

- Use JavaScript to add Google AdSense advertisements, PayPal buttons, and other goodies to your pages

- Add a custom header to your web site

Learning to Use an IFRAME

A browser window typically displays one web page at a time. If you want to display multiple pages in a single browser window, you can use *frames*. Frames are HTML constructs that divide a browser window into zones, each of which holds a web page.

Frames are laid out like the cells of a table. Therefore, two frames never overlap. However, there might be times when you'd like to place a web page inside a "window" on another web page. Frames aren't useful in such situations, because the page in the window must superimpose a section of the web page it sits on. HTML has another construct just for such a need. It's called IFRAME (pronounced *eye-frame*).

IFRAME Basics

An `IFRAME` is a "floating" frame. You can place it on a web page just like tables, text boxes, buttons, and other HTML elements. I won't get into murky details of HTML syntax, but placing an `IFRAME` on your page is as easy as typing the following line of code in an HTML module:

```
<iframe src="http://www.somedomain.com/somepage.html"></iframe>
```

When you bring up your web page in your browser, `somepage.html` appears in a little window where you placed the `IFRAME` code.

Why go through this trouble? Because you can add features to your site that Office Live doesn't support natively. Take blogs, for example. You can't create a blog with Office Live, but you can create one at a popular blogging site such as Blogger (`www.blogger.com`) or WordPress (`www.wordpress.org`) and display it in an `IFRAME` on one of the web pages on your site.

Figure 11-1 shows my Blogger blog.

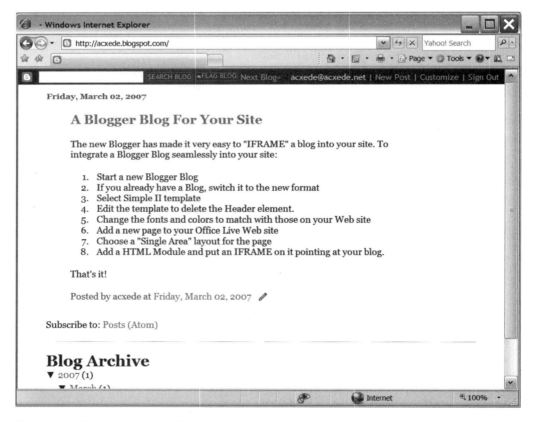

Figure 11-1. *This is my Blogger blog.*

I could easily enclose it in an `IFRAME` and show it on my Office Live–generated web site, and that's exactly what I did. You can see the result in Figure 11-2.

Figure 11-2. *Here's my Blogger blog in an* IFRAME *on my Office Live–generated web site.*

You can't even see the "window" in Figure 11-2. The entire page appears to be just another run-of-the-mill web page. That's the beauty of using an IFRAME. However, if you'd like to integrate an IFRAME on your pages as seamlessly as I've done in Figure 11-2, you'll have to do a little more work.

The line of code you saw earlier merely puts a "window" on your web page. You can make it taller and wider to fit its content, and you can add a border to it or remove the border if it already has one. To add such cosmetic effects, you need additional specifications for your IFRAME. In HTML, these specifications are called *attributes*.

Each attribute has a name and a value. An attribute called `frameborder`, for example, has two possible values, 0 and 1. A value of 0 means "don't show a border"; a value of 1 means "show a border." If you want to hide the border around your IFRAME, you can add the `frameborder` attribute to your code as follows:

```
<iframe src="http://www.somedomain.com/somepage.html" frameborder="0"></iframe>
```

I've shown the attribute in bold font to show you where to place it. You don't have to make it bold when you type the code. You must place an = sign between the attribute and its value, and you must enclose the value between double quotation marks.

■Note   src is an attribute too. It specifies the address of the web page you'll display in the IFRAME.

You can add as many attributes as you want to your IFRAME, as long as you leave a blank space before each and you place all of them before the first > symbol in the code. Here's an example of an IFRAME with two additional attributes:

```
<iframe
src="http://www.somedomain.com/somepage.html"
frameborder="0" scrolling="no">
</iframe>
```

Table 11-1 lists the IFRAME's most important attributes.

Table 11-1. *Attributes of* IFRAME

Attribute	What It's for and Which Values It Can Take
frameborder	A value of 1 places a border around the IFRAME. A value of 0 removes the border so that you can integrate the IFRAME seamlessly with your page, as I've done in Figure 11-1. For example: frameborder="0".
scrolling	A value of yes allows you to scroll a web page inside the IFRAME. A value of no disables scrolling. A value of auto lets the browser decide when to show scrollbars. For example, scrolling="no".
width	You can specify the width of the IFRAME in two ways: as a percentage of the width of the parent web page, or as an absolute value in pixels. For example, width="80%" of width="400".
height	Like its width, you can specify the height of the IFRAME in two ways: as a percentage of the height of the parent web page, or as an absolute value in pixels. For example, height="40%" or width="500".
align	The possible values of top, middle, and bottom specify the IFRAME's position with respect to the content surrounding it on the parent web page. For example, align="left".
name	You don't really have to specify a name, but if you want to manipulate the frame using JavaScript, as you'll shortly see, your IFRAME will need a name. For example, name="blogframe".
longdesc	Like name, longdesc is a discretionary attribute. However, it's a good idea to include it to make your web site accessible. For example, longdesc="This frame encloses my blog at http://www.myblog.com".

Adding an IFRAME to Your Pages

Follow these steps to add a page with an `IFRAME` to your web site:

1. Add a new page to your site or open a page to which you'd like to add the `IFRAME` in edit mode.

2. Add a new `HTML` module to the zone in which you want the `IFRAME` to be in.

3. Right-click on the `HTML` module and select `Properties`. The `HTML` dialog pops up.

4. Enter your `IFRAME` code and click `OK`. The dialog closes, and you return to the web page in Page Editor, which displays the web page you specified in your `IFRAME` code (see Figure 11-3).

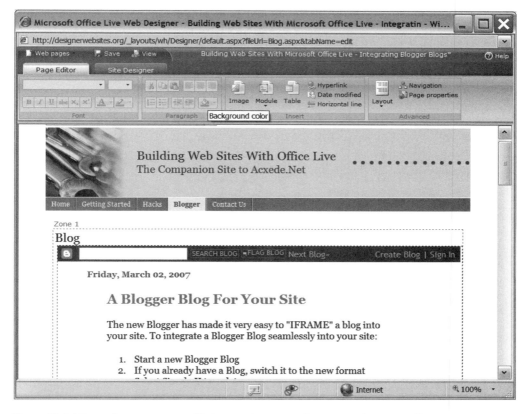

Figure 11-3. *The web page you specify in your* `IFRAME` *code appears in Page Editor.*

5. Adjust the `height`, `width`, or other attributes of the frame if necessary by adding additional attributes from Table 11-1.

What you can do with `IFRAME`s is limited only by your imagination. You could display a PDF document from your `Document Gallery` in an `IFRAME`, or you could even pull in a video clip from YouTube.

Adding Dynamic Behavior with JavaScript

Content you see on Office Live pages is mostly static. You can add life to it with the help of a script. The prevalent scripting language on the Web is JavaScript. I won't be teaching you JavaScript; that's beyond the scope of this book. I'll just show you how to add JavaScript to your pages. Once you know the technique, you can use it to customize your pages with scripts that service providers such as Google and PayPal make freely available to their users.

Google AdSense, for example, provides you with a little script that you can put on any web page to show advertisements from AdSense. You could display these advertisements on your pages too.

Adding JavaScript Using HTML Modules

The easiest way of adding JavaScript code to web pages is to add it just like HTML markup—that is, drop an HTML module on a page and just type your script in it.

The problem is it may not always work. Office Live isn't very fond of JavaScript, and for good reason. When used indiscriminately, JavaScript can wreak havoc and bring web servers to their knees. In fact, Office Live's technology has several safeguards against malicious or ignorant people trying to add potentially harmful JavaScript to their web pages.

These safeguards might prevent the script you add from executing as expected. When that happens, your web page might just freeze in a visitor's browser or throw an error, causing your web page to look like the one shown in Figure 11-4.

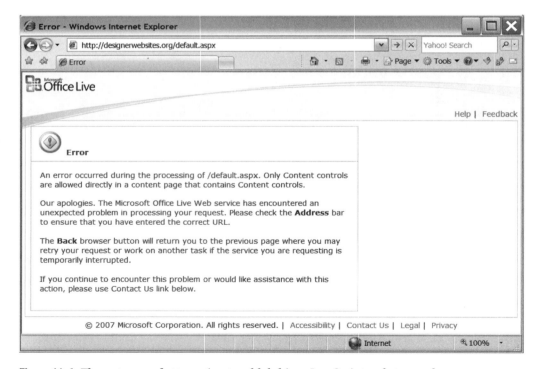

Figure 11-4. *The outcome of attempting to add dubious JavaScript code to a web page*

Don't worry if you can't understand the message. In plain English, it means "Don't add weird stuff to your pages, you doofus!"

■**Note** Something else you should keep in mind is that even if your page seems to work just fine after adding JavaScript to it in an HTML module, it may not work in the future. I've personally experienced the problems with JavaScript in an HTML module. When Office Live was in beta, I had injected JavaScript into several of my test pages. Many of these pages stopped working later.

So how do you add JavaScript to your web pages if adding it using an HTML module doesn't work? Using IFRAMEs, of course.

Adding JavaScript Using IFRAMEs

Although the content of an IFRAME seems to belong to your web page, you now know it doesn't. Therefore, Office Live couldn't care less about what's actually on the page in an IFRAME. You can take advantage of this fact and inject JavaScript indirectly into your pages without offending Office Live. Let's see a few examples of this technique.

■**Note** Another advantage of adding scripts using IFRAMEs is that the scripts stay in the Document Gallery, separate from your web pages. As you'll see in Chapter 14, you can't back up your web pages directly. Having scripts in separate documents makes it easier to restore pages if you mess them up unintentionally.

Displaying Google AdSense Ads

Let's say you want to add Google AdSense advertisements to your web page. Google supplies you with the JavaScript code, which looks something like this:

```
<script type="text/javascript">
<!--
google_ad_client = "pub-82645557679XXXXX";
google_ad_width = 728;
google_ad_height = 90;
google_ad_format = "728x90_as";
google_ad_type = "text_image";
google_ad_channel = "";
//-->
</script>
<script type="text/javascript"
  src="http://pagead2.googlesyndication.com/pagead/show_ads.js">
</script>
```

To show advertisements on your web page, follow these steps:

1. Type the code in a text editor such as Notepad.

2. Save the file with a name such as textads.html. Use an htm or html extension for your file.

3. Upload the file to your Document Gallery.

4. Add a new page to your site or open a page in edit mode to which you'd like to add advertisements.

5. Add a new HTML module to the zone in which you want the advertisements to display.

6. Right-click on the HTML module and select Properties. The HTML dialog pops up.

7. Enter your IFRAME code as follows:

```
<iframe src="http://www.yourdomain.com/documents/textads.html"
width="740" height="300" frameborder="0" align="left"
marginwidth="0px" marginheight="0px"
scroll="auto">Loading Blog...</iframe>
```

8. The values for height and width are shown in bold font in the code. You don't have to type them in bold font. They're bold just to show you what to alter if you want to change the dimensions of your IFRAME. Alter them to suit your design, and click OK. The dialog closes and you return to the web page in Page Editor, which displays the advertisements from AdSense, as shown in Figure 11-5.

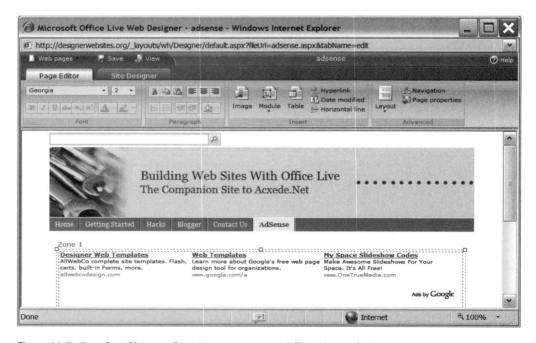

Figure 11-5. *Google AdSense advertisements on my Office Live web site*

As with IFRAMEs, what you can do with JavaScript is limited only by your imagination.

FAQ

Can I Use This Technique Instead of Using HTML Modules?

Yes, you can. Using IFRAMEs is also a better approach in a way, because the HTML module "forgets" the formatting of your HTML markup when you try to edit it, as you saw in Chapter 10. Using IFRAMEs preserves the formatting, because the markup stays in a physical file in your Document Gallery. As a result, it's easier to edit.

Can I Place Multiple IFRAMEs on One Page?

You sure can. An IFRAME is just another HTML element. Just as you can place any number of text boxes on your page, you can place as many IFRAMEs as you want as well.

Once I Write a Script and Upload It to Document Gallery, Can I Use It on Multiple Pages?

Absolutely. In fact, that's one of the advantages of this approach. If you decide to change how the AdSense advertisements on your site should look, for example, you only have to change the script at a single location instead of messing around with 50 pages individually.

Note that the script in Document Gallery determines *which* content will be displayed, and attributes of the IFRAME on each page determine *how* the content will appear on that page.

Hiding the Search Box at the Top of Your Pages

You can see the infamous search box at the top of the web page in Figure 11-4. If you're an Office Live Basics subscriber, you're stuck with it; the option to hide it is disabled. But you can get around it, at least partially, using JavaScript. To do so, use this script in the HTML page you'd upload to the Document Gallery:

```
<script language=javascript>
top.document.getElementById("SearchInputBoxId").style.visibility="hidden";
top.document.getElementById("SearchButtonId").style.visibility="hidden";
</script>
```

The steps remain exactly the same as those in the AdSense example; only the script changes.

Redirecting to Another Page or Web Site Automatically

Use this script with the address of wherever it is that you want to redirect your users, and replace the web address shown in bold font:

```
<script language="javascript">
parent.document.location.href='http://www.yourdestination.com';
</script>
```

Again, the steps remain exactly the same as those in the AdSense example; only the script changes.

Doing Almost Anything That's Possible to Do with JavaScript

Want to add PayPal buttons to your pages? No problem. Just add the JavaScript that PayPal provides you.

Now this is getting more and more interesting. Once you know the technique and write (or have someone write for you) the script to achieve your goal, you can easily incorporate almost any JavaScript functionality into your web pages.

■**Tip** You'll find plenty of tips and ideas on improving your web pages on my site, www.acxede.net. If you ask a question on the forums, chances are I'll reply to it.

Adding a Custom Header

If you don't like Office Live's built-in themes for your site's header, you can replace the header with a single image. To make this hack work, you'll have to play with the site themes, color themes, and possibly the background color of your header image as well. But with some trial and error and a dash of patience, you can make it work. Here's how:

1. Create a header image (preferably as a GIF) 641 pixels wide by 112 pixels high. These are the default measurements of the header area. Figure 11-6 shows the pretty header image I created to demonstrate this hack.

Figure 11-6. *The custom header image I want to put on my web site*

2. Upload the header image to the Image Gallery of your site.

3. Go to Site Designer and click on the Header button on the Ribbon. The Customize Header -- Webpage Dialog pops up.

4. Erase the Site Title.

5. Erase the Site Slogan.

6. Click OK to save the header settings, close the Customize Header -- Webpage Dialog, and return to Site Designer.

7. Click on the Logo button on Site Designer's Ribbon. The Change your Logo -- Webpage Dialog pops up.

8. Click on the header image you just uploaded.

9. Click OK to save the logo, close the Change your Logo -- Webpage Dialog, and return to Site Designer.

10. Click on the Theme button on Site Designer's Ribbon. The Themes menu appears.

11. Scroll down and select the General(no photos) option.

12. Click on the little *x* on the top right-hand corner of the Site themes menu to close it.

13. Click on the Style button on Site Designer's Ribbon. The Site headers menu appears.

14. Scroll down to the bottom of the menu, and select the second option from the bottom, as shown in Figure 11-7.

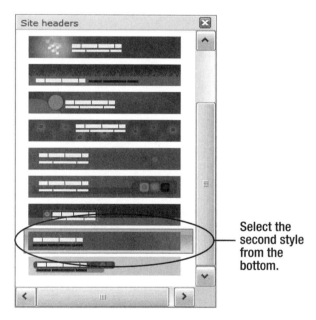

Figure 11-7. *Select the second style from the bottom on the* Site headers *menu.*

15. Click on the little *x* on the top right-hand corner of the Site headers menu to close it.

16. Click on the Color button on Site Designer's Ribbon. The Site color themes menu appears.

17. Try a few color themes until you find one that matches the background color of your header image.

18. Click on the little *x* on the top right-hand corner of the Site color themes menu to close it.

19. Click the Save button on the Quick Access Toolbar to save your changes.

20. Bring up your web site in a new browser window. You should see your site in its new garb. Figure 11-8 shows how my site looks with its new header image.

Figure 11-8. *My web site with the new custom header*

Don't Go Overboard

If you're already feeling like a lesser god with your newfound power, here's a word of caution. *Avoid doing things with your web pages simply because you can.*

There are sensible hacks, and there are senseless hacks. Here's an example of a senseless one. While playing with Office Live's features in its early days, I discovered a way to change the site's style sheet. Terrific! I went to town changing styles in the default style sheet and overrode almost all of Office Live's default styles. It was tedious work. It took a long time, but the results were worth the trouble.

A few months later, though, the internal structure of Office Live changed, causing my style sheet to stop working as intended. Because my custom styles were deeply ingrained within my site's design, I had to practically redesign the entire site using the default styles again.

How do you determine which hacks are the senseless ones? Follow Pitre's First Law of Web Design.[1] *If something feels silly to you while building your site, then it probably is.* I'll even add a corollary. *If a workaround for your design problems appears too convoluted, don't use it.*

---

1. See Chapter 6.

Summary

In this chapter, I discussed ways of enhancing Office Live's capabilities. Here are the notable points from the discussion:

- Contrary to common belief, hackers are honorable people. *Crackers* are the villains.

- It's possible to extend Office Live's features with IFRAMEs and JavaScript without having to resort to nefarious techniques.

- IFRAMEs are floating "windows" that you can place on your web pages and display external web pages in.

- JavaScript allows you to add dynamic functionality to your web pages.

- You can easily integrate content such as external blogs and AdSense advertisements in your web pages using IFRAMEs and JavaScript.

- JavaScript is a powerful tool, but don't go overboard with it and create nonsensical web pages.

You now know enough about spicing up your web pages with goodies that Office Live doesn't support right out of the box. Go right ahead and hack your site! When you're done, proceed to the next section, where I'll give you practical advice on taking your site live and being your own webmaster.

PART 3

■■■

Being Your Own Webmaster

■■■

CHAPTER 12

Lights, Camera, Action!

Once your web site is ready, the next step is to roll it out—or *go live*, as the pros like to say.

Going live can give site designers a few gray hairs. There are many things to check. Does the FTP password work? Does the directory structure on the server match that of the computer the site was designed on? Do relative paths work? Is the domain name pointing to the web server? No matter how carefully you plan the rollout, something or other invariably goes wrong, and the National Guard has to be summoned.

Unlike other site-building tools, taking an Office Live site live is deceptively simple. You don't really have to do anything in particular. Whatever you do to your site goes live instantaneously.[1] Still, it's prudent to check and double-check a few items before proclaiming your web site live.

In this chapter, I'll walk you through the "going live" checklist. The goal of the checklist is to ensure that

- Individual web pages on your site are functionally complete, factually accurate, and project a professional image to prospective visitors

- Site-wide settings on your web site, such as headers, footers, and contact forms, are configured correctly

- Your web site functions well with different computers, operating systems, and browsers

- Search engines know about your site and will display it in their results one day

Checking Individual Web Pages

Even if you take great care while building your web pages, you'll almost always find that you left out a few little details or got a few facts wrong. It's a good idea, therefore, to go over your pages once again before going live.

Checking Text

Start checking your web pages by going over the text. Confirm that

- The text is factually and grammatically correct

- The hyperlinks in the text point to their intended destinations

---

1. Now you know why Microsoft decided to call the service Office Live!

- The references to downloadable documents point to the intended documents

- The hacks, if any, that you introduced on your pages work as intended

Proofreading Text

I don't mean to sound like your fifth-grade English teacher, but reading the text on each page carefully for accuracy, spelling, and grammar is a very good idea. Bring up every page on your site in your browser, and check its copy. Correct all factual errors that you find.

When you write copy for individual pages, you tend to forget about the copy on other pages. Go over your pages as if you're visiting the site for the first time, and get rid of redundant and duplicate copy.

Ask a friend or two for a critique of the copy on your web site. Copy that seems crystal clear to you may be barely comprehensible to your friends. When you ask other people to view your site, you may find that they look at it in a whole different light.

Checking All Hyperlinks

Every once in a while, you end up changing the names of pages as you build them. If the text on your pages contains hyperlinks to those pages, the hyperlinks may still refer to the old page names. Click on every hyperlink as you read through the copy. Does the right page come up? Correct all incorrect references that you find.

I must confess that advising people to click on all links on their web site is easier said than done. It's actually quite tedious. Luckily, there's an easier way: *link validators*.

Link validators are programs that locate every link on a web page and then verify that it leads somewhere. Unfortunately, you can't use them with 100% accuracy with Office Live–generated sites.

Office Live–generated web sites have three kinds of links:

- Those that Office Live generates for you—navigation links, for example

- Those that you add to the pages by writing HTML markup yourself in Page Editor's HTML module

- Those that you add to the pages using the Hyperlink button on Page Editor's Ribbon

Link validators can catch broken links generated by the first two methods but not the third. Still, they're worth a try. The "Hands-On Lab" sidebar shows you how to use the link validator on the World Wide Web Consortium (W3C) web site.

Adding hyperlinks to your pages using the Hyperlink button on Page Editor's Ribbon has another drawback: you don't get an option to add a *title* attribute to your link. As I mentioned in Chapter 6, missing title attributes aren't desirable if you want your site to be accessible.

You can work around these limitations by writing your own HTML markup for the affected hyperlinks using Page Editor's HTML module. Refer to the discussion on the HTML module in Chapter 10 if you need to jog your memory about writing HTML markup yourself.

HANDS-ON LAB

Find Broken Links with Link Validator

A good tool for finding broken links on your pages quickly is the W3C Link Checker tool at `http://validator.w3.org/checklink`. Follow these steps to find broken links on your pages with Link Checker:

1. Point your browser at `http://validator.w3.org/checklink`. The web page shown in the following figure appears.

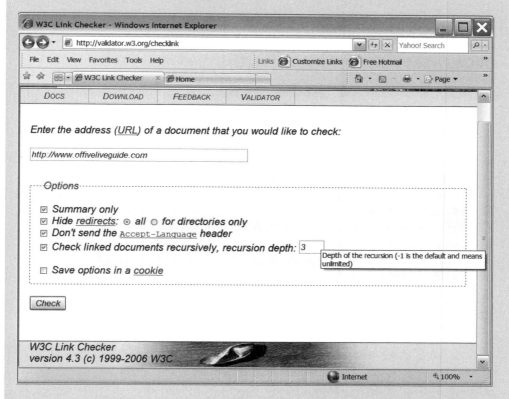

2. Enter the full address of your web site (for example, `http://www.officeliveguide.com`).

3. Under `Options`, check these boxes:

   - `Summary only`

   - `Hide redirects`

   - `Don't send the Accept-Language header`

   - `Check linked documents recursively`

4. Type 3 in the `recursion-depth` box.

5. Click the `Check` button. After what seems to be an eternity, you get a detailed report, such as the one shown in the following figure.

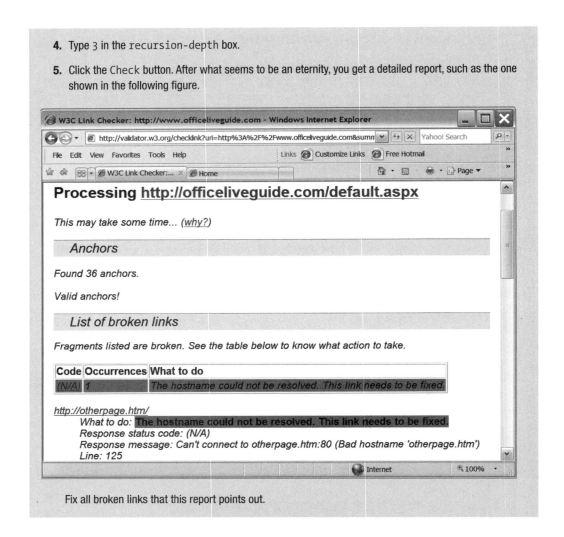

Fix all broken links that this report points out.

Checking References to Downloadable Files

If your pages have hyperlinks that point to files in the Document Gallery, click on each hyperlink and confirm that the right document opens.

Ensuring That Your Hacks Work

If you hacked your way around your web pages using hacks from Chapter 11, you must verify that your hacks work as intended. Pay special attention to PayPal buttons and JavaScript you added to your pages.

Follow these steps to verify that PayPal buttons work:

1. "Buy" an item by clicking each button. Confirm that the item is added to the cart.

2. Confirm that you can place an order from the shopping cart.

3. Ask a friend to place an order to make doubly sure.

Confirm that JavaScript you added to your pages works. Scripts that *should* work on run-of-the-mill web pages may not work with Office Live–generated pages because each module on the pages is displayed in an `IFRAME` element. You may need to tweak the scripts to include a reference to the parent frame or the top frame.

If you know JavaScript, you can easily do this yourself. However, if you obtained the script from a book or from the Web, you may need a helping hand from someone who can program.

Checking Images

After you work through the text on your web pages, check the images to verify that

- No images are missing

- Their img HTML tags have `height`, `width`, and `alt` attributes, whenever possible

- You have optimized them to reduce their size

Checking for Missing Images

Verify that none of the images are missing. If an image is missing when you view a page in the browser, you may have forgotten to upload it to the Image Gallery, or you may have misspelled its name.

If you find a spelling error, don't change the name of the image in the Image Gallery; it may break links to it from other places. Correct the spelling in the `src` attribute of the hyperlink instead.

Checking Image Attributes

Every image on your site should have the `alt`, `height`, and `width` attributes.

FAQ

Why Do My Web Pages Have a Few Images Without the `alt`, `height`, and `width` Attributes?

Your web pages will always have a few images without the `alt`, `height`, and `width` attributes because of the way Office Live assembles web pages. There are two situations in which you can't control how Office Live renders images, and therefore, you can't control the attributes of the `img` tag:

- When Office Live inserts header images for you depending on the theme and style you select

- When you place an image on your page using the `Image` button on Page Editor's Ribbon

You can't do a thing about the images in the header. However, you can alleviate the problem in the second situation if you hand-code the HTML markup that renders the image. To hand-code HTML, you must use the HTML module in Page Editor instead of the Image button on its Ribbon. This substitution, although always possible, is not necessarily straightforward. To render an image at a precise location on your web page with HTML, you must be well versed with HTML's nuances. As a beginning web designer, you may not be able to manipulate HTML to achieve the desired visual effect.

Your top priority as a designer is to ensure that the page appears in a browser the way it's supposed to. The attributes on the img tag are nice to have, given the circumstances. The rule of thumb, therefore, should be to code HTML markup for as many images as you can without getting an aneurism.

The easiest way to check for missing alt attributes is to turn the image display off in your browser. When you load a page in the browser with images turned off, the text specified in the alt attribute of the image will appear in place of the image. If you don't see text where an image should have been, add it to its img tag. Refer to the discussion on the HTML module in Chapter 10, if you don't remember offhand how to add these attributes.

HANDS-ON LAB

Turning the Image Display Off and On in Internet Explorer

Chances are, the image display is turned on in your browser. To turn it off while testing your site, follow these steps:

1. Open Internet Explorer. I'm assuming you're using Internet Explorer 7. If you're still using an older version of Internet Explorer, links in it may have slightly different names.

2. Pull down the Tools menu and click on the Internet Options… menu item. The Internet Options window pops up.

3. Click on the Advanced tab. You should see the details shown in the following figure.

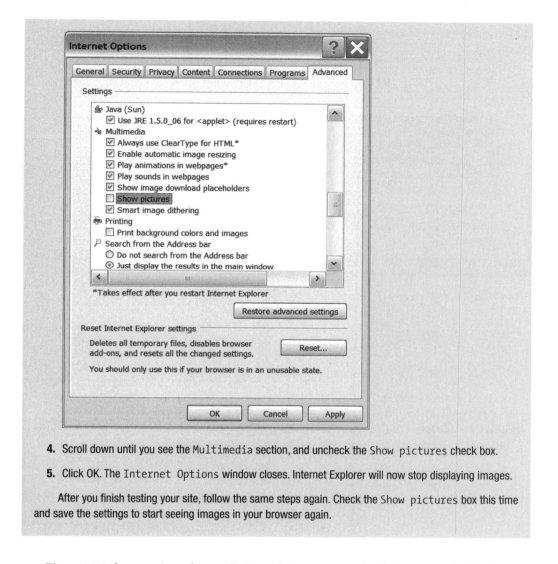

4. Scroll down until you see the Multimedia section, and uncheck the Show pictures check box.

5. Click OK. The Internet Options window closes. Internet Explorer will now stop displaying images.

After you finish testing your site, follow the same steps again. Check the Show pictures box this time and save the settings to start seeing images in your browser again.

Figure 12-1 shows a view of my web site with images turned off. Notice, under the heading First Steps Towards Search Engine Optimization, that the browser displays the text Print this page, which is the text specified in the alt attribute of the missing image. The two images in the header, on the other hand, don't show any text because their img tags don't have any text in the alt attribute.

But the missing text isn't my doing. Office Live inserts those images in the header on my site without specifying the alt attribute. What's worse, it doesn't let me correct the problem.

You can't do much about missing tags that you have no control over. But you can at least check that the img tags of images *you place* on your web pages have alt attributes.

Also, check whether you have specified height and width attributes for the images on your web pages. If you don't specify the dimensions, a visitor's browser will have to determine them on the fly. As a result, your page will take longer to load.

An easy way to check whether any of the three attributes is missing is to use an online tool.

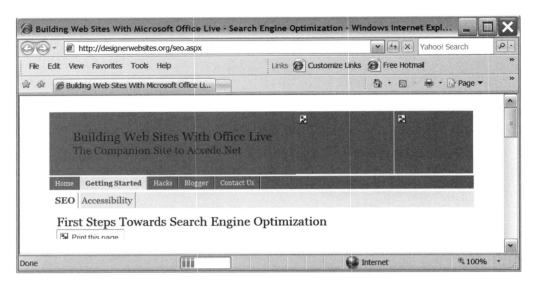

Figure 12-1. *Turn off images in your browser to look for missing* alt *tags on images.*

HANDS-ON LAB

Checking for Missing Image Attributes

Several online tools can help you find missing image attributes quickly. One called *Alt Tag Checker*, which you can find at www.clarity-media.co.uk/alttagchecker.php, checks pages only one at a time. However, for small sites, I find it easier to use than many others.

To check a page for missing image tags with Alt Tag Checker, follow these steps:

1. Point your browser at www.clarity-media.co.uk/alttagchecker.php. The web page shown in the following figure appears.

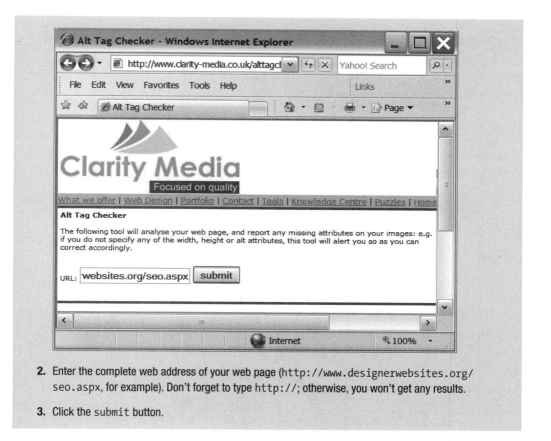

2. Enter the complete web address of your web page (`http://www.designerwebsites.org/seo.aspx`, for example). Don't forget to type `http://`; otherwise, you won't get any results.

3. Click the `submit` button.

After a few seconds, a report, such as the one shown in the following figure, appears in your browser.

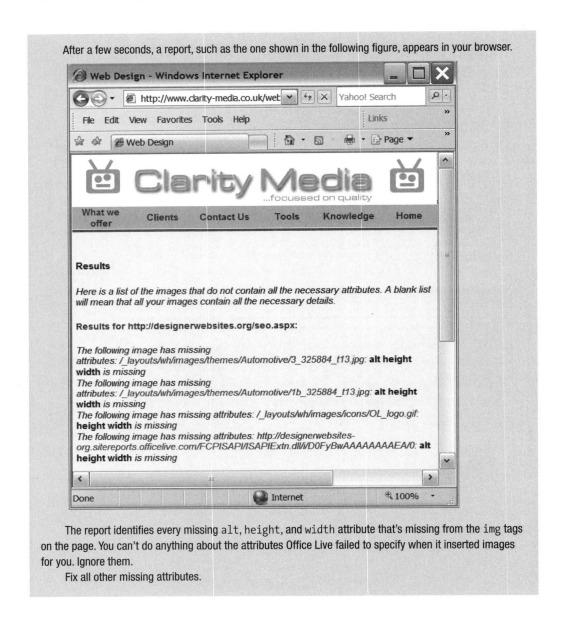

The report identifies every missing `alt`, `height`, and `width` attribute that's missing from the `img` tags on the page. You can't do anything about the attributes Office Live failed to specify when it inserted images for you. Ignore them.

Fix all other missing attributes.

Optimizing Large Images

Do your pages seem to take forever to load in the browser? The culprit may be the high-quality pictures you snapped with your digital camera. You may be able to reduce their size by cropping or compressing them using the techniques discussed in Chapter 8.

Reducing the Number of Images on a Page

Too many pictures on a page can delay the loading of your pages. When you find a page with too many images on it, you may be able to speed it up by distributing the images over several pages.

Let's say you have a product page with four views of the product. If the page takes too long to load, you may be able to break up the content on that page into two, or even four, pages.

Checking the Ownership of Images and Text

While building a page, you may have "borrowed" placeholder images or text from other web sites. Some of those images or text snippets might have remained on the finished site. It doesn't sound like a really big deal, but it amounts to violating copyrights. If you haven't bought an image or generated it yourself, check if someone else holds rights to it. If so, you may either have to pay the copyright holder for using it or find a replacement image that's not copyrighted. Make sure that you have either bought or created *every* image on your site.

And don't forget that text on the Web or in print is copyrighted too, even if you don't see a copyright notice with it. If you've borrowed text, ensure that it is not copyrighted.

Checking Site-Wide Settings

Some settings on your web site apply to the entire site, not to individual pages. Check that they are correct by verifying the following items:

- The text in the site's headers

- The links in the site's footer

- The e-mail address on the Contact Us page

- The "look and feel" settings, such as fonts, background colors, and width

Checking the Site Header

This may sound silly to you, but I've seen many a site with a misspelled name or tag line. Because you see your business name and tag line all the time, it's difficult to catch errors you make while typing them. Go over them letter by letter to verify that they're correct.

Checking the Links in the Site's Footer

If you've placed hyperlinks in your web site's footer, click on each one and verify that it points to the right page.

Checking the Contact Us Page

All you need to specify to make the Contact Us page work is the Contact Us e-mail address. Right-click on the form in the page in Page Editor and chose Properties from the pop-up menu. Verify that you've entered the correct e-mail address.

Then verify that the page actually shoots you an e-mail. Pretend to be a visitor and bring up the contact form in your browser. Enter your own e-mail address in the Your e-mail address box, write yourself a message, and click the Submit button. You should receive the message in your mailbox.

If you don't receive it, verify that you entered the correct e-mail address in the properties of the form. If the address is correct but you still don't receive a message, verify that you're checking the right mailbox. If the e-mail address is from your domain, verify that you created it to begin with!

Repeat these steps, this time using an e-mail address that's *not* from your domain—a Yahoo! or an MSN address, for example.

Nonworking contact forms are a big nuisance—the sender gets the impression that he sent you a message, but you never bothered to answer it. Don't let that happen to you.

Checking the Site's Look and Feel

If the width of all your pages is not the same, your pages will appear to "jump around" as you move from page to page. This typically happens when you place an image that's wider than the page width, add a really long hyperlink, or add some other kind of content that overflows the declared width of the page. Adjust the width of the offending elements to fit on the page.

Check whether any of the pages have a different set of fonts or a different color scheme. Office Live applies most font or color settings in Office Live across the entire site, but look for anomalies in the HTML code that you've added using the HTML module in Page Editor.

Checking the Web Site from Another Computer

Once you've checked all pages and confirmed that all is well, view your site on a friend's computer. When you build the site from a single computer, it always looks good from that computer. Anomalies show up only when someone else views the site from a different computer.

Take fonts, for instance. You may have used some esoteric font that's installed on your computer, but if it's not a core Windows font, other computers may not have it installed. Yes, Office Live only gives you a selection of core fonts in Site Designer, but if you've added any custom HTML, you may have succumbed to the temptation of using a "cool" noncore font.

The site may look different in other ways too. Be on the lookout for anything that looks different from what you are used to while viewing the site on your computer. In the same vein, you should view the site in other browsers and at different screen resolutions.

Letting the World Know

Now that you've gone through all this trouble, it's time to let everyone know about your new web site. You don't have to go overboard, but here are a couple of things you can do:

- Submit your site to search engines.

- Promote your site offline.

Submitting Your Site to Search Engines

If you've dutifully followed the guidelines mentioned in Chapter 6, your site will already be optimized for search engines. All you need to do now is to submit it to the top three directories and search engines by visiting these sites:

- Google: www.google.com/addurl/?continue=/addurl

- Yahoo!: http://search.yahoo.com/info/submit.html

- MSN: http://search.msn.com/docs/submit.aspx

It takes a few days for the search engines to index your site, but there are no hard-and-fast rules. If you submit two sites at the same time, one may get indexed overnight, and the other may mysteriously languish for a couple of months.

Typically, your site will appear fairly quickly on MSN and Yahoo!. However, Google often takes agonizingly long to index it. So don't panic if you can't find your site in Google's search results the next morning.

FAQ

How Will I Know When a Search Engine Has Indexed My Site?

To see whether Google has indexed your site, type site:yourdomain.com in Google's search box and press Enter. If your site is indexed, you'll see one or more of your web pages in the results. If it's not indexed, you'll see a message that says, Your search - site:yourdomain.com - did not match any documents.

To do the same with Yahoo!, go to http://search.yahoo.com/search/options. The page has a plethora of search options. The one you need is Site/Domain. Check the last radio button next to the option that says only search in this domain/site:. Then type yourdomain.com in the text box next to it and press Enter. If your site is indexed, you'll see a link to your home page in the results. If it's not indexed, you'll see a message that says, We were unable to find any results for the given URL in our index: http://yourdomain.com.

Finally, to check the status of your site with MSN, just type the yourdomain.com in the MSN search box and press Enter. If your site is indexed, a link to your home page will appear in the results. If it's not indexed, you'll see a message that says, We did not find any results for yourdomain.com.

Promoting Your Site Offline

Add your new web address and e-mail address to your stationery. If you print your own letterheads and business cards, the additions should be trivial matter. If you buy printed stationery, you'll have to order a new version with these details. I just hope you don't have 10,000 old letterheads left!

Updating Site Documentation

Yes, it's that time again!

If you've done everything I asked you to do in this chapter, you'll have made at least a few changes to your site. Update the documentation you've created for your site in the staging area to reflect these changes.

Sit Back and Relax

You've earned it!

Type `www.yourdomain.com` in your browser and press the Enter key on your keyboard. Yes, that's *your* web site.

Summary

This chapter presented a last-minute to-do list of things you should check before your site goes live. If you've followed this book's advice religiously thus far, you should have breezed through the checklists. Remember these important points from this chapter:

- Double-check your web pages for spelling mistakes and grammatical errors.

- Ensure that the text on you web pages is void of factual errors.

- Check for broken links and missing images.

- Test all the scripts and hacks you introduce on your web pages.

- Verify the site-wide settings such as headers and footers.

- Test the contact form by sending a message to yourself.

- Have a friend go over your site to point out potential problems you may have missed.

- View your web site at different screen resolutions, in different browsers, and from as many different computers as you can.

- Submit your site to the top three search engines: Google, Yahoo!, and MSN.

- Promote your web site online and offline.

Now bring in the band, roll your site out, and pat yourself on the back for a job well done. But if you think you can rest on your laurels, you have another thing coming. Web sites require ongoing monitoring, updates, and maintenance. That'll be the topic of discussion in the final two chapters.

CHAPTER 13

■■■

Lies, Damned Lies, and Site Statistics

Not long ago, the only people even remotely interested in web site statistics were bored server administrators looking for something—anything—to do during long night shifts. They would scan web server logs to look for unusual activity, such as attempts to vandalize web servers and attempts to flood them with a deluge of automated requests in order to bring them to their knees.

Reading *raw logs*, as the server logs are called, is about as interesting an activity as reading a differential calculus textbook. To dissuade server administrators from quitting their jobs and taking up farming, a few enterprising people wrote applications, called *log analyzers*, to read raw logs and present data in a more easily understandable tabular format. Log analyzers made life a lot easier. The server administrators were grateful, and that was the end of the matter.

Until 2005. In mid 2005, Google bought a company that wrote a popular log-analysis application, *Urchin*. Urchin used a somewhat different mechanism to gather visitor data. The technique allowed administrators to track of any web site and store the traffic statistics on a central server. Google built upon Urchin by adding a killer user interface, adding support for Google's popular AdWords advertising program, giving it a new name of Google Analytics, and making it available at no charge to anyone who wanted it.

One of Google Analytics' strengths is its interactive graphical interface, as shown in Figure 13-1. This is exactly the kind of stuff that impresses marketing types. Almost overnight, everyone true to his salt began analyzing web site statistics, and the discipline got a new name that does marketing folks proud—*web analytics*.

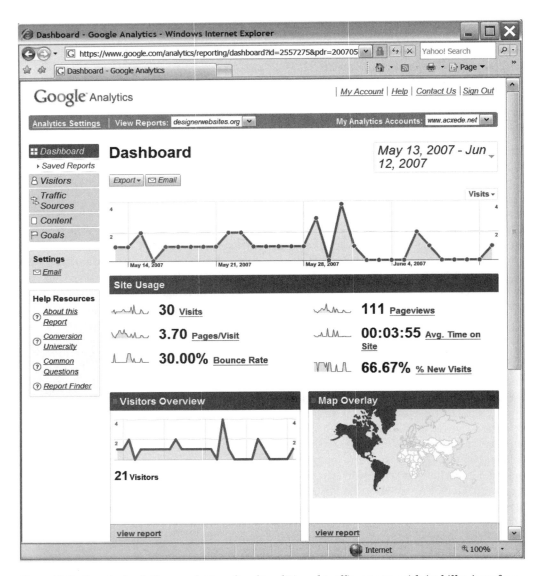

Figure 13-1. *Google Analytics revolutionized traditional traffic reports with its killer interface.*

Naturally, every self-respecting hosting service now includes traffic reports of some sort. Office Live has them too. They're called, simply, *Site Reports*.

In this chapter, you will learn to work with Office Live's Site Reports. After reading it, you'll

- Understand what Site Reports are

- Understand what Site Reports can and can't do for you

- Learn how to customize Site Reports to your liking

- Learn how to use Site Reports rationally to increase traffic to your web site and make it more appealing to visitors

- Systematically take apart marketing types who talk about *pairs of eyeballs, click-through rates, cost per click,* and other such marketese

What Are Site Reports?

Site Reports are graphical and tabular views of the traffic to your web site. They quantify the actions of your site's visitors and present the data to you in an easy-to-understand format. You can then analyze that data to draw conclusions about your visitors' intentions and behavior. The conclusions you draw can give you pointers for tweaking or improving your site and making it more appealing to your visitors.

Viewing Site Reports isn't some mysterious ritual that you perform once every full moon and then forget about. It's a continuous, four-step process:

1. Collect web site traffic data.

2. Sort and group the data to generate metrics.

3. Analyze the metrics to determine whether what your web site offers is what your visitors want.

4. Make changes to your web site to account for variations, and go back to step 1.

FAQ

Are Site Reports Accurate?

Site Reports are based on visitor statistics. Gathering visitor statistics isn't an exact science. The numbers can get distorted, as the following examples illustrate:

- If two people who visit your web site are behind the same proxy server, they may not be recorded as two visitors. An AOL subscriber, on the other hand, may be recorded as many distinct visitors. Consecutive requests from AOL subscribers don't necessarily come from the same IP address, because AOL often routes them through different proxy servers.

- The term *visit* doesn't have an all-encompassing, universally accepted definition. What constitutes a single visit to a person may appear to be two different visits to a web server. For example, you may get a call from a friend soon after you visit a web site. You may chat with your friend for an hour and then continue on the web site from where you left off. From your perspective, you visited the web site only once. The site's web server, however, may have stopped keeping track of you after, say, 30 minutes. When you resume your interrupted visit, the server then records it as a distinct visit.

- Semantic issues may muddle the statistics as well. Take three people huddled over a monitor looking at the same web page. Is that one visit or three? The server records only one.

- Sometimes, web servers record visitors based on a unique cookie that they issue to each visitor. This approach has two advantages: visits by robots are ignored because they don't accept cookies, and multiple visits by the same person can be tracked to get a more accurate count of unique visitors. But this system is not foolproof either. If you visit a site from your work computer as well as from your home computer, the web server may count you as two distinct visitors.

Such distortions tend to even out as the volume of the data increases. It's difficult, or even pointless, to analyze data that consists of all of five visits, but as the volume grows, you can consider Site Reports accurate enough for all practical purposes.

What Site Reports Do for You

Site Reports give you insight into how visitors find your site and what they do once they navigate to it. They provide answers to questions like these:

- How did a visitor arrive at your site?

- Did he click on an advertisement or did a search engine direct him to it?

- Which keyword did he use in the search engine to find your site?

- Once on the site, how many pages did he view before leaving?

- Which was the first page he viewed? Which was the last?

- What's the resolution of his monitor?

- Which browser did he use?

Site Reports log information about each visit to your web site. Information about a single visit isn't very useful, but if you consolidate information from 50,000 visits, you begin to notice trends. That's exactly what Site Reports do for you: they slice and dice visitor information into a format that helps you notice trends. With concrete figures in hand, you can take educated guesses at what visitors like about your web site and what they don't. You can then go on and make changes to your site to fix what you think turns the visitors off.

Let's say you see from Site Reports that 30% of your visitors leave your site from the Contact Us page. You can then argue, reasonably, that something on that page turns visitors off. If you go check the page, you may find that the contact form doesn't work and that your phone number isn't listed.

You then make a hypothesis that people want to contact you, but they can't because of the missing phone number or the malfunctioning contact form. If your hypothesis is correct, you should start receiving more e-mail or more telephone calls once you fix those problems. If you don't, you need start looking into what else may be turning your visitors off.

Of course, not all conclusions will be this simple and straightforward, but you get the idea.

FAQ

How Often Should I View Site Reports?

Statistics of any kind make sense only when sufficient data is available for analysis. If you analyze daily statistics of a popular community site that gets tens of thousands of visits every day, you can draw meaningful conclusions from them right away. The same is not true of a small web site, like my test site, which has a significantly lower viewership. I might have to wait a good six months before I have enough data to analyze meaningfully.

Site Reports aren't an antibiotic; you don't need a dose of it at fixed intervals. It may make sense to work on some metrics on a daily basis. Some others may warrant a yearly review. There are no hard-and-fast rules.

New site owners tend to pore over their Site Reports several times a day and tweak a few settings here and there. Doing so won't double the traffic to your site anytime soon. For small sites, analyzing statistics too frequently serves little purpose. Heck, it may even lead you to the wrong conclusions!

What Site Reports *Won't* Do for You

Ideally, nothing would make me happier than receiving a bulleted list from Site Reports every day that says something like this:

- Add two more pages to your site with such-and-such content.

- Change the background color to white and use Garamond font.

- There's a spelling error on line 64 of the `Products` page.

- Your prices are too high. Reduce them across the board by 10%, and your sales will increase by 23%.

Unfortunately, Site Reports can neither provide such a list nor prescribe the magic elixir that would cause people all over the world to ditch their favorite web sites and flock to yours.

Statistical reports, no matter how sophisticated, can be twisted any which way to support just about any hypothesis. It's very easy to draw nonsensical conclusions from them. Statistically speaking, a man with his head in the oven and his feet in the refrigerator is, on an average, at room temperature. In reality, he is dead.

■Tip If you're serious about using Site Reports, or any other statistical web analytics package for that matter, I suggest reading a wonderful little book called *How to Lie With Statistics* by Darrell Huff (W. W. Norton & Company, [1954] 1993). The book was written decades before the Web was invented, so you won't find anything about web analytics in it. What you'll find instead is an outrageously funny yet very informative treatise on how *not* to interpret statistics—web or not.

Site Reports merely present relevant information to you in a metrics form. How effectively you use this information is up to you.

Viewing Site Reports

You can view Site Reports only if you're signed in to Office Live as the owner or as an administrator. Other users of your web site who try to access Site Reports will see a page such as the one shown in Figure 13-2. If you want to grant them access to Site Reports, you must make them administrators.[1]

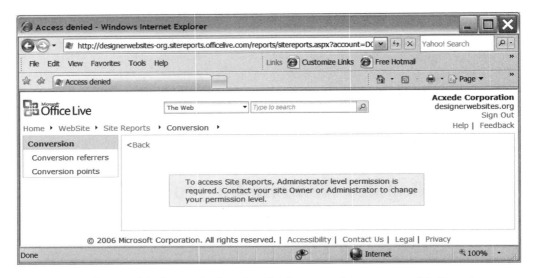

Figure 13-2. *Right out of the box, only the subscriber's account has acccess to Site Reports.*

To view Site Reports, click on the Site Reports link in Page Manager's left navigation pane. Office Live serves up the Web Site statistics summary page, as shown in Figure 13-3.

---

1. See Chapter 5 for instructions.

Figure 13-3. *The* Web Site statistics summary *page provides an overview of important statistics at a glance.*

Web Site Statistics Summary

The Web Site statistics summary page gives you an overview of the traffic to your site and sheds some light on where it comes from.

You can think of this page as the dashboard of Site Reports. Its left navigation pane has links to subsections that focus on a specific category or feature of Site Reports. Most subsections have summary pages of their own that show excerpts of reports from that section.

SPEAKING THE LANGUAGE

Web Analytics Jargon

To interpret the Site Reports, you should be familiar with basic web analytics terminology. If you're new to web analytics, here's the vernacular.

- **Search engines**: Search engines help you find web pages on a topic that interests you. Google, MSN, and Yahoo! are the most popular search engines. (Technically speaking, Yahoo! is a *directory*, not a search engine, but for this discussion, the difference between a search engine and a directory isn't relevant. Therefore, I'll lump directories under a broader category of search engines.)

- **Crawlers**: Crawlers are automated programs that search engines employ to scour web sites across the Internet to index their content and store it in a database. They're sometimes called *spiders*, *robots*, or *bots*. The most well-known robot is Googlebot, which Google uses to index web sites.

- **Keywords**: Keywords are the words, terms, or phrases people search using search engines. If you search for the words *Paris Hilton* (while no one is looking over your shoulder), they are the keywords.

- **Hits**: The term *hits* refers to the number of files requested from a web site. It's the most commonly cited statistic and the most useless as well. Let's say you have a single all-text web page on your web site. If people request it 200 times, your web site will get 200 hits. If you add 5 images to your page, every request for your page will send down 6 files to the requester's browser—one web page and 5 images. Now if people request your page 200 times, your web site will have a healthier hit-count of 1,200.

- **Page views**: The term *page views* refers to the number of web pages downloaded from a web site. It's a more useful statistic than hits because it takes into account only the actual web pages viewed. It ignores images, cascading style sheets, include files, and other such secondary elements that a viewer doesn't request specifically.

- **Visits and visitors**: Visitors are people (or crawlers) that request a file from a web server. Visitors are tracked based on their IP address or by giving them a cookie. If the same person visits a web site at five different times, the site will record five visits. Everything that a visitor does on a web site before leaving constitutes a visit. A visit results in one or more page views. A single visitor may pay many visits to a web site.

- **Unique visitors**: The term *unique visitors* refers to the number of distinct people (or crawlers) that visit a web site. If a person visits a web site five times, the web server will record five visitors and five visits, but only one unique visitor.

- **Referrers**: Referrers are web sites or web pages from where people click links to arrive at your site. If a person searches for a keyword with Google and clicks on a link in the search results to come to your site, www.google.com is the referrer site for that visit and Google's search result page is the referrer page.

- **Entry pages**: An entry page is the first page on your web site that a visitor views during a given visit. Say you have three pages on your web site: Home, Products, and Services. If a visitor clicks on a link in search-engine results that brings him to the Services page, then the Services page is the entry page for that visit.

- **Exit pages**: An exit page is the last page on your web site that a visitor views during a given visit. Continuing with the example in the previous entry, if the visitor views the Products page after entering your site at the Services page and then surfs away to another site, the Products page is the exit page for that visit.

- **Conversion points**: The purpose of a web site is to lure visitors into taking an action, whether that's to buy an item, ask for a quote, give feedback, or take some other identifiable action. When a visitor takes an action that the site owner wants him to take, he reaches a conversion point. You may want visitors to your site to buy a specific item on your site, for example. Every time someone reaches the "Thank you for your order" page after buying that item, he takes the action you want him to take. Therefore, reaching the "Thank you for your order" page is a conversion point. Other examples of conversion points could be subscribing to a newsletter or initiating contact from the contact form on your web site.

Figure 13-3 shows the following six key statistics:

- **Unique visitors over the last four months**: This graph tells you how many people visited your site over a four-month period. In Figure 13-3, you can see that the number of unique visitors to my site increased slightly from January to February and then increased significantly in March. Whatever it is that I did with my site in February apparently worked like a charm, and I should work along the same lines from now on. By the way, the number of unique visitors in April is quite small, because I took the screen shot on April 1, 2007.

- **Page views over the last four months**: This graph shows you how many pages your visitors viewed. In Figure 13-3, you can see that roughly 75 visitors viewed some 400 pages on my site in February. In March, 500-odd visitors viewed 2,000 or so pages. Although the number of visitors increased significantly, the average number of pages that each visitor viewed remained about the same. I can infer from these graphs that I need to do more to engage a visitor's attention and try to keep him on my site longer.

- **Top search engines this month**: This graph tells you which search engines sent traffic your site's way. Figure 13-3 shows that Google is the only search engine that sent traffic to my site. Normally, I would expect to see Yahoo! and MSN on the list as well. Yahoo! is a directory; it is indexed by people, not by robots. Its absence in the list may mean that my site has either been cataloged incorrectly or not cataloged at all in Yahoo!'s directory. Similarly, MSN's absence may be the result of incorrect indexing of my site by its robot. The graph tells me that I must look into this issue.

- **Top keywords this month**: This table tells you which search terms the visitors to your site used to find it. Figure 13-3 indicates that visitors to my test site tried to look for "Office Live hacks." My site is indeed about Office Live hacks, and I should be quite proud of myself that I speak the same language as my visitors. However, my site is also about designing web sites with Office Live. The absence of design-related keywords indicates that I must try harder at convincing the indexing robots that my site is the prime destination for people who want help in designing their web sites with Office Live. Perhaps I should write more content to emphasize the design aspect and tweak a few metatags.

- **Top referring domains this month**: Once people find your web site useful, they tend to mention it on their own web sites and link to it. This table lists the sites that sent visitors to your site. Figure 13-3 shows that in April, four visitors came to my site from Acxede.Net and two from Google. The table tells me that I should find more sites like Acxede.Net and try to have links to my site placed on them. Visiting Acxede.Net may give me a better insight into what kinds of visitors are interested in my site. It may even be worthwhile placing advertisements on Acxede.Net and other similar sites.

- **Top referring pages this month**: This table drills down on the details in the preceding table. Figure 13-3 indicates that the page node/165 at Acxede.Net sent all four visitors who came from that site. I can now go check what that page is all about and gain some insight into what the visitors were thinking when they visited my site.

Notice that each of the graphs or tables has a View all link next to the title. You can click on it to get a more detailed version of that graph or table.

Tracking Code

Click on the Get code link in the left navigation panel of the Web Site statistics summary page. The Tracking Code page, shown in Figure 13-4, loads in your browser. It's not really a report; rather, it displays the JavaScript that drives Site Reports.

Site Reports work by issuing a cookie with every page request to your site. The cookie has a unique tracking code in it. The script to issue and track the cookie is embedded in every page that Site Reports track. When someone visits your web site, the cookie and the JavaScript code work in tandem to gather information such as where the visitor came from and what she did on your web site. The information is sent back to Office Live's web servers. The servers analyze the information and present it in an easy-to-understand graphical format in the form of Site Reports.

The script you see on the Tracking Code page contains the JavaScript code. If you're building your web site with Office Live's Web Designer, this code will be embedded on each of your site's pages automatically. Therefore, you can ignore this page for all practical purposes.

FAQ

How Can I Verify That the Tracking Code Is Embedded in My Pages?

You can easily confirm that your pages indeed have this code.

Point your browser to any page on your web site. Right-click on any free area of the page and select View Source. A new Notepad window containing the HTML markup for the page pops up. Scroll to the bottom of the Notepad window. You should see the code beginning with this comment line:

```
<!-- BEGIN TRACKING CODE -->
```

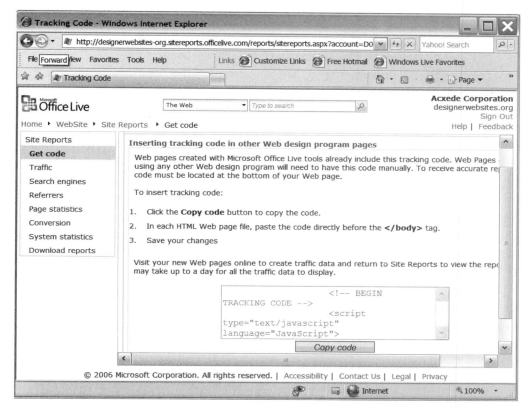

Figure 13-4. *The* Tracking Code *page shows the code that drives Site Reports.*

Why, then, do you need this page at all? For two reasons:

- The code is added automatically only to pages that you create in Page Manager. You may want to add a custom page in the documents folder and track it just like all the other pages. You can then copy the code from this page and paste it at the bottom of your custom page.

- If you subscribe to Office Live Essentials or Office Live Premium, you may decide at some point to stop using Office Live's Site Designer and use another design tool instead. To continue using Site Reports under this scenario, you'll need to copy this code and paste it at the bottom of each of your custom-designed pages.

Google Analytics uses a similar mechanism to gather visitor statistics.

FAQ

Should I Be Using Google Analytics Instead of Site Reports?

Google Analytics is perhaps the best web analytics tool. Feature-wise, it leaves Site Reports behind in the dust. It produces slick interactive reports that illuminate every imaginable statistic about traffic to your web site. Besides, it has an unbeatable price tag: *free*.

The greatest strength of Google Analytics is its integration with AdWords, Google's advertisement-placement service. If you advertise with AdWords, you can easily track the effectiveness of each ad campaign with Google Analytics. For anyone who spends advertising dollars on AdWords, Google Analytics is an indispensable tool. AdWords is the most popular advertisement-placement service, so naturally Google Analytics is the most popular web analytics tool.

Google Analytics has a lot to offer even if you don't use AdWords. The traffic and user-statistics reports it produces are useful in tailoring your site's content to the visitor's requirements.

If you monitor web statistics faithfully, it makes sense to filter out visits from you and your employees. This is one area where Google Analytics is vastly superior to Site Reports. Site Reports have no settings to filter out internal users. If you expect your web site to have a significant amount of internally generated traffic, you may want to look into Google Analytics.

However, keep in mind that Site Reports are quite comprehensive for the needs of a small web site. Like Google Analytics, Site Reports are free too. And if you use adManager, Microsoft's AdWords-like service, you're better off with Site Reports, which have built-in support for tracking adManager campaigns.

My advice is to use Site Reports if you're just starting out with web analytics; Google Analytics can be somewhat overwhelming in the beginning. Also, it's extremely difficult to integrate Google Analytics with your Office Live web site. However, if you're a seasoned Google Analytics pro and don't mind the hassles of integrating it with your web site, there's no reason not to use it.

Traffic Summary

Unlike the Tracking Code section, the Traffic section of Site Reports has real reports. The Traffic summary page in Figure 13-5 shows excerpts of some of those reports. Traffic data highlights two important metrics—the number of unique visitors and the number of page views. Various traffic reports in this section are merely different views of the same underlying data. You can see some of the views by clicking on the links in the left panel, and others by clicking on one of the several View all links next to the headers of the reports on this page.

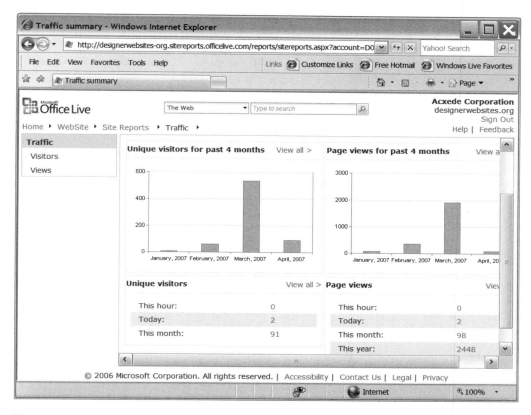

Figure 13-5. *The* Traffic summary *page*

For instance, clicking on the View all link above the Unique visitors graph lets you view the Unique visitors by month report, as shown in Figure 13-6.

The graph in this report shows monthly visitors over a one-year period instead of the four-month period used in the summary graphs. Below it, in tabular form, is the data underlying the graph. At the top of the page is a drop-down for you to select the reporting period. The final option in the drop-down is Custom. If you select that option, a control bar appears alongside the drop-down where you can choose a reporting interval of your choice to generate a graph of unique visitors over that period. It's just another way of tailoring the data to your specific needs.

What's the point in showing so many different representations of the same data? It appears to serve no purpose other than fluffing up the number of available reports. But as it turns out, the multiple representations do have a purpose.

No two people interpret statistical data exactly the same way. Each person uses it in his own unique way of thinking. Site Reports attempt to provide custom views tailored to each person's specific needs through these apparently repetitive links.

In the beginning, you may find these reports confusing. With time, though, you'll learn to focus on a metric and not on a report. With that in mind, I'll avoid a running commentary of every page in this and every other section of Site Reports; it would serve little purpose. I'll focus instead on the metrics they represent and on how to interpret them.

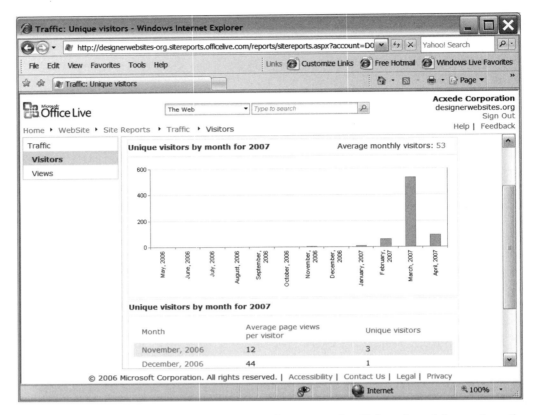

Figure 13-6. *The* Traffic: Unique visitors *page has a more detailed version of the graph on the* Traffic summary *page.*

Interpreting Traffic Statistics

If you think about it, the entire paradigm of web analytics is based on two simple facts:

- People visit web pages.

- You can count how many people visit a web page.

If you're running a well-designed web site, you should notice the following trends over time:

- The number of visitors to the site increasing

- The number of page views increasing

- The number of page views per user increasing

The traffic statistics reports in this section show you, at a glance, whether that's true. If you don't see one or more of these trends, corrective measures are in order.

But what exactly should you correct? That's not an easy question to answer. You'll have to dig deeper into the statistics. The reports in this section merely give you a high-level view. The rest of the Site Reports help you drill down on the statistics and arrive at the answer to the question.

Search Engine Summary

Click on the Search engines link on the Web Site statistics summary page. You'll come to the Top search engines page shown in Figure 13-7.

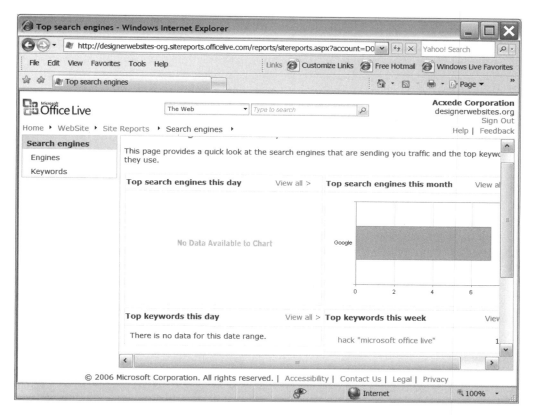

Figure 13-7. *The* Top search engines *page provides insight on how people find your site on the Web.*

This section of Site Reports deals with two metrics: search engines and keywords. The summary page tells you at a glance which search engines send traffic to your site and which keywords your visitors searched for before arriving at your site. Like the Traffic summary page, each graph or table on this page has a View all option too, which you can click to view a more detailed version of that graph or table.

Interpreting Search Engine Statistics

Search engine statistics tell you which search engines are sending traffic to your web site. For example, Figure 13-7 shows that only Google sends traffic to my web site. While it could mean that visitors to my site prefer Google over other search engines, a more likely explanation is that my site hasn't been indexed by Yahoo! or MSN. Since I rolled out my site just a few days ago, MSN and Yahoo! may not have gotten around to indexing it yet. The report tells me that I should look out for signs of recognition by Yahoo! and MSN over the next few days. If they fail to show up in the report, I may have to resubmit my sites to those search engines.

Keyword reports tell you which terms your visitors used to find your web pages with search engines. If the reports indicate that users seldom find some of the most important pages on your site, you may want to double-check the text on those pages. For instance, you may be using terms in your text that are too technical. If you sell insecticides, your products will no doubt exterminate Periplaneta Americana, but people who are searching for something in Google to "kill cockroaches" will never find your page, if that's what your page calls cockroaches. Keyword reports can help you identify pages that need your attention.

Referrers Summary

Click on the Referrers link on the Web Site statistics summary page, and you'll come to the Referrers summary page shown in Figure 13-8.

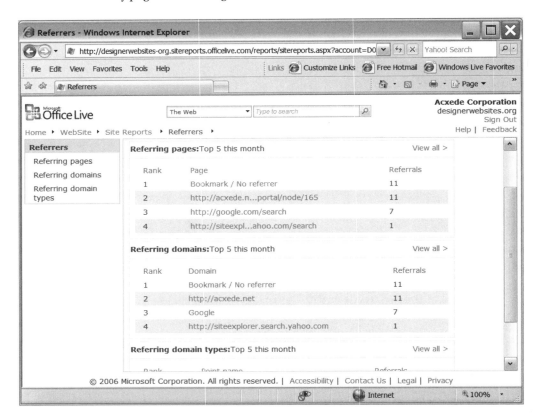

Figure 13-8. *The* Referrers *summary page lists web sites that direct traffic to your site.*

The `Referrers` section displays details on three metrics: referring pages, referring domains, and referring domain types. Reports here give you an insight into how visitors arrived at your site. They list the web sites your visitors arrived from and the names of specific pages they clicked on to arrive at your site.

Interpreting Referrer Statistics

Referrer statistics shed light on how people find your site. You can see who links to your site and whether the search engines are sending traffic your way.

Referrers are ranked based on the number of hits they produced. You'll find pages from your own site among the top referrers. This is expected, because the text on your pages has (or, at least, *should* have) links to other pages on your site. It simply means that visitors clicked on many pages once they came to your site.

Notice that the `Bookmark / No referrer` entry is the top-ranked entry under both `Referring pages` and `Referring domains` in Figure 13-8. It shows the number of hits that visitors initiated by typing your site's URL in their browsers or navigating from bookmarks in their browsers.

Early in your web site's life, you'll often find this to be the top-ranking entry. The reason is simple: you'll likely be the person visiting your site the most! Besides, once you give your site's address to people, many will visit for the first time by entering your site's web address in their browsers.

Referrer statistics are also useful in determining if someone is stealing your bandwidth and your intellectual property by linking to the images on your pages, or even encasing entire pages into frames on their sites. If you see a suspiciously high number of visits from a seemingly unrelated site, you can click on its link to see if your images or pages appear there.

If you've placed paid links on other web sites, referrer statistics will tell you which of them have sent more people your way and which are simply a waste of money.

Page Statistics Summary

When you click on the `Page statistics` link on the `Web Site statistics summary` page, you come to the `Page statistics summary` page shown in Figure 13-9.

This section is home to three key metrics: the most requested pages, the top entry pages, and the top exit pages.

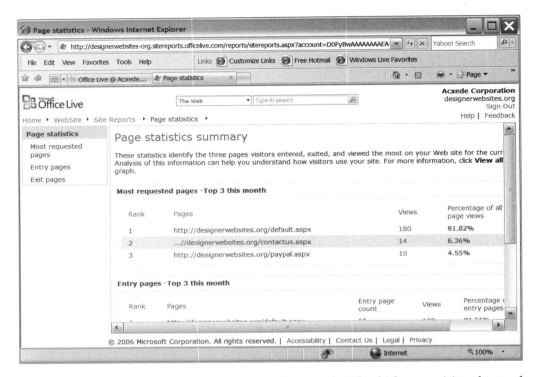

Figure 13-9. *The* Page statistics summary *page helps you identify which pages visitors love and which pages they hate.*

Interpreting Page Statistics

Page statistics tell you what visitors like about your web site and what turns them off. The most requested pages are obviously the most popular ones. The way their content is structured, or the way they are optimized for search engines, may be a clue to their popularity. You may want to emulate the same strategy on other pages.

Top entry pages tell you how people enter your site. You normally would expect your home page to be the top entry page, but don't be surprised if it isn't. For instance, people may be coming to your site because they search for a product that you sell whose page readily appears at the top of search-engine results. Or many people may have liked the content of a particular page and may have linked to it from their web sites or blogs. Looking at top entry pages gives you a clue as to what attracts visitors. You can then try and make the other pages on your site like those pages.

Top exit pages tell you the other side of the story. They tell you which pages drive away visitors. You can check those pages to see if they contain factual errors, offensive language, obnoxious pictures, or some other trigger that causes visitors to go find another site.

You don't have to be Sherlock Holmes to unearth the reasons why your site's visitors bolt from a page. Something as simple as the size of the page may be the culprit. For example, if you stuff a page with several large images, it will take forever to display. Few people have the patience to put up with a delay, and this may be the reason they're going elsewhere.

The clues you gather by analyzing page statistics can help you decide the course of action to take in order to keep visitors on your site longer.

Conversion Manager

Clicking on the Conversion link on the Web Site statistics summary page brings you to the Conversion manager page shown in Figure 13-10. In this section, you can define your own metrics, called conversion points, and track them.

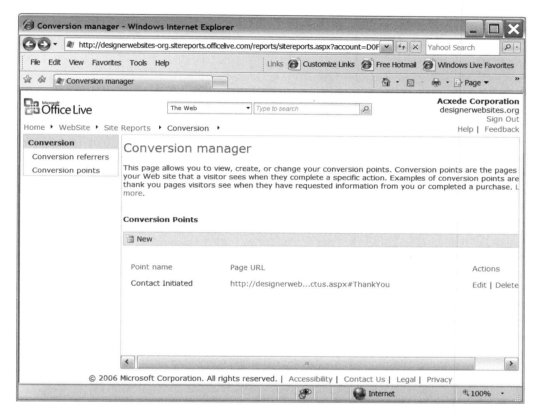

Figure 13-10. *You can define custom metrics on the* Conversion manager *page.*

Adding Conversion Points

A conversion point indicates that a visitor has taken an action you want him to take. Let's say you want visitors to get in touch with you using the Contact Us page on your site, so you embed a link to the Contact Us page in the text of several of your pages. After a user fills out the form and clicks Send, he sees a Thank you page.

Every time someone reaches the Thank you page, he has taken the action you want him to take. Therefore, reaching the Thank you page is a conversion point. Other examples of conversion points could be the sale of a particular product or the subscription to a newsletter.

Take these steps to define a conversion point:

1. Click the New icon on the blue toolbar in the content area of the Conversion manager page. You'll see the page shown in Figure 13-11.

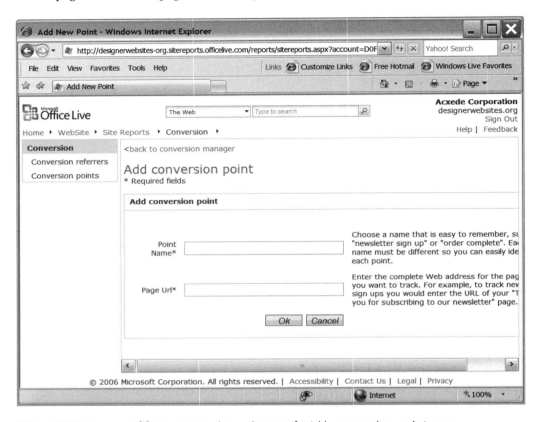

Figure 13-11. *You can add new conversion points on the* Add conversion point *page.*

2. Enter a name for your conversion point in the first text box.

3. Enter the URL of the page that indicates a conversion point in the second text box. In our little example, it's the URL of the Thank you page.

4. Click OK.

After you define conversion points, you can edit or delete them using the Edit and Delete links to the right of the conversion point on the Conversion manager page. Tracking of conversion points begins right after you define them.

Interpreting Conversion Statistics

You can see how your conversion points perform by clicking on the Conversion referrers link in the left navigation pane of the Conversion manager page.

I defined the Thank you page conversion point on my test site. Figure 13-12 shows its results.

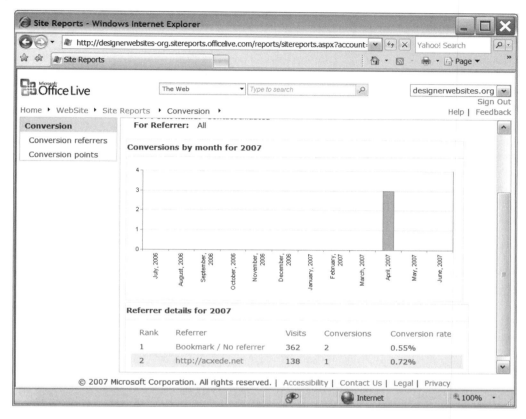

Figure 13-12. *The* Conversion referrers *page show how visitors took an action you wanted them to take.*

As you can see, 362 people visited the Contact Us page, but only 2 initiated contact. That may mean that something on that page isn't right. Either it doesn't coax people enough into filling out the form, or it doesn't work every time as expected. I'll have to look into it.

The second entry shows that the link to the Contact Us page on another site, Acxede.Net, generated 138 page views but only 1 conversion. It supports the conclusions I drew from the first entry and presents a stronger case for me to look into the workings of the Contact Us page.

System Statistics

The next section of Site Reports is System statistics. Click on the System statistics link on the Web Site statistics summary page. You'll see the Operating Systems page shown in Figure 13-13.

This section doesn't have a summary page; you see one of the reports instead. The reports elaborate on three metrics: operating systems, browsers, and screen resolutions. These metrics are a bit different from those you've seen so far. They take into account all visits since you signed up for Office Live rather than keeping track of daily, weekly, or monthly figures.

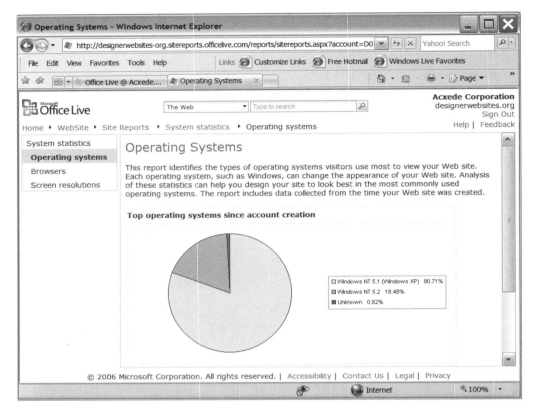

Figure 13-13. *The* System statistics *section of Site Reports doesn't have a summary page; you see the* Operating Systems *report instead.*

Interpreting System Statistics

Your site may look different to visitors with different hardware/software configurations. Operating systems, browsers, and screen resolutions give you a glimpse of the kind of computers and software your visitors use. You can use these metrics to tweak design parameters of your site.

Operating systems can affect design parameters such as fonts. For example, some fonts, such as Verdana, Tahoma, and Trebuchet MS, are supported on Windows and Mac OS X operating systems but not on Mac Classic and Unix. Helvetica, on the other hand, is a core font on all of Apple's operating systems and Unix-based operating systems. The Operating Systems report shows you which operating systems your visitors use and in what proportion. If 30% of your users have Linux, you may want to reconsider the choice of Verdana as your default font.

Your visitors' choices of browsers can also affect the features your site can provide. Office Live typically generates browser-agnostic pages. But remember that it forces you to use Internet Explorer while designing your pages. If you add JavaScript to a page or use Internet Explorer–specific HTML markup, you won't know whether it will work with, say, Mozilla Firefox. If statistics indicate that 98% of your visitors use Internet Explorer, you may not want to bother with checking every page in Firefox or Opera. But if only 80% of your visitors use Internet Explorer, you may be forced to.

Screen resolution of your visitors' desktops can help you determine the ideal width settings for your site. Let's say you've designed your site for 1024 × 768 resolution. If the screen-resolution report tells you that 50% of your visitors prefer 800 × 600 resolution, you might have some serious redesigning on your hands.

Download Reports

The final section of Site Reports is `Download reports`. Click on the `Download reports` link in the left navigation pane of the `Web Site statistics` summary page. You'll arrive at the `Download reports` page shown in Figure 13-14.

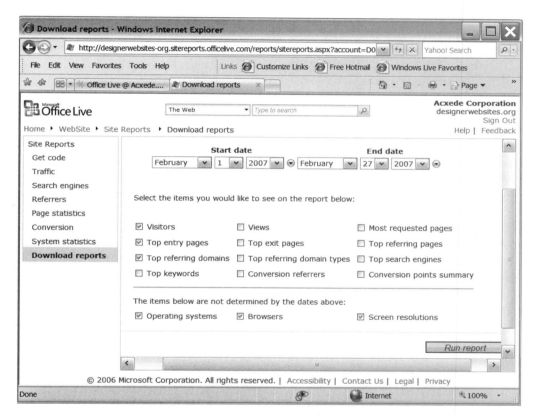

Figure 13-14. *You can download raw statistics from the* Download reports *page.*

Downloading raw data is yet another way of viewing your site statistics in a different light. You can download raw data from any number of reports from Site Reports in a single downloadable file in comma-separated values (CSV) format. To do so, take these steps:

1. Select a date range.

2. Select the items you want in your download.

3. Click the Run report button at the bottom.

4. Office Live generates a CSV file with all the data you requested. You can save the file to your hard disk. CSV files have a .csv extension, which is associated with Microsoft Excel if you have Excel installed on your computer. When you open the file, it looks like the Excel spreadsheet shown in Figure 13-15.

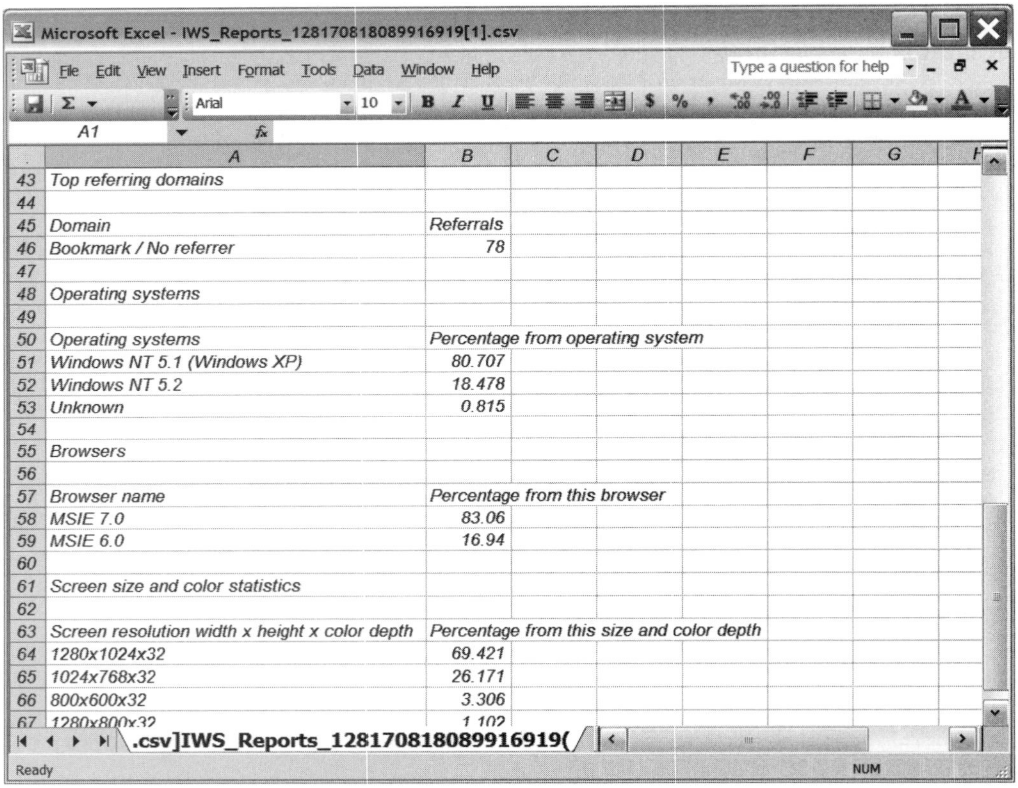

Figure 13-15. *Downloaded raw statistics in Microsoft Excel*

Why on earth would you export raw statistics data? Well, if you're a geek, you could write a custom application to slice and dice the exported data and generate reports that Site Reports can't produce. Owners of large web sites do exactly that. But if you're building a small identity web site with Office Live, a custom reporting application is probably overkill. In all likelihood, Site Reports should suffice for all your analytics needs.

Summary

In this chapter, I gave you a tour of Office Live's Site Reports and explained how to interpret them effectively to improve your web site.

Web analytics may confuse and overwhelm you if you've never used them before. You may feel compelled to take some action every day. You don't have to. Start with simply viewing your Site Reports periodically. With time, you'll be able to draw meaningful conclusions and make suitable changes to your web site. Here are the main points to remember from this chapter:

- Statistics by themselves are simply numbers. What you get out of them depends on how logically and rationally you analyze them.

- Drawing conclusions from a single number is rather difficult, but when you look at several different statistics over a period of time and they all lead you to the same conclusion, you get an insight into what you're getting right and where you're going wrong.

- Site Reports aren't, by any stretch of the imagination, the best possible site statistics reports known to mankind. But they suffice for the needs of most small web sites—the kind that Office Live subscribers are likely to build.

- Google Analytics is a much more comprehensive and sophisticated analysis package as compared to Site Reports. But most Office Live–generated web sites don't need that level of sophistication. Unless you use Google's AdWords, Site Reports should serve you well.

Like maintaining an attractive garden, maintaining an impressive web site is an ongoing process. Web analytics is an important aspect of it, but there are other aspects that warrant your attention as well. In the next chapter, I'll introduce you to the chores of tending to your web site on a regular basis.

■■■

CHAPTER 14

Maintaining Your Web Site

Your web site is finally live! Sit back, relax, and admire it—only for about five minutes, though. Then you've got to start thinking about ways of improving it and tending to everyday maintenance chores.

In this chapter, I'll give you a few pointers on how to

- Update the content on your web site periodically

- Monitor your web site for uptime and response (or downtime and lack of response, if you're a pessimist)

- Restore your site from backup if disaster strikes

- Submit a technical support request if you encounter a problem

Updating Content

Building a web site is only half the battle. If the content on it never changes, visitors will have little reason to come back. One way to keep them interested is to update the appearance and content on your site periodically.

The first question people ask upon learning this is, "How often is periodically?" Like so many other aspects of maintaining a web site, the question doesn't have a one-size-fits-all answer. When you should update your site depends on a couple of things:

- **The type of site you have**: If you publish news on your site, it's reasonable to expect daily or weekly updates. If you have a calling-card web site, on the other hand, you may not need to update it all that often—once a month, or even once a quarter, may be just what the doctor ordered.

- **How critical an update is**: Once in a while, you may come across a situation where you must put aside whatever you're doing and fix an issue right away. If the price of a product on your site is wrong, for example, or your contact e-mail address is misspelled, you'll need to fix these problems at the first opportunity. Nonessential updates, on the other hand, can wait until you have some free time.

The sequel to the "How often" question is, "What exactly do you mean by update?" This one doesn't have a one-size-fits-all answer either. Doing an update doesn't necessarily mean adding new pages. It simply means keeping the site current. Therefore, what you should update depends again on what kind of a site you have.

If you run a news portal, for example, you'll have several new pages to add to your site every time you update it. But if all you do is sell three models of concrete mixers, the only updates your site may need are periodic changes to prices, documentation, and appearance.

Here's another example: If you're a careful worker, you'll have very few design mistakes on your site that need to be fixed. However, if you're a design-as-you-go type of person, you may find the need to make changes to the design every day.

Updating your site, therefore, may mean one or more of the following things:

- Fixing design flaws and anomalies

- Updating outdated information

- Adding new content as and when it becomes available

- Correcting errors reported by visitors

- Improving content based on visitor feedback

- Making your site friendlier, easier to use, and more appealing to your target audience based on analysis of Site Reports (see Chapter 13)

- Giving your site a face-lift, such as changing the design and colors according to the season or an upcoming holiday

TIPS FROM THE TRENCHES

Don't Forget to Document Your Updates

Don't forget to update your site documentation whenever you make *any* change to your web site. Doing so may be a royal pain (in several parts of your anatomy), but in some situations, described later in this chapter, you may have to resort to your documentation to restore your site.

Managing Updates

A good way to manage site updates is to classify them as critical or scheduled. You need to perform critical updates as soon as you get a chance, but you can set a timetable for scheduled updates—every Sunday or the first of every month, for example. If you decide on a monthly update schedule, you should accumulate updates over a month and update the site on the first of the next month.

An update timetable has two advantages over ad-hoc updates:

- Visitors get used to your timetable and visit the site when they expect the site to be updated.

- You don't have to fight fires by signing in to Office Live every time you find trivial problems.

FAQ

When Is a Good Time to Update My Site?

Update your site when you expect the least traffic. An important point to remember about the timing of your updates is that Office Live doesn't have a preview mode. The moment you save a page in the Page Editor, the page is visible to the world. If you make a mistake, that too is visible to the world.

Therefore, a good time to update your site is when the fewest people are likely to visit it. You can find out when the fewest people visit your site by checking your Site Reports. You may find, for example, that Friday nights are low-turnover nights for your site. You would do well, in that case, to update your site on Friday nights.

What If I Can't Find Time for Updates?

Okay, you may agree in principle that you need to update your site regularly, but finding time to do so is often difficult. After all, you have a business to run. The solution is to do as much as you can to give an impression that you've updated the site recently. Follow these tips:

- **Update the last-updated date**: But don't do it too often without actually updating the site. If you claim to have updated the site earlier in the day and the information is two years old, people can see through the shenanigan.

- **Change color schemes**: Google changes its logo to match seasons or events; you can change color schemes. Choosing a different color scheme is a matter of just a few clicks with Office Live. A green scheme for St. Patrick's Day and a pink one for Valentine's Day would lead your visitors to believe that the site gets updated frequently.

- **Change text on the home page**: If the home page stays the same week after week, your site will appear unchanged to visitors even if you change other pages daily.

- **Make an entry on the** `What's New` **page, if you have one**: Update whatever you can, whenever you can.

The key is to keep your visitors under the impression that you update your site frequently.

Monitoring Your Web Site for Uptime and Response

Has this ever happened to you? All of a sudden, your car develops an audible squeak. Everyone can hear it. Your friends, most of whom have never opened the hood of a car, give you advice that ranges from changing the oil to changing the engine gasket. So you take the car to the mechanic.

When the mechanic steps within 50 feet of the car, the squeak stops and the car purrs along nicely. You swear by your firstborn that the car squeaks. The mechanic nods sympathetically and walks away. As soon as he steps out of earshot, your car starts squeaking again.

Web sites are like that too. No, they don't actually squeak, but they go down from time to time when you aren't looking. They can go down because of hardware, software, or connectivity problems. Most web sites experience outages—to use the technical term—some time or another. If an outage is a one-off occurrence, it's understandable. But if your site goes down repeatedly, the folks over at Office Live will have to do something about it.

In my experience, Office Live is extremely reliable. I've run automated checks on three Office Live web sites for more than a year at 15-minute intervals. Not once have any of them ever been down. That's pretty impressive.

But that's not to say that a web site built with Office Live will never go down. If and when yours does, you can have Office Live support correct the situation quickly if you have a record of when your site was down and for how long.

To build such a record, you need to monitor your site periodically to check whether it's up and running. This task begs automation. Several automated services available on the market monitor your web site for downtime. The one I recommend is Site24x7 (`www.site24x7.com`). It checks the status of your web site every 60 minutes and sends you a nice report. Best of all, the service is free for up to two web sites.

Site24x7 is an industrial-strength site monitoring service. To start using it, register online at `www.site24x7.com`, create an account, and set up a *monitor*. A monitor is a set of parameters to check on your web site. The only mandatory parameter you need to choose is the *polling frequency*—the interval at which the service should check the status of your site. The polling frequency is set at 60 minutes for free accounts. You can reduce the frequency to as low as every 5 minutes for a small fee. But for most sites designed with Office Live, the free service should suffice.

If you're a savvy user, you can increase the granularity of the checks by monitoring form-submission methods, URL changes, and maximum response time, among others.[1] Once you set up your monitor, the service will start polling your site.

Site 24x7 considers your site to be unavailable if

- The site doesn't respond at all

- The home page doesn't come up in 30 seconds

- The site throws an error

The service can send you a detailed monitoring report in two ways: through alerts when the site goes down (and when it comes back up again), or through daily, weekly, or monthly reports. You can choose to get the alerts by e-mail or by Short Message Service (SMS). Figure 14-1 shows a report that displays the uptime of my site. As you can see, my web site hasn't been down in the 30-day reporting period.

You'll start getting such alerts regularly. The alerts consist of graphs and tables that shed light on the time at which your site was unavailable, the time at which it became available again, and the percentage of time your site was available. The service catalogs the response time for each request and also calculates the average response time. You can log in to your account at any time and view historical reports online.

---

1. If you don't have a clue as to what these terms mean, relax. That's a sign you don't need to monitor them.

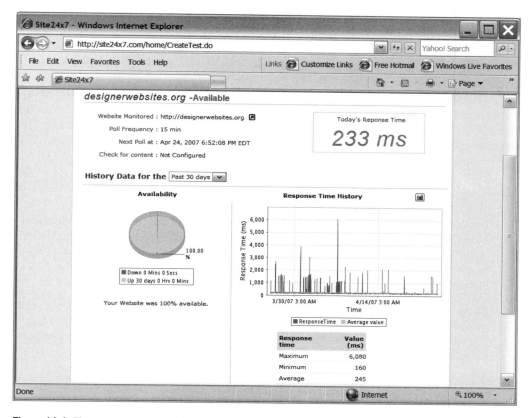

Figure 14-1. *You can get a monthly site-downtime report like this from Site24x7.*

The service can send you a daily report if you wish, but that becomes a nuisance after the novelty wears off. I like the 30-day report instead, because it's a long enough interval to conclude whether the outages are occasional or chronic. If you see more than a couple of outages, you should contact Office Live tech support with a copy of your report and ask them to look into it.

Restoring Your Web Site from a Disaster

Getting a site up and running again from a software-related downtime usually requires only a reboot of the server. Once in a while, though, more serious hardware-related problems can bring your site to its knees.

Hardware-related downtimes are usually more serious than their software-related counterparts. Thankfully, most data centers, including Office Live's, are well equipped to deal with them. As long as the actual files on the disk that make up your web site aren't harmed, your site will be back up after the hardware problem is fixed.

However, if the hard disk on the server that houses your web site or the database that stores critical information fails, you'll have a problem on your hands. Unless you have a backup copy of your web site stored somewhere, you can kiss your web site goodbye.

A backup copy of your site is very useful in one other situation. If you make wholesale changes to your web site and then decide to discard them, your only option is to restore your site from the most recent backup.

Office Live automatically makes a backup copy of your web site every 24 hours. The entire backup and restore process is transparent to you—you don't have to worry about it at all.

But there's a catch.

You don't get to decide when to make a backup; Office Live does. In fact, you can't back up your web site yourself at all. You can only restore it from the backup that Office Live makes for you automatically.

This solution for backing up your web site is inelegant for several reasons:

- **Even if you mess up just one page, you must restore the entire site**: The restore has absolutely no granularity. It's all or nothing.

- **You have a maximum of 24 hours to decide whether you want to scrap your changes**: If you don't decide within 24 hours, your changes will automatically get backed up the next day. Office Live maintains only one copy of the backup, so if you decide after 24 hours that you don't like your changes, the copy of your site before you made the changes will be gone and you'll be stuck with the site you don't want.

- **There's no set time for Office Live's backup**: This means that 24 hours in practice could actually be 18 or 36. You'll have to wait for Office Live to finish the day's backup before you can start making changes to your site. Otherwise, your changes will get backed up in less than 24 hours.

Not allowing users to make their own backups is one of Office Live's most serious limitations. Hopefully, Microsoft will address it sooner rather than later.

FAQ

Why Can't I Make My Own Backups?

The web pages in Office Live aren't static web pages. They aren't even files, which you can make copies of. When you design your pages in the Site Designer using Office Live's modules, your "design" is really stored in a database. When someone requests your page over the Web, Office Live constructs it on the fly by extracting the data stored in the database.

So a backup, in Office Live terms, is not a copy of HTML files on the disk, but rather a copy of the data in the database. To restore your site, Office Live has to overwrite the current data in its database with the data in the backup copy.

It isn't technologically impossible to allow you to make your own backups. However, it's not as straightforward as simply copying files. Hopefully, as Office Live matures, you will be able to do so.

In the meantime, prayers and Office Live's tech support are your only options. Now you can appreciate why back in Chapter 11, I was harping about keeping a copy of all your content in a Microsoft Word document.

Restoring Your Site from Office Live's Backup

To restore your site from the last backup, follow these steps:

1. Go to Page Manager.

2. You'll see the Site actions tile in the top right-hand corner of the page. Click on it to reveal the pull-down menu shown in Figure 14-2.

Figure 14-2. *The* Restore Site *link is hidden under the* Site actions *tile.*

3. Click Restore Site. You'll see the page shown in Figure 14-3, which displays the date and time of your last backup.

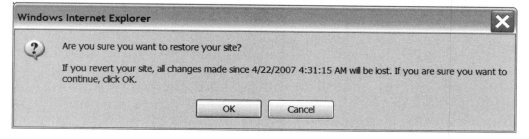

Figure 14-3. *Office Live displays the date and time of the last backup and asks you to confirm that you want to restore from this backup.*

4. Remember that once you click OK, all the changes you made since the time of the backup are toast. Click Cancel if you aren't sure. Click OK if you want to restore. You will see the page shown in Figure 14-4.

5. Although the page informs you that the restore will take several hours, it usually finishes in 30 or so suspense-packed minutes. While a restore is in progress, you can't start another restore, which is a reasonable expectation.

Tip Sometimes the page shown in Figure 14-4 will keep on showing even after your site has been restored. If you still see the page after an hour or so, try refreshing it.

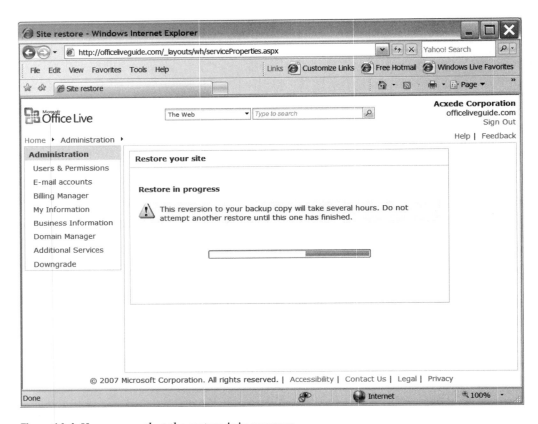

Figure 14-4. *You can see that the restore is in progress.*

When Things Go Wrong

Once in a while, the restore process presents proof for Murphy's Law. Instead of the page shown in Figure 14-4, you'll see the one shown in Figure 14-5.

Figure 14-5. *The restore process can report an error once in a while, but it doesn't necessarily mean anything is wrong. Try again, as the message suggests.*

You don't have to panic at the "File Not Found" error. This is just the kind of error you can expect because of the very nature of the Web. Simply click your browser's back button and try to start the restore again.

If you're lucky, you'll be on your way to the confirmation page shown in Figure 14-4. But if Mr. Murphy is having a particularly good day, you may get the "File Not Found" error again, or worse yet, you'll see a page like the one in Figure 14-6.

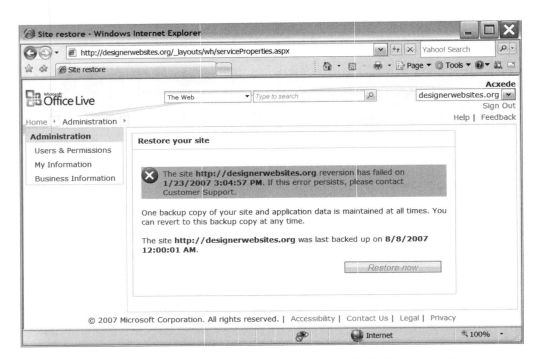

Figure 14-6. *Now something is really wrong with the restore. Get help from Office Live's tech support.*

Okay. *Panic!* Contact Office Live's technical support folks on the double. In the meantime, cross your fingers, promise the Almighty that you'll be a good boy (or girl) for the rest of your life if your site is restored to an acceptable state, and hope for the best.

All joking aside, if god forbid you're ever faced with this situation, your *only* way out is to re-create your site from a well-documented copy of your web site—the copy I've insisted that you maintain in your staging area all along.

My intent here is not to scare the living daylights out of you, but instead to make you aware that such disasters can and do happen. Very rarely, of course, but they do happen. And you should be prepared if you happen to be the victim of this unlikely event.

Getting Technical Support

I've mentioned several times that links to Office Live's technical support aren't easy to find. Let me walk you through the process of submitting a support ticket:

1. Click the Contact Us link at the bottom of any page in Member Center. Office Live may ask you to enter your Windows Live ID and password again. Do so if you're asked to. You should see the Contact Us page shown in Figure 14-7.

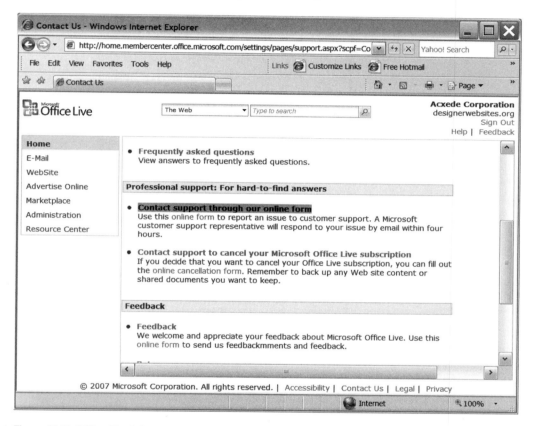

Figure 14-7. *Office Live's* Contact Us *page*

2. Click on the Contact support through our online form link toward the middle of the page. The page shown in Figure 14-8 appears.

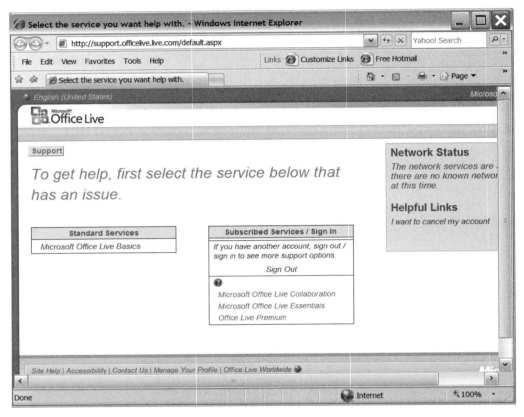

Figure 14-8. *The level of support you're entitled to depends on your subscription.*

3. Under Standard Services, click on your subscription level. A page with available support options appears, as shown in Figure 14-9. Office Live Essentials and Office Live Premium subscribers will see a telephone number. Office Live Basics subscribers will only see an E-mail button.

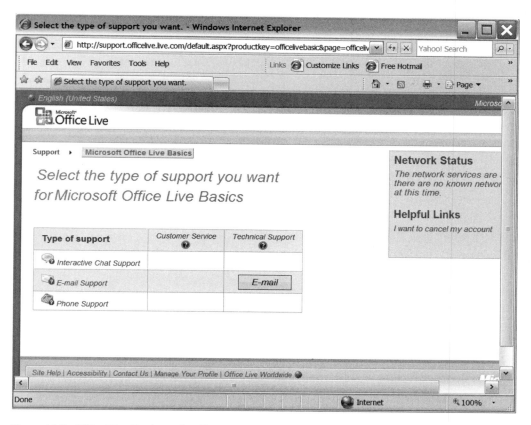

Figure 14-9. *Office Live Basics only offers support by e-mail.*

4. If you subscribe to Office Live Essentials or Office Live Premium, grab the nearest telephone and call the toll-free number listed next to Phone Support. If you're an Office Live Basics subscriber, you can only vent your frustration via e-mail. Click on the E-mail button. You should see the web page shown in Figure 14-10.

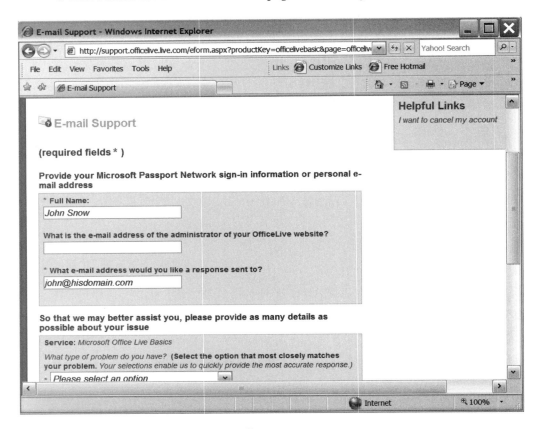

Figure 14-10. *The actual support form. Finally!*

5. Fill out the form and click the Submit button at the bottom. You should see a page like the one shown in Figure 14-11. Write down the ticket number or print the page for your reference.

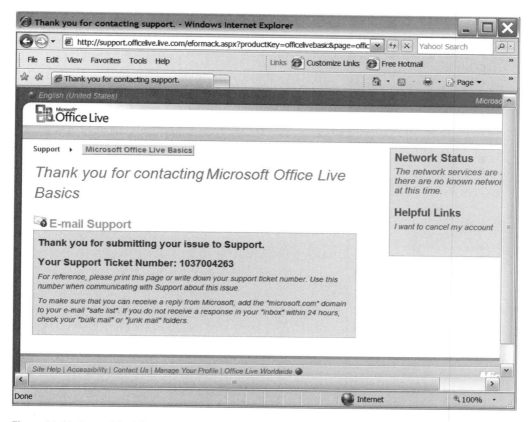

Figure 14-11. *Save this ticket number for reference until your issue is resolved.*

6. Wait for a reply. Office Live's tech support is quite efficient. You should hear from them in less than four hours.

TIPS FROM THE TRENCHES

A Five-Point Maintenance Check for Your Web Site

Like your car, your web site will perform better over the long run with preventive maintenance. Whenever you update the content on your site, take a few minutes to do the following:

- **Verify that Office Live has made a backup of your site since you last updated it**: If a backup copy isn't available, you'll see the following figure, which mentions that your site "does not have any backups yet," instead of Figure 14-6. This is not a good situation to be in. Contact Office Live's technical support and have the issue addressed as soon as you can.

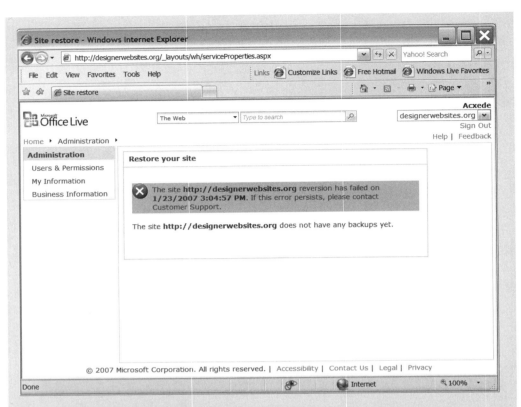

- **Verify that the Contact Us page works**: Office Live's contact form has a habit of dying on you if you're not on your toes. Send an e-mail to yourself after every update.

- **Check all external hyperlinks**: Pages on other sites change too. You may have to update links to them on your site. Make it a habit to check external links periodically.

- **Check your site-monitoring report for persistent downtime problems with the site**: As I mentioned earlier, Office Live is very reliable. If your site reports show persistent downtime, it could be the harbinger of more serious problems. Contact Office Live's technical support to get the problem fixed as soon as you can.

- **Tweak site-wide settings periodically**: Is any holiday or event on the horizon? You may want your site to reflect that. You could try changing the Theme, Style, or Color of your site—pastel colors in the fall and bright colors in the summer, for example.

Summary

After your site goes live, you'll begin a new career as a part-time webmaster. In this chapter, I gave you a few practical tips on fulfilling your new duties. In particular, you learned how to

- Update your site periodically
- Monitor it for uptime
- Restore it from backup if disaster strikes

Although you're no longer a web site newbie, you probably realize that you have a lot more to learn about building and maintaining web sites. You'll find more information about improving your webmastering skills on the companion sites[2] to this book. These sites feature:

- A complete list of the resources I've referred to in this book
- Links to other Office Live resources on the Web
- Bonus content about Office Live's features not covered in this book

I hope this book has helped you use Office Live to build a user-friendly web site that you're proud of. Good luck with it!

2. See the Introduction.

Index

You Need the Companion eBook

Your purchase of this book entitles you to buy the companion PDF-version eBook for only $10. Take the weightless companion with you anywhere.

We believe this Apress title will prove so indispensable that you'll want to carry it with you everywhere, which is why we are offering the companion eBook (in PDF format) for $10 to customers who purchase this book now. Convenient and fully searchable, the PDF version of any content-rich, page-heavy Apress book makes a valuable addition to your programming library. You can easily find and copy code—or perform examples by quickly toggling between instructions and the application. Even simultaneously tackling a donut, diet soda, and complex code becomes simplified with hands-free eBooks!

Once you purchase your book, getting the $10 companion eBook is simple:

❶ Visit **www.apress.com/promo/tendollars/**.

❷ Complete a basic registration form to receive a randomly generated question about this title.

❸ Answer the question correctly in 60 seconds, and you will receive a promotional code to redeem for the $10.00 eBook.

THE EXPERT'S VOICE™